EXPERT **RESUMES** for
Health Care Careers

Wendy S. Enelow and
Louise M. Kursmark

jist
Works
America's Career Publisher

Expert Resumes for Health Care Careers

© 2004 by Wendy S. Enelow and Louise M. Kursmark

Published by JIST Works, an imprint of JIST Publishing, Inc.
8902 Otis Avenue
Indianapolis, IN 46216-1033
Phone: 1-800-648-JIST   Fax: 1-800-JIST-FAX   E-mail: info@jist.com

Visit our Web site at www.jist.com for information on JIST, free job search tips, book chapters, and how to order our many products!

Quantity discounts are available for JIST books. Please call our Sales Department at 1-800-648-5478 for a free catalog and more information.

Acquisitions and Development Editor: Lori Cates Hand
Copy Editor: Stephanie Koutek
Cover Designer: Katy Bodenmiller
Interior Designer and Page Layout: Trudy Coler
Proofreaders: Jeanne Clark, David Faust
Indexer: Kelly Henthorne

Printed in Canada
10 09 08 07 06 05   9 8 7 6 5 4 3

We have been careful to provide accurate information in this book, but it is possible that errors and omissions have been introduced. Please consider this in making any career plans or other important decisions. Trust your own judgment above all else and in all things.

Trademarks: All brand names and product names used in this book are trade names, service marks, trademarks, or registered trademarks of their respective owners.

ISBN 1-59357-000-7

CONTENTS AT A GLANCE

TABLE OF CONTENTS

ABOUT THIS BOOK

If you're already employed in the health care industry or considering a career in health care, you've made a wise decision! Health care is one of the largest industries in the U.S., employing over 11 million people in 2000 (according to the U.S. Department of Labor's Bureau of Labor Statistics).

Health care is one of the fastest-growing sectors of the U.S. economy, projected to increase at a rate of 25 percent through 2010. According to the Bureau of Labor Statistics, *9 out of the 20 occupations projected to grow the fastest between 2000 and 2010 are concentrated in health services,* ranging from highly trained medical personnel and registered nurses to aides, orderlies, and attendants.

What this means to you is that health care is one of the few industries in today's economy that is virtually "recession-proof." Unlike many of the other major industries that have been hard hit by the downward economic spiral, health care remains a stable industry offering tremendous employment opportunities.

If you're currently employed in health care, you probably already know this. Nursing, for example, is always a "hot" profession; in fact, many hospitals and health care facilities offer nurses sign-on bonuses, three- or four-day work weeks, and numerous other incentives to attract high-quality care providers. Virtually every position in home health care is growing at a phenomenal rate, as are positions in allied health care, biomedical technology, specialty care, and health care management/administration.

To take advantage of all of these opportunities, you must develop a powerful, performance-based resume. To be a savvy and successful job seeker, you must know how to communicate your qualifications in a strong and effective written presentation. Sure, it's important to let employers know essential details, but a resume is more than just your job history and academic credentials. A winning resume is a concise yet comprehensive document that gives you a competitive edge in the job market. Creating such a powerful document is what this book is all about.

We'll begin with a thorough discussion of the top nine strategies for getting your resume noticed and getting an interview. Then, we'll follow with a thorough discussion of each of the key components of a winning resume. Next, we'll explore the changes in resume presentation that have arisen over the past decade and the similarities and differences between print, e-mail, scannable, and Web-based resumes.

Finally, you can review more than 100 outstanding resume samples contributed by some of the best resume writers in the world. Then, use the samples and our tips to create your own winning resume.

INTRODUCTION

According to the U.S. Department of Labor's Bureau of Labor Statistics, the U.S. should expect to see a **25 percent increase in the number of health care positions** between 2000 and 2010 (compared to only 16 percent for all other industries). What does that mean to you? What it means is that, by 2010, there will be approximately 14 million health care positions in the U.S. And all you want is one!

Those of you in the health care field already know that you're in one of the few industries that is considered recession-proof. Of course, there may be downsizings, mergers, acquisitions, changes in ownership, and other reorganizations, but largely, health care is "safe" from the dramatic and pervasive layoffs that have crippled other professions and industries.

If, on the other hand, you're considering entering the health care field for the first time, you can be certain that you have made an excellent decision. Health care can and will provide you with years and years of outstanding employment opportunities.

Consider these other statistics from the U.S. Department of Labor:

- Approximately 13 percent of all *new* jobs created between 2000 and 2010 will be in the health care industry. This translates to 2.8 million *new* health care positions.

- The single largest segment of growth in the industry is in home health care. Employment is projected to increase more than 60 percent by 2010, largely as a result of the increasing longevity of the U.S. population.

- Other health care occupations projected to grow by 30 percent or more include medical assistants, physical therapists, medical and health services managers, medical records and health information technicians, and dental assistants.

- The mean (similar to an average) annual income for an individual employed in health care is $49,930. For those paid on an hourly wage or salary basis, mean hourly earnings range from $8 to $27 an hour, depending on the position, amount of training required, and level of responsibility.

- Hospitals employ more workers than any other sector within the health care industry (approximately 40 percent).

- The largest percentage of jobs in health care require less than a four-year college education.

Considering Entering the Health Care Field?

If you're currently evaluating a variety of job and career opportunities, health care might be just the right choice for you. Consider just a sampling of the positions that are available in health care:

Cardiovascular Technologists and Technicians

Chiropractors

Clinical Laboratory Technologists and Technicians

Dental Assistants

Dental Hygienists

Dental Laboratory Technicians

Dentists

Diagnostic Medical Sonographers

Dietitians and Nutritionists

Emergency Medical Technicians and Paramedics

Licensed Practical and Licensed Vocational Nurses

Medical and Health Services Managers

Medical Assistants

Medical Records and Health Information Technicians

Medical Secretaries

Medical Transcriptionists

Nuclear Medicine Technologists

Nursing, Psychiatric, and Home Health Aides

Occupational Therapist Assistants and Aides

Occupational Therapists

Ophthalmic Laboratory Technicians

Opticians

Optometrists

Personal and Home Care Aides

Pharmacists

Pharmacy Aides

Pharmacy Technicians

Physical Therapist Assistants and Aides

Physical Therapists

Physician Assistants

Physicians and Surgeons

Podiatrists

Psychologists

Radiologic Technologists and Technicians

Receptionists and Information Clerks

Recreational Therapists

Registered Nurses

Respiratory Therapists

Social and Human Service Assistants

Social Workers

Speech-Language Pathologists and Audiologists

Surgical Technologists

Veterinarians

EDUCATIONAL CONSIDERATIONS

After you've decided that health care is your preferred career choice, you'll need to evaluate the various levels of education required for each position; a vast array of programs provide specialized training. Some, such as certificate and associate-degree programs, require only one or two years of training. Others, such as baccalaureate, professional, or graduate degrees, require four or more years of specialized training and education.

The health-services industry also provides many job opportunities for people without specialized training. In fact, 56 percent of the workers in nursing and personal-care facilities have a high school diploma or less, as do 25 percent of the workers in hospitals.

Some health-services establishments provide on-the-job or classroom training as well as continuing education. For example, in all certified nursing facilities, nursing aides must complete a state-approved training and competency evaluation program and participate in at least 12 hours of in-service education annually. Hospitals, more so than any other segment within health care, have the resources and incentive to provide training programs and advancement opportunities to their employees. In other segments, staffing patterns tend to be more fixed and the variety of positions and advancement opportunities more limited. Larger establishments usually offer a broader range of opportunities.

Some hospitals provide training or tuition assistance in return for a promise to work for a particular length of time in the hospital after graduation. Many nursing facilities have similar programs. Some hospitals have cross-training programs that train their workers—through formal college programs, continuing education, or in-house training—to perform functions outside their specialties.

EDUCATIONAL RESOURCES

We recommend the following additional resources related to employment within the health care industry and particular employment opportunities.

For detailed information on specific careers in health care, job requirements, training requirements, working conditions, salaries, and more, refer to

Occupational Outlook Handbook at www.bls.gov/oco, or purchase a copy of the book from JIST Publishing at www.jist.com.

For referrals to hospital human resources departments about local opportunities in health care facilities, contact

American Hospital Association/American Society for Hospital Human Resources Administrators, One North Franklin, Chicago, IL 60606.

For additional information on specific health-related occupations, contact

American Medical Association/Health Professions Career and Education Directory, 515 N. State St., Chicago, IL 60610; or visit its Web site at www.ama-assn.org/ama/pub/category/2322.html.

For information on health care scholarship opportunities, contact

U.S. Department of Health and Human Services at (301) 443-4776. Be sure to ask about both the National Health Services Corps and the Undergraduate Education of Professional Nurses Grant Program.

There is also a wealth of information on health care careers and job opportunities available through the Internet, schools, colleges and universities, libraries, professional associations, medical associations, and employers. And be sure to closely review the appendix in the back of this book for a detailed listing of job-related Web sites.

If You're Already in Health Care, Where Are the Jobs?

In 2000, there were more than 469,000 health care establishments in the U.S., varying greatly in size, staffing patterns, and organizational structure. Of those 469,000 establishments, more than 65 percent were privately owned offices of physicians, dentists, and other health care practitioners. The remaining establishments included medical and dental laboratories, nursing and personal care facilities, home health care services, and hospitals. Interestingly, although hospitals constitute only 2 percent of all health care establishments, they ranked #1 as the largest employer in the industry, with over 40 percent of all health care workers.

OCCUPATIONS WITHIN THE HEALTH CARE INDUSTRY

Here is how the U.S. Department of Labor breaks down the various occupations within the health care industry:

Professional Occupations

Sample Positions: Physicians and Surgeons, Dentists, Registered Nurses, Social Workers, Physical Therapists

Educational Requirements: Usually require at least a bachelor's degree in a specialized field or higher education in a specific health field (although registered nurses also enter through associate-degree or diploma programs).

Allied Health Care Professionals and Technicians

Sample Positions: Radiology Technicians, Medical Records Technicians, Dental Hygienists, Health Information Technicians, Emergency Medical Technicians

Educational Requirements: Usually a one- or two-year training or certificate program.

Service Occupations

Sample Positions: Nursing Aides, Home Health Aides, Dental Assistants, Medical Assistants, Laboratory Technologists

Educational Requirements: Usually little or no specialized education; training is provided on-the-job.

Administrative and Management Occupations

Sample Positions: Health Care Administrators, Hospital Administrators, Medical Service Managers, Billing Clerks, Medical Transcriptionists, Food Services Directors

Educational Requirements: Vary based on level of position, from no formal training or education to four-year degrees and higher.

WHERE HEALTH CARE WORKERS ARE EMPLOYED

Now that you know how health care positions are classified, let's explore the eight different segments of the health care industry to understand which type of establishments employ which type of health care workers. This information is critical to understand so that you know where the best employment opportunities are for you.

Hospitals

Hospitals employ workers with all levels of education and training to provide a wider variety of services than any other segment within the health-services industry. About one in four hospital workers is a *registered nurse*. Hospitals employ many *physicians* and *surgeons*, *therapists*, and *social workers*. Hospitals also employ large numbers of *office* and *administrative* personnel.

Nursing and Personal Care Facilities

More than 60 percent of all nursing-facility jobs are in service occupations, primarily *nursing, psychiatric*, and *home health*. Professional and administrative support occupations make up a much smaller percentage of employment in these facilities than in other parts of the health-services industry.

Physicians' Offices and Clinics

Many of the jobs in private physician offices are in professional and related occupations, primarily *physicians, surgeons*, and *registered nurses*. A large number of positions, however, are in the office and administrative-support occupations, such as *receptionists, billing clerks*, and *office managers*, which comprise more than 30 percent of all workers in physicians' offices.

Home Health Care Services

More than 50 percent of the jobs in home health care are in service occupations, mostly *home health aides* and *personal care aides. Nursing* and *therapist* jobs also account for substantial shares of employment in this segment.

Dentists' Offices and Clinics

More than 33 percent of the jobs in this segment are in service occupations, mostly *dental assistants*. The typical staffing pattern in dentists' offices consists of one professional with a support staff of *dental hygienists* and *dental assistants*. Larger practices are more likely to employ *office managers* and *administrative personnel*, as well as *dental laboratory technicians*.

Offices and Clinics of Other Health Care Practitioners

Professional and related occupations account for about two out of five jobs in this segment, including *physical therapists, occupational therapists, dispensing opticians*, and *chiropractors. Office and administrative-support occupations* also accounted for a significant portion of all jobs (almost one-third).

Medical and Dental Laboratories

Professional and related workers accounted for more than one-third of all jobs in this segment, primarily *clinical laboratory* and *radiologic technologists and technicians*. Unlike the other health care segments, many jobs are also in production occupations, most notably *dental laboratory technicians*.

Health and Allied Services (not Elsewhere Classified)

This segment of the health-services industry employs the highest percentages of professional and related workers including *counselors, social workers,* and *registered nurses.*

You should now have a good sense of "where the jobs are" in the health care industry. More importantly, you can use this information to determine where the best opportunities are for the type of position that you are seeking. Remember, "smart and savvy" health care professionals control their own careers, charting a strong and steady course to reach their ultimate career goals.

A Step-by-Step Action Plan for Finding Your Next Great Job

An action plan will keep you moving steadily toward your goal of finding a new position. We've outlined the major steps in the job-finding process in the following sections. Use these steps to create—and follow—your own detailed action plan.

STEP 1: WRITE A POWERFUL RESUME

All job seekers in the 21st century have a unique challenge. As the workforce has grown and employers have undergone massive changes, job search has become increasingly competitive, even in an industry like health care where opportunities abound. In turn, job seekers must know how to position themselves above the crowd of other candidates applying for similar opportunities. And the best way to achieve that is with a powerful resume that clearly communicates your accomplishments and the value you bring to a prospective employer. That is what this book will teach you. You must always remember…

Your resume is a marketing tool written to sell YOU!

If you're a nurse manager, *sell* the fact that you've improved quality of care and reduced length of stay while curtailing excessive payroll costs. If you're a social worker, *highlight* your success in developing new programs, facilitating community-outreach projects, and enhancing coordination between various care-delivery organizations. If you're a hospital purchasing manager, *market* your successes in cost reduction, inventory control, and loss prevention. If you're a laboratory technician, prominently *display* your achievements in the design, development, and delivery of innovative new laboratory procedures.

When writing your resume, your challenge is to create a picture of knowledge, action, and results. In essence, you're stating "This is who I am, this is what I know, this is how I've used it, and this is how well I've performed." Success sells, so be sure to highlight yours. If you don't, no one else will.

STEP 2: BECOME A SAVVY JOB SEEKER

Just as important, you must be an educated job seeker. This means you must know what you want in your career, where the hiring action is, what qualifications and credentials you will need to attain your desired career goals, and how best to market your qualifications. It is no longer enough to be a competent radiologic technician, dental assistant, licensed practical nurse, or surgical assistant. Now, you must be a strategic marketer, able to package and promote your experience to take advantage of this wave of employment opportunity.

There's no doubt that the employment market has changed dramatically from only a few years ago. According to the U.S. Department of Labor (2000), you should expect to hold between 10 and 20 different jobs during your career. No longer is stability the status quo. Today, the norm is movement, onward and upward, in a fast-paced and intense employment market. And to stay on top of all the changes and opportunities, you must proactively control and manage your career.

STEP 3: LAUNCH A SUCCESSFUL SEARCH CAMPAIGN

The single most important thing to remember is that **job search is marketing!** You have a product to sell—yourself—and the best way to sell it is to use all appropriate *marketing channels* just as you would for any other product.

Suppose you wanted to sell televisions. What would you do? You'd market your products using newspaper, magazine, and radio advertisements. You might develop a company Web site to build your e-business, and perhaps you'd hire a field sales representative to market to major retail chains. Each of these is a different *marketing channel* through which you're attempting to reach your audience.

The same is true for job search. You must use every marketing channel that's right for you. Unfortunately, there is no single formula. What's right for you depends on your specific career objectives—position, preference for type of health care practice or institution, geographic restrictions, compensation, and more.

Following is a recommended Job Search Marketing Plan for health care professionals. These items are rank ordered, from most effective to least effective, and should serve as the foundation on which you build your own search campaign.

1. **Referrals.** There is nothing better than a personal referral to a hospital, health care practice, or other type of health care institution, either in general or for a specific position. Referrals can open doors that, in most instances, would never be accessible any other way. If you know anyone who could possibly refer you to a specific organization, contact that person immediately and ask for their assistance.

2. **Networking.** Networking is the backbone of every successful job search. Although you might consider it an arduous task, it is essential that you network effectively with your professional colleagues and associates, past employers, past co-workers, suppliers, neighbors, friends, and others who might know of opportunities that are right for you. Another good strategy is to attend meetings of professional associations (for example, medical, nursing, health care administration, technical) in your area to make new contacts and expand your network. And particularly in today's nomadic job market—where you're likely to change jobs every few years—the best strategy is to keep your network "alive" even when you're *not* searching for a new position.

3. **Responses to newspaper, magazine, and periodical advertisements (in print).** So much of job search has transitioned to the Internet and e-mail, as you'll read later, that people now often overlook a great hiring resource—the help-wanted ads. Do not forget about this "tried and true" marketing strategy. If they've got the job and you have the qualifications, it's a perfect fit. We've seen it work hundreds of times.

4. **Responses to online job postings.** One of the greatest advantages of the technology revolution is an employer's ability to post job announcements and a job seeker's ability to respond immediately via e-mail. It's a wonder! In most (but not all) instances, these are bona fide opportunities, and it's well worth your while to spend time searching for and responding to appropriate postings. However, don't make the mistake of devoting *too* much time to searching the Internet. It can consume a huge amount of your time that you should spend on other job search efforts that will yield even better results.

   Generally speaking, the higher the level of position you are seeking, the less value the Internet and electronic job search will be to you. Most very senior-level medical, health care, management, and executive positions are filled through networking, referrals, and other person-to-person contact.

   Refer to the appendix for a listing of the largest and most widely used online job posting sites for health care professionals. In addition, you'll find Web sites with information on interviewing and salary negotiation, along with some of our favorite sites for researching information on companies (a must-do before any interview!).

5. **Targeted e-mail campaigns (resumes and cover letters) to recruiters.** Recruiters have jobs, and you want one. It's pretty straightforward. The only catch is to find the "right" recruiters who have the "right" jobs. Therefore, you must devote the time and effort to preparing the "right" list of recruiters. There are many resources on the Internet where you can access information about recruiters (for a fee) and sort that information by industry and position specialization. This allows you to identify just the "right" recruiters who would be interested in a health care candidate with your qualifications. What's more, because these campaigns are transmitted electronically, they are easy and inexpensive to produce.

   When working with recruiters, it's important to realize that they *do not* work for you! Their clients are the hospitals and health care institutions that pay their fees. They are not in business to "find a job" for you, but rather to fill a specific position with a qualified candidate, either you or someone else. To maximize your chances of finding a position through a recruiter or agency, don't rely on just one or two, but distribute your resume to many that meet your specific criteria.

6. **Targeted e-mail and print campaigns to employers.** Just as with campaigns to recruiters (see item 5), you must be extremely careful to select just the right employers that would be interested in a health care candidate with your qualifications. The closer you stick to "where you belong" in relation to your specific experience, the better your response rate will be. We believe that print campaigns (paper and envelopes mailed the old-fashioned way) are the most

appropriate and effective presentation for health care professionals when they are contacting employers directly.

7. **In-person "cold calls" to employers and recruiters.** We consider this the least effective and most time-consuming marketing strategy for health care positions. It is extremely difficult to just walk in the door and get in front of the right person, or any person who can take hiring action. You'll be much better off focusing your time and energy on other, more productive channels (for example, networking, referrals, and advertisements).

8. **Online resume postings.** The 'Net is swarming with reasonably priced (if not free) Web sites where you can post your resume. It's quick, easy, and the only *passive* thing you can do in your search. All of the other marketing channels require action on your part. With online resume postings, once you've posted, you're done. You then just wait (and hope!) for some response.

Conclusion

Health care is one of the most stable industries in today's global economy, currently employing more than 11 million and projected to employ almost 14 million by 2010. Whether you're looking for a clinical nursing position in a hospital, a technology position with a biomedical engineering laboratory, an administrative assignment with a home health care provider organization, or a position as Chief of Medicine with a leading teaching hospital, opportunities abound.

Your challenge is to write a top-flight resume, identify the most appropriate job search channels for the type of position you are seeking, and mount a well-targeted and professionally managed job search campaign. With such great employment statistics in your favor, you can't help but be successful in your job search and find the position of your dreams!

PART I

Resume Writing, Strategy, and Formats

CHAPTER 1

Resume-Writing Strategies for Health Care Careers

If you're reading this book, chances are you've decided to make a career move. It might be because

- You're ready to leave your current position and move up the ladder to a higher-paying and more responsible management or executive-level position.

- You've decided to pursue new occupational opportunities within your industry (health care).

- You're unhappy with your current employer or senior management team and have decided to pursue opportunities elsewhere.

- You've completed a contract assignment and are looking for a new "free agent" job or perhaps a permanent position.

- You've decided to resign your current position to pursue an entrepreneurial opportunity.

- You're relocating to a new area and need to find a new position.

- You're returning to the workforce after several years of unemployment or retirement.

- You've just completed additional education (for example, training, certification, an undergraduate degree, or an advanced degree) and are ready to make a step upward in your career.

- You've been laid off, downsized, or otherwise left your position and you must find a new one.

- You're simply ready for a change.

There might even be other reasons for your job search besides these. However, regardless of the reason, a powerful resume is an essential component of your search campaign. In fact, it is virtually impossible to conduct a search without a resume. It is your calling card that briefly, yet powerfully, communicates the skills, qualifications, experience, and value you bring to a prospective employer. It is the document that will open doors and generate interviews. It is the first thing people will learn about you when you forward it in response to an advertisement, and it is the last thing they'll remember when they're reviewing your qualifications after an interview.

Your resume is a sales document, and you are the product! You must identify the *features (what you know* and *what you can do)* and *benefits (how you can help an employer)* of that product and then communicate them in a concise and hard-hitting written presentation. Remind yourself over and over, as you work your way through the resume process, that you are writing marketing literature designed to sell a new product—YOU—for a new position.

Your resume can have tremendous power and a phenomenal impact on your job search. So don't take it lightly. Rather, devote the time, energy, and resources that are essential to developing a resume that is well-written, visually attractive, and effective in communicating *who* you are and *how* you want to be perceived.

Resume Strategies

The following sections outline the nine core strategies for writing effective and successful resumes.

RESUME STRATEGY #1: WHO ARE YOU AND HOW DO YOU WANT TO BE PERCEIVED?

Now that you've decided to look for a new position, the very first step is to identify your current career interests, goals, and objectives. *This task is critical* because it is the underlying foundation for *what* you include in your resume, *how* you include it, and *where* you include it. You cannot write an effective resume without knowing, at least to some degree, what type or types of positions you will be seeking. This requires more than the simple response of "I'm looking for a new position within the health care industry." You must be more specific in terms of your objectives in order to create a document that powerfully positions you for such opportunities.

There are two concepts to consider here:

- **Who you are:** This relates to what you have done professionally and academically. Are you a physician, surgeon, nurse, occupational therapist, phlebotomy technician, lab manager, or board-certified hearing instrument specialist? Are you a clinical nutritionist, medical assistant, health records administrator, or licensed acupuncturist? Are you a nurse educator responsible for designing and delivering training programs, or a cardiac surgeon with a world-renowned reputation? Perhaps you're a hospice counselor, CT scan technologist, or ER orderly. Have you just graduated with your BSN degree or chemistry lab certificate? Who are you?

- **How you want to be perceived:** This relates to your current career objectives. If you're a physician looking for your first departmental management position, don't focus solely on your medical skills. Put an equal emphasis on your success in training other physicians and medical personnel, managing budgets and resources, coordinating emergency response, designing and administering new health care programs, and the like. If you're a lab technician seeking a promotion to the next level of responsibility, highlight your accomplishments in developing new lab procedures, streamlining existing procedures, purchasing new equipment, training staff, managing record keeping, and other administrative and management-type responsibilities.

The strategy, then, is to connect these two concepts by using the *Who You Are* information that ties directly to the *How You Want to Be Perceived* message to determine what information to include in your resume. By following this strategy, you're painting a picture that allows a prospective employer to see you as you want to be seen—as an individual with the qualifications for the type of position you are pursuing.

> **WARNING:** If you prepare a resume without first clearly identifying what your objectives are and how you want to be perceived, your resume will have no focus and no direction. Without the underlying knowledge of "This is what I want to be," you do not know what to highlight in your resume. In turn, the document becomes a historical overview of your career and not the sales document it should be.

RESUME STRATEGY #2: SELL IT TO ME...DON'T TELL IT TO ME

We've already established the fact that resume writing is sales. You are the product, and you must create a document that powerfully communicates the value of that product. One particularly effective strategy for accomplishing this is the "Sell It to Me...Don't Tell It to Me" strategy that impacts virtually every word you write on your resume.

If you "tell it," you are simply stating facts. If you "sell it," you promote it, advertise it, and draw attention to it. Look at the difference in impact between these examples:

Tell It Strategy: Supervised staffing and scheduling for all nursing aides and assistants in the hospital.

Sell It Strategy: Full responsibility for managing a 245-person staff of nursing aides and assistants at a 650-bed acute-care hospital. Coordinated new-staff orientation, staff scheduling, an ongoing training and development program, and the annual recertification process. Maintained staffing levels at near 100%, with less than 5% turnover.

Tell It Strategy: Managed a large-scale reorganization of the entire medical records department.

Sell It Strategy: Spearheaded hospital-wide reorganization and full computerization of all medical records. Project impacted more than 100 employees at the hospital, adjacent nursing home, ambulatory care facility, and off-premise laboratory. Following year-long implementation, reduced staffing and payroll by 21%, virtually eliminated errors, and introduced virtual reporting and analytical capabilities.

Tell It Strategy: Supervised development of next-generation prosthetic devices at The Johns Hopkins Hospital Biomedical Lab.

Sell It Strategy: Led 4-person project team in the design, prototyping, testing, and introduction of next-generation prosthetic device technology. Earned worldwide recognition for project success, honored with several industry awards, and selected as keynote presenter for the 2003 Annual Conference of the American Prosthetics Association. Long-term revenue projections for new products forecasted at better than $500 million within 2 years.

What's the difference between "telling it" and "selling it"? In a nutshell…

Telling It	Selling It
Describes features.	Describes benefits.
Tells what and how.	Sells why the "what" and "how" are important.
Details activities.	Includes results.
Focuses on what you did.	Details how what you did benefited your employer, department, team members, patients/clients, the body of medical knowledge, and so on.

RESUME STRATEGY #3: USE KEYWORDS

No matter what you read or who you talk to about job search, the concept of keywords is sure to come up. Keywords (or, as they were previously known, buzz words) are words and phrases that are specific to a particular industry or profession. For example, keywords for health care occupations can include *case management, acute care, chronic care, patient scheduling, billing, reimbursement, community outreach, P&L management, efficiency improvement, quality assurance, length of stay, resource management, patient/physician relations, peer review, occupational health, holistic care, rehabilitation, medical instrumentation, lab analysis,* and hundreds more.

When you use these words and phrases—in your resume, in your cover letter, or during an interview—you are communicating a very specific message. For example, when you include the words *primary care* in your resume, your reader will most likely assume that you have experience in direct patient care, assessment and diagnosis, patient teaching/education, medication administration, emergency response, crisis intervention, third-party referrals, and more. As you can see, people will make inferences about your skills based on the use of just one or two individual words.

Here are a few other examples:

- When you use the words *lab management,* people will assume you have experience with staffing, budgeting, resource management, equipment management, purchasing, instrumentation calibration, and more.

- By referencing *managed care* in your resume, you convey that you most likely have experience in coordinating patient care through a network of providers, administering all required documentation and reporting, coordinating third-party reimbursement, facilitating provider referrals, and other actions specific to the managed-care arena.

- When you mention *health care education,* readers and listeners will infer that you have experience in curriculum planning and development, instructional materials design, technology-based learning, teacher selection and training, continuing professional education, and more.

- When you include *regulatory affairs* as one of your areas of expertise, most people will assume you are experienced in regulatory compliance and reporting, regulatory agency affairs, JCAHO standards, and more.

Keywords are also an integral component of the resume scanning process, whereby employers and recruiters electronically search resumes for specific terms to find candidates with the skills, qualifications, and credentials for their particular hiring needs. In organizations where it has been implemented, electronic scanning has replaced the more traditional method of an actual person reading your resume (at least initially). Therefore, to some degree, the *only* thing that matters in this instance is that you have included the "right" keywords to match the organization's or recruiter's needs. Without them, you will most certainly be passed over.

Although keyword scanning is not as prevalent throughout the health care industry (particularly in private offices) as in other industries, it is increasing in popularity because of its ease and efficiency. What's more, for those of you in technology-related industries, resume scanning and other electronic hiring systems are often the preferred method of application. Just like any other job seekers, health care professionals must stay on top of the latest trends in technology-based hiring and employment as these trends relate directly to them.

Of course, in virtually every instance your resume will be read at some point by human eyes, so it's not enough just to throw together a list of keywords and leave it at that. In fact, it's not even necessary to include a separate "keyword summary" on your resume. A better strategy is to incorporate keywords naturally into the text within the appropriate sections of your resume.

Keep in mind, too, that keywords are arbitrary; there is no defined set of keywords for a nurse, lab technician, surgeon, cardiologist, or health care program administrator. Employers searching to fill these positions develop a list of terms that reflect the specifics they desire in a qualified candidate. These might be a combination of professional qualifications, skills, education, length of experience, and other easily defined criteria along with "soft skills," such as leadership, problem-solving, and communication.

> **NOTE:** Because of the complex and arbitrary nature of keyword selection, we cannot overemphasize how vital it is to include in your resume *all* of the keywords that represent your experience and knowledge!

How can you be sure that you are including all the keywords—and the right keywords? Just by describing your work experience, achievements, educational credentials, technical qualifications, and the like, you will naturally include most of the terms that are important in your field. To cross-check what you've written, review online or print job postings for positions that are of interest to you. Look at the precise terms used in the ads and be sure you have included them in your resume (if they are an accurate reflection of your skills and qualifications).

Another great benefit of today's technology revolution is our ability to find instant information, even information as specific as keywords for the health care industry. Refer to the appendix for a listing of Web sites that list keywords, complete with descriptions. These are outstanding resources.

RESUME STRATEGY #4: USE THE "BIG" AND SAVE THE "LITTLE"

When deciding what you want to include in your resume, try to focus on the "big" things—new health care programs, innovative public health training and outreach programs, revenue and profit growth, new ventures, special projects, cost savings, improvements in quality of care, improvements in diagnostic capabilities, technology implementations, and more. Here's an example:

CEO/Administrator of a 28-bed long-term acute-care hospital and a 79-bed skilled nursing facility accredited by JCAHO. Lead a medical staff of 70 physicians, 140 nurses, and 25 support staff. Services include intensive case management, social service programs, medical nursing care, rehabilitation, and respiratory therapy.

- Increased operating profits 100% in one year by developing new revenue channels and implementing effective cost controls.

- Met/exceeded all regulatory requirements.

- Reorganized hospital and skilled nursing management structure to capitalize on the changing health care marketplace, and launched a number of innovative marketing programs.

- Spearheaded effort to introduce onsite patient-care training programs for non-skilled nursing staff.

- Authored 250-page policies and procedures manual to ensure consistency between the different facilities, eliminate redundancy, and improve reporting capabilities.

Then, save the "little" stuff—the details—for the interview. With this strategy, you will accomplish two things: You'll keep your resume readable and of a reasonable length (while still selling your achievements), and you'll have new and interesting information to share during the interview, rather than merely repeating what is already on your resume. Using the preceding example, when discussing this experience during an interview, you could elaborate on your specific achievements; namely, how you increased revenues and profits so dramatically, what unique marketing programs you created and their results, the specific training programs you launched, regulatory obstacles you overcame, procedures you streamlined, and more.

RESUME STRATEGY #5: MAKE YOUR RESUME "INTERVIEWABLE"

One of your greatest challenges is to make your resume a useful interview tool. After the employer determines that you meet the primary qualifications for a position (you've passed the keyword scanning test or initial review) and you are contacted for a telephone or in-person interview, your resume becomes all-important in leading and prompting your interviewer during your conversation.

Your job, then, is to make sure the resume leads the reader where you want to go and presents just the right organization, content, and appearance to stimulate a productive discussion. To improve the "interviewability" of your resume, consider these tactics:

- Make good use of Resume Strategy #4 (*Use the "Big" and Save the "Little"*) to invite further discussion about your experiences.

- Be sure your greatest "selling points" are featured prominently rather than buried within the resume.

- Conversely, don't devote lots of space and attention to areas of your background that are irrelevant or about which you feel less than positive; you'll only invite questions about things you really don't want to discuss.

- Make sure your resume is highly readable—this means plenty of white space, an adequate font size, and a logical flow from start to finish.

RESUME STRATEGY #6: ELIMINATE CONFUSION WITH STRUCTURE AND CONTEXT

Keep in mind that your resume will be read *very quickly* by hiring authorities! You might agonize over every word and spend hours working on content and design, but the average reader will skim quickly through your masterpiece and expect to pick up important facts in just a few seconds. Try to make it as easy as possible for readers to grasp the essential facts:

- Be consistent: for example, put job titles, company names, and dates in the same place and format them the same for each position.

- Make information easy to find by clearly defining different sections of your resume with large, highly visible headings.

- Define the context in which you worked (for example, the organization, your department, and the specific challenges you faced) before you start describing your activities and accomplishments.

RESUME STRATEGY #7: USE FUNCTION TO DEMONSTRATE ACHIEVEMENT

When you write a resume that focuses only on your job functions, it can be dry and uninteresting and will say very little about your unique activities and contributions. Consider the following example:

> Responsible for managing a turnaround of the behavioral health division of Pima Healthcare.

Now, consider using that same function to demonstrate achievement and see what happens to the tone and energy of the sentence. It becomes alive and clearly communicates that you deliver results.

> Recruited to plan and orchestrate a profitable turnaround of the behavioral health division of Pima Healthcare, a full-service, 400-bed community hospital. Delivered total cost savings of more than $25 million annually by reducing FTEs 50%, salaries and wages 48%, physician fees 30%, and total expenses 50%. Concurrently, renegotiated managed-care contracts with 12% weighted average increase, resolved longstanding Medicare compliance issues, and achieved a personal performance rating of 95%.

Try to translate your functions into achievements and you'll create a more powerful resume presentation.

RESUME STRATEGY #8: REMAIN IN THE REALM OF REALITY

We've already established that resume writing is sales. And, as any good salesperson does, one feels somewhat inclined to stretch the truth, just a bit. However, be forewarned that you must stay within the realm of reality. Do not push your skills and qualifications outside the bounds of what is truthful. You never want to be in a position where you have to defend something that you've written on your resume. If that's the case, you'll lose the opportunity before you ever get started.

RESUME STRATEGY #9: BE CONFIDENT

You are unique. There is only one individual with the specific combination of employment experience, qualifications, achievements, education, and technical qualifications that you have. In turn, this positions you as a unique commodity within the competitive job search market. To succeed, you must prepare a resume that is written to sell *you*, one that highlights *your* qualifications and *your* success. If you can accomplish this, you will have won the job search game by generating interest, interviews, and offers.

There Are No Resume-Writing Rules

One of the greatest challenges in resume writing is that there are no rules to the game. There are certain expectations about information that you will include: principally, your employment history and your educational qualifications. Beyond that, what you include is entirely up to you and what you have done in your career. What's more, you have tremendous flexibility in determining how to include the information you have selected. In chapter 2, you'll find a complete listing of each possible category you might include in your resume, the type of information that you should include in each, preferred formats for presentation, and sample text you can edit and use.

Although there are no rules, there are a few standards to live by as you write your resume. The following sections discuss these standards in detail.

CONTENT STANDARDS

Content is, of course, the text that goes into your resume. Content standards cover the writing style you should use, the items you should be sure to include, items you should avoid including, and the order and format in which you should list your qualifications.

Writing Style

Always write in the first person, dropping the word "I" from the front of each sentence. This style gives your resume a more aggressive and more professional tone than the passive third-person voice. Here are some examples:

First Person:

Manage 12-person team responsible for the global market launch of new OTC pharmaceuticals for Bayer's Consumer Division.

Third Person:

> Mr. Glenwood manages a 12-person team responsible for the global market launch of new OTC pharmaceuticals for Bayer's Consumer Division.

By using the first-person voice, you are assuming "ownership" of that statement. You did such-and-such. When you use the third-person, "someone else" did it. Can you see the difference?

Phrases to Stay Away From

Try *not* to use phrases such as "responsible for" or "duties included." These words create a passive tone and style. Instead, use active verbs to describe what you did.

Compare these two ways of conveying the same information:

> Duties included scheduling, job assignment, and management of over 200 health care workers, nurses, and medical assistants for a 152-bed chronic care and rehabilitation facility.

OR

> Revitalized and strengthened the entire human resource management function for a 152-bed chronic care and rehabilitation facility. Restructured staffing patterns and assignments impacting over 200 health care workers, nurses, and medical assistants. Facilitated a double-digit increase in productivity and performance.

Resume Style

The traditional **chronological** resume lists work experience in reverse-chronological order (starting with your current or most recent position). The **functional** style de-emphasizes the "where" and "when" of your career and instead groups similar experience, talents, and qualifications regardless of when they occurred.

Today, however, most resumes follow neither a strictly chronological nor strictly functional format; rather, they are an effective mixture of the two styles that is usually known as a "combination" or "hybrid" format.

Like the chronological format, the hybrid format includes specifics about where you worked, when you worked there, and what your job titles were. Like a functional resume, a hybrid emphasizes your most relevant qualifications—perhaps within chronological job descriptions, in an expanded summary section, in several "career highlights" bullet points at the top of your resume, or in achievement summaries. Most of the examples in this book are hybrids and show a wide diversity of organizational formats that you can use as inspiration for designing your own resume.

Resume Formats

Resumes, principally career summaries and job descriptions, are most often written in a paragraph format, a bulleted format, or a combination of both. Following are three job descriptions that are very similar in content yet presented in each of the three different writing formats. We also address the advantages and disadvantages of each format.

Paragraph Format

Physical Therapist
1996 to 2003

Albany Veterans Hospital, Albany, New York

Albany Memorial Hospital, Albany, New York

Crescent County Nursing Facility, Rochester, New York

Promoted through a series of increasingly responsible positions providing physical therapy to children, adults, and seniors. Advanced based on excellence in therapeutic diagnosis and intervention, case management, and patient relations. To date, managed and/or participated in the successful rehabilitation of more than 360 patients.

Highly effective in diagnosing and preparing treatment plans for patients living with neurological, degenerative, and geriatric orthopedic conditions, resulting in increased independence. Heavily involved with designing discharge plans and follow-up instructions.

Performed prosthetic training with amputee patients. Knowledge in E-STEM for wound healing and pain management, and with knee and hip replacement. Experience with technologies and techniques required for effective treatment of cardiac rehabilitation, sports injuries, and cervical and pelvic traction. Used ultrasound, gait belt training equipment, therabands, swimming pools, stretching exercises, and hot and cold packs.

Trained PTAs, CNAs, and family members in infection control, injury prevention, and proper rehabilitative care, including wheelchair positioning, proper use of exercise equipment, and methods to assist patients without affecting independence or self-confidence.

Trained/precepted newly hired physical therapists and therapy aides. Designed and led in-house training programs for the entire PT staff on new diagnostic and therapeutic procedures.

Advantages

Requires the least amount of space on the page. Brief, succinct, and to-the-point.

Disadvantages

Achievements get lost in the text of the multiple paragraphs. They are not visually distinctive, nor do they stand alone to draw attention to them.

Bulleted Format

Physical Therapist
1996 to 2003

Albany Veterans Hospital, Albany, New York

Albany Memorial Hospital, Albany, New York

Crescent County Nursing Facility, Rochester, New York

- Promoted through a series of increasingly responsible positions providing physical therapy to children, adults, and seniors. Advanced based on excellence in therapeutic diagnosis and intervention, case management, and patient relations. To date, managed and/or participated in the successful rehabilitation of more than 360 patients.

- Highly effective in diagnosing and preparing treatment plans for patients living with neurological, degenerative, and geriatric orthopedic conditions, resulting in increased independence. Heavily involved with designing discharge plans and follow-up instructions.

- Performed prosthetic training with amputee patients. Knowledge in E-STEM for wound healing and pain management, and with knee and hip replacement. Experience with technologies and techniques required for effective treatment of cardiac rehabilitation, sports injuries, and cervical and pelvic traction. Used ultrasound, gait belt training equipment, therabands, swimming pools, stretching exercises, and hot and cold packs.

- Trained PTAs, CNAs, and family members in infection control, injury prevention, and proper rehabilitative care, including wheelchair positioning, proper use of exercise equipment, and methods to assist patients without affecting independence or self-confidence.

- Trained/precepted newly hired physical therapists and therapy aides. Designed and led in-house training programs for the entire PT staff on new diagnostic and therapeutic procedures.

Advantages

Quick and easy to peruse.

Disadvantages

Responsibilities and achievements are lumped together with everything of equal value. In turn, the achievements get lost further down the list and are not immediately recognizable.

Combination Format

Physical Therapist
1996 to 2003

Albany Veterans Hospital, Albany, New York

Albany Memorial Hospital, Albany, New York

Crescent County Nursing Facility, Rochester, New York

Promoted through a series of increasingly responsible positions providing physical therapy to children, adults, and seniors. Advanced based on excellence in therapeutic diagnosis and intervention, case management, and patient relations. To date, managed and/or participated in the successful rehabilitation of more than 360 patients.

- Highly effective in diagnosing and preparing treatment plans for patients living with neurological, degenerative, and geriatric orthopedic conditions, resulting in increased independence. Heavily involved with designing discharge plans and follow-up instructions.

- Performed prosthetic training with amputee patients. Knowledge in E-STEM for wound healing and pain management, and with knee and hip replacement. Experience with technologies and techniques required for effective treatment of cardiac rehabilitation, sports injuries, and cervical and pelvic traction. Used ultrasound, gait belt training equipment, therabands, swimming pools, stretching exercises, and hot and cold packs.

- Trained PTAs, CNAs, and family members in infection control, injury prevention, and proper rehabilitative care, including wheelchair positioning, proper use of exercise equipment, and methods to assist patients without affecting independence or self-confidence.

- Trained/precepted newly hired physical therapists and therapy aides. Designed and led in-house training programs for the entire PT staff on new diagnostic and therapeutic procedures.

Advantages

Our recommended format. Clearly presents overall responsibilities in the introductory paragraph and then accentuates each achievement as a separate bullet.

Disadvantages

If you don't have clearly identifiable accomplishments, this format is not effective. It also might shine a glaring light on the positions in which your accomplishments were less notable.

E-Mail Address and URL

Be sure to include your e-mail address prominently at the top of your resume. As we all know, e-mail has become one of the most preferred methods of communication in job search.

We advise against using your e-mail address at your place of business on your resume. Not only does this present a negative impression to future employers, it will become useless after you make your next career move. And because your resume might exist in cyberspace long after you've completed your current job search, you don't want to direct interested parties to an obsolete e-mail address. Instead, obtain a private e-mail address that will be yours permanently. A free e-mail address from a provider such as Yahoo!, Hotmail, or NetZero is perfectly acceptable to use on your resume.

In addition to your e-mail address, if you have a URL (Web site) where you have posted your Web resume, be sure to also display that prominently at the top of your resume. For more information on Web resumes, refer to chapter 3.

PRESENTATION STANDARDS

Presentation regards the way your resume looks. It has to do with the fonts you use, the paper you print it on, any graphics you might include, and how many pages your resume should be.

Typestyle

Use a typestyle (font) that is clean, conservative, and easy to read. Stay away from anything that is too fancy, glitzy, curly, and the like. Here are a few recommended typestyles:

Tahoma	Times New Roman
Arial	Bookman
Krone	Book Antiqua
Soutane	Garamond
CG Omega	Century Schoolbook
Century Gothic	Lucida Sans
Gill Sans	Verdana

Although it is extremely popular, Times New Roman is our least preferred typestyle simply because it is overused. More than 90 percent of the resumes we see are typed in Times New Roman. Your goal is to create a competitive-distinctive document; to achieve that, we recommend an alternative typestyle.

Your choice of typestyle should be dictated by the content, format, and length of your resume. Some fonts look better than others at smaller or larger sizes; some have "bolder" boldface type; some require more white space to make them readable. After you've written your resume, experiment with a few different typestyles to see which one best enhances your document.

Type Size

Readability is everything! If the type size is too small, your resume will be difficult to read and difficult to skim for essential information. Interestingly, a too-large type size, particularly for senior-level professionals, can also give a negative impression by conveying a juvenile or unprofessional image.

As a general rule, select type from 10 to 12 points in size. However, there's no hard-and-fast rule, and a lot depends on the typestyle you choose. Take a look at the following examples:

Very readable in 9-point Verdana

Won the 2002 "Employee of the Year" award at Crest Hills Memorial Hospital. Honored for innovative contributions to cost reduction, patient care, and employee satisfaction.

Difficult to read in too-small 9-point Gill Sans

Won the 2002 "Employee of the Year" award at Crest Hills Memorial Hospital. Honored for innovative contributions to cost reduction, patient care, and employee satisfaction.

Concise and readable in 12-point Times New Roman

Senior Training & Development Manager specializing in the design, development, and presentation of training and orientation programs for health-care workers.

A bit overwhelming in too-large 12-point Bookman Old Style

Senior Training & Development Manager specializing in the design, development, and presentation of training and orientation programs for health-care workers.

Type Enhancements

Bold, *italics*, underlining, and CAPITALIZATION are ideal to highlight certain words, phrases, achievements, projects, numbers, and other information to which you want to draw special attention. However, do not overuse these enhancements. If your resume becomes too cluttered, nothing stands out.

> **NOTE:** Resumes intended for electronic transmission and computer scanning have specific restrictions on typestyle, type size, and type enhancements. We discuss these details in chapter 3.

Page Length

Our recommendation to the "average" job seeker is to keep his or her resume to one or two pages. The same is true for many professionals in the health care industry. Keep it short and succinct, giving just enough to catch your readers' interest. However, for others, particularly senior executives, doctors, surgeons, and other highly skilled medical practitioners, it can be difficult to include all the relevant information in just two pages. In situations like this, your health care career might simply warrant a longer resume, and that's okay!

In countless situations, we've prepared health care resumes that were multiple pages in length, anywhere from three to four to more than 15 pages (a longer resume is more commonly referred to as a *curriculum vitae*, hereinafter referred to as a *CV*). Let the amount of quality information you have to share be the determining factor in the length of your resume. Do *not* feel as though it must remain on two pages. All it really *must* do is attract prospective employers.

Here are some specific situations in which a resume might be longer than two pages:

- You are a physician, surgeon, or other highly degreed medical professional who is expected to submit a CV that includes all of your medical experience (professional positions, professional and hospital appointments, board appointments, internships, residencies, research, publications, presentations, grants, and so on), all of your educational credentials, your medical licenses, public-speaking engagements, honors and awards, scholarships and grants, professional affiliations, and more. A CV is really an entirely different type of document than a resume. You'll read much more about this in chapter 2.

- You have an extensive list of technical qualifications that are relevant to the position for which you are applying. (You can include these either on your resume or on a separate page as an addendum.)

- You have extensive educational training and numerous credentials/certifications, all of which are important to include. (You can include these either on your resume or on a separate page as an addendum.)

- You have an extensive list of special projects, task forces, and committees to include that are important to your current career objectives. (You can include these either on your resume or on a separate page as an addendum.)

- You have an extensive list of professional honors, awards, and commendations. This list is tremendously valuable in validating your credibility and distinguishing you from the competition.

- You have an extensive list of publications. Again, this list is extremely valuable in validating your credibility and distinguishing you from the competition. You must include it.

If you create a resume that's longer than two pages, make it more reader-friendly by carefully segmenting the information into separate sections. For instance, begin with your career summary and your work experience. This will most likely take one or two pages. Then follow with education, any professional or industry credentials, honors and awards, technology and equipment skills, publications, public-speaking engagements, professional memberships, civic memberships, technology skills, volunteer experience, multiple language skills, and other relevant information you want to include. Put each into a separate category so that your resume is easy to peruse and your reader can quickly see the highlights. You'll read more about each of these sections in chapter 2.

Paper Color

Be conservative. White, ivory, light blue, or light gray are ideal. Other "flashier" colors are inappropriate for individuals in the health care industry.

Graphics

For entry-level or mid-level health care positions, an attractive, relevant graphic can enhance your resume. When you look through the sample resumes in chapters 4 through 12, you'll see some excellent examples of the effective use of graphics to enhance your resume's visual presentation. Just be sure not to get carried away; be tasteful and relatively conservative.

For those of you at the senior management or executive level, we do not recommend graphics on your resume. Clean, crisp, and conservative is our motto for resumes at this level.

White Space

We'll say it again: Readability is everything! If people have to struggle to read your resume, they simply won't make the effort. Therefore, be sure to leave plenty of white space. It really does make a difference.

ACCURACY AND PERFECTION

The very final step, and one of the most critical in resume writing, is the proof-reading stage. It is essential that your resume be well written, visually pleasing, and free of any errors, typographical mistakes, misspellings, and the like. We recommend that you carefully proofread your resume a minimum of three times, and then have two or three other people also proofread it. Consider your resume an example of the quality of work you will produce on a company's behalf. Is your work product going to have errors and inconsistencies? If your resume does, it communicates to a prospective employer that you are careless, and this is the "kiss of death" in job search.

Take the time to make sure that your resume is perfect in all the little details that do, in fact, make a big difference to those who read it.

CHAPTER 2

Writing Your Resume

For many health care professionals, resume writing is *not* at the top of the list of fun and exciting activities! How can it compare to saving a person's life, discovering a cure for a disease that has plagued the human race, or improving the quality of care delivered to thousands of patients each year? It can't!

However, resume writing can be an enjoyable and rewarding task. When your resume is complete, you can look at it proudly, reminding yourself of all that you have achieved. It is a snapshot of your career and your success. When it's complete, we guarantee you'll look back with tremendous self-satisfaction as you launch and successfully manage your job search.

The very first step in finding a new position or advancing your career, resume writing can be the most daunting of all tasks in your job search. If writing is not one of your primary job functions, it might have been years since you've actually sat down and written anything other than notes to yourself. Even for those of you who write on a regular basis, resume writing is unique. It has its own style and a number of peculiarities, as with any specialty document.

Therefore, to make the writing process easier, more finite, and more efficient, we've consolidated it into four discrete sections:

- **Career Summary.** Think of your Career Summary as the "head" of your resume. It is the accumulation of everything that you know and everything that you are.

- **Professional Experience.** Professional Experience is the "backbone" of your resume. It is all the finite pieces that, when "stacked" together, create the whole of who you are.

- **Education, Licenses, and Certifications.** Think of this section as the "bones," giving your resume structure and integrity. These third-party validations attest to the quality of your qualifications, knowledge, and expertise.

- **The "Extras."** These extra sections can include Hospital Affiliations, Board Affiliations, Professional Appointments, Publications, Public Speaking, Honors and Awards, Technology Qualifications, Training and Public Speaking, Professional Affiliations, Civic Affiliations, Research Projects, Foreign Languages, Personal Information, and so on. You can think of these as facial features that give each resume its distinctive flair. These items further validate your experience and help you stand out from the crowd of other applicants.

Making the Right Choice: Resume or Curriculum Vitae (CV)

Before you start writing your resume, you have to determine whether a resume or a CV is the right document for you. As discussed in chapter 1, certain health care professionals—such as physicians, surgeons, dentists, and other highly degreed medical professionals—are expected to submit a CV in certain circumstances (generally for hospital, university, and other "institutional" positions).

A CV is a much longer document than a resume. It includes a comprehensive listing of the following:

- Medical experience (professional positions, internships, residences, and more)
- Professional appointments (generally, hospital or academic)
- Professional, board, and hospital affiliations (including leadership positions)
- Medical degrees, licenses, and other educational credentials
- Publications (books, papers, abstracts, conference proceedings, and more)
- Professional presentations (keynotes, lectures, seminars, and more)
- Research projects
- Honors and awards (professional, medical, academic, and others)
- Scholarships and grants

A good rule of thumb to determine whether you should prepare a resume or CV is the following:

- Prepare a CV if your best "marketing tool" is a conservative document that lists *all* of your medical experience and credentials.
- Prepare a resume if your best "marketing tool" is a document that sells the *highlights* of your career in a more succinct presentation than a CV.

A CV is most often the right tool in circumstances such as these:

- You're applying for a position on the teaching faculty at a prominent university.

- You're applying for a position as a Chief of Medicine at a large city hospital.

- You're pursuing a medical research position.

- You're a nurse seeking a role with a clinical study.

On the other hand, you will most likely use a resume if

- You are applying for a medical position in a private health care practice.

- Your professional focus has shifted from direct health care to business performance—for instance, if you are a surgeon seeking a position as CEO of a hospital.

- You are an allied health technologist or technician, pharmacist, or health care administrator or manager.

If you're a recent medical graduate, base your decision on the type of position you are seeking and the type of medical environment in which you work.

Use the following chart as your guide to determine which document is right for you. (Chart reprinted with the permission of Hal Flantzer, Career Planning Resources, Kew Gardens, NY.) And keep in mind, as the distinction between resume and CV continues to blur, the best solution might be a "hybrid"—a CV that is enhanced by a few resume elements. You can see examples of hybrids on pages 72–73 and 77–78.

Topic/Area	Resumes	CVs
Accomplishments?	State accomplishments and transferable skills that pertain to your job target.	**Avoid** stating accomplishments—use credentials and selectively use headings that will showcase the attractive features of your work. CVs are based more on credentials than performance.
Education?	Usually used as an adjunct to a work history and, except for recent graduates, is placed at the end. Dates of degrees might or might not be stated.	**An essential feature of the CV:** Degrees and credentials must be described in detail, and dates of degrees should *always* be stated.
Chronology?	**Important!** Experience should always be in reverse-chronological order with all time covered. One chronology per resume is almost always the rule.	Experience should be in reverse-chronological order, but there might be chronologies for various headings; therefore, time coverage is not quite as important as on a resume.
Appearance and Length?	**Important!** The first page must grab the reader's attention, and the most important information should be found and read in *ten seconds flat!* Hardly ever longer than two pages.	**Important!** The first page must grab the reader's attention, but it should also entice him/her to spend time reading it through. Depending on experience, it can be much longer than two pages.
How Useful for Career Changers?	**Quite useful:** A resume allows for the flexibility to adapt your skills to new career tracks using a functional or a reverse-chronological format.	**Not very useful:** Although headings can be arranged to somewhat direct the information to a different career track, a CV is predicated upon formal education that is applicable to your job target.
Summary Statement ("Job Objective")?	**A summary statement is often used,** informing the employer of what your target is and what you have to offer in terms of skills that are attractive to the employer, as well as accomplishments.	**A summary statement is never used.** Education is always listed just below the name and address. Occasionally, a job objective is used, but only if the goal is different than an employer would expect.
Headings?	A more or less standard set of ordered headings, with several optional headings available.	A standard set of headings, with some variance in the order, and with more optional ones available to allow for a more individualized and tailored document.

Step-by-Step: Writing the Perfect Resume and CV

In the preceding section, we outlined the four core resume sections. Now, we'll detail the particulars of each section—what to include, where to include it, and how to include it.

CONTACT INFORMATION

Before we start, let's briefly address the very top section of your resume: your name and contact information.

Name

You'd think writing your name would be the easiest part of writing your resume! But there are several factors you might want to consider:

- Although most people choose to use their full, formal name at the top of a resume, it has become increasingly more acceptable to use the name by which you prefer to be called.

- Bear in mind that it's to your advantage to have readers feel comfortable calling you for an interview. Their comfort level might decrease if your name is gender-neutral, difficult to pronounce, or very unusual; they don't know who they're calling (a man or a woman) or how to ask for you. Here are a few ways you can make it easier for them:

> Lynn T. Cowles (Mr.)
>
> (Ms.) Michael Murray
>
> Tzirina (Irene) Kahn
>
> Ndege "Nick" Vernon

Address

You should always include your home address on your resume. If you use a post office box for mail, include both your mailing address and your physical residence address.

Telephone Number(s)

You should include your home telephone number. If you're at work during the day, when you can expect to receive most calls, consider including a work phone number (if it's a direct line and you can receive calls discreetly). Or, you can include a mobile phone number (refer to it as "mobile" rather than "cellular") or a pager number (however, this is less desirable because you must call back to speak to the person who called you). You can include a private home fax number (if it can be accessed automatically), but do not include your work fax number. *Never* include your employer's toll-free number. This communicates the message that you are using your employer's resources and budget to support your own personal job search campaign. Not a wise idea!

E-mail Address

Without question, if you have a private e-mail address, include it on your resume. E-mail is now often the preferred method of communication in job search, particularly in the early stages of each contact. Do not use your employer's e-mail address, even if you access e-mail through your work computer. Instead, obtain a free, accessible-anywhere address from a provider such as Yahoo!, Hotmail, or NetZero.

As you look through the samples in this book, you'll see how resume writers have arranged the many bits of contact information at the top of each resume. You can use these as models for presenting your own information. The point is to make it as easy as possible for employers to contact you!

Now, let's get to the nitty-gritty of the four core content sections of your resume.

CAREER SUMMARY

The Career Summary is the section at the top of your resume that summarizes and highlights your knowledge and expertise.

You might be thinking, "But shouldn't my resume start with an Objective?" Although many job seekers still use Objective statements, we believe that a Career Summary is a much more powerful introduction. The problem with Objectives is that they are either too specific (limiting you to a "pediatric nursing position") or too vague (doesn't everyone want "a challenging opportunity with a progressive organization offering the opportunity for growth and advancement"?). In addition, Objective statements can be read as self-serving because they describe what *you* want instead of suggesting what you have to offer an employer.

In contrast, an effective Career Summary allows you to position yourself as you want to be perceived and immediately "paint a picture" of yourself as it relates to your career goals. It is critical that this section focus on the specific skills, qualifications, and achievements of your career that are related to your current objectives. Your summary is *not* a historical overview of your career. Rather, it is a concise, well-written, and sharp presentation of information designed to *sell* you into your next position.

This section can have various titles, such as the following:

Career Summary	Management Profile
Career Achievements	Professional Qualifications
Career Highlights	Professional Summary
Career Synopsis	Profile
Executive Profile	Summary
Expertise	Summary of Achievements
Highlights of Experience	Summary of Qualifications

Or, as you will see in the first example format that follows (Headline Format), your summary does not have to have any title at all.

Here are five sample Career Summaries. Consider using one of these as the template for developing your Career Summary, or use them as the foundation to create your own presentation. You will also find some type of Career Summary in just about every resume included in this book.

Headline Format

NURSE MANAGER ▶ CASE MANAGER ▶ DIRECTOR OF NURSING

15+ Years' Experience in Inpatient & Outpatient Settings

Skilled Project Manager, Team Builder & Staff Trainer

Expertise in Patient, Nurse & Physician Relations

Paragraph Format

CAREER SUMMARY

BIOMEDICAL INSTRUMENT TECHNICIAN with 10+ years' progressive experience. Precision craftsmanship applied throughout design, engineering, production, and repair of sophisticated devices and instrumentation. Set new benchmarks for quality, efficiency, and productivity. Considered a solid communicator—a first point of contact for technical troubleshooting and customer support.

Core Competencies Summary Format

MEDICAL TECHNOLOGIST

AMT-Certified Medical Laboratory Technologist with experience in histopathology, microbiology, chemistry, serology/immunology, hematology, phlebotomy, blood banking, and microscopy. Able to work calmly and accurately under pressure. Team-oriented with strong interpersonal skills. Well-developed troubleshooting ability. Equipment experience includes:

☑ Clinical laboratory analyzers	☑ Cell counters
☑ Automatic staining consoles	☑ Cell washers
☑ Blood gas analyzers	☑ Cryostats
☑ Tissue processors	☑ Sonicators
☑ Microscopes	☑ Centrifuges

Eisenhower Quality Award, Eisenhower Hospital, 2002
Technologist of the Year, Eisenhower Hospital, 2001

Bullet List Format

PROFESSIONAL QUALIFICATIONS

Health Trainer / Coach / Program Developer

- **Certified health trainer & coach** delivering customized training to public/private businesses to help meet employee health challenges. Effectively train diverse audiences on health topics, facilitate practical goal-setting and solutions, and address both mental and physical limitations and challenges.

- **Training specializations** include communication, one-on-one and group problem-solving, goal setting and achievement, conflict resolution, life skills and coaching, psychological and physical ergonomics, stress management, wellness, and occupational therapy.

- **Teaching style** integrates auditory, visual, and tactile learning with holistic, mind-body-spirit connection.

- **Creative program developer** with a passion for out-of-the-box thinking and motivation through personal empowerment. Blend health and metaphysical therapies with coaching and training. Skillfully coach toward acceptance of meaningful choice and change. Enthusiastic, high-energy, and intuition-based leader.

Category Format

Professional Career Highlights

Experience	**Clinical Pharmacist** with 15 years of experience managing large-scale, hospital-based pharmacy operations.
Education	**Doctor of Pharmacy**—Rutgers University **BS Microbiology**—University of Pennsylvania
Licensure	Licensed in New Jersey and California.
Publications	"Evaluating & Identifying the Effects of Asthma," *Annals of Asthma & Immunology*, 2001. "How to Use Claims Database to Document Cost Centers," *Archives of Asthma Medicine*, 1999.
Presentations	ABC's BreathRightPrograms: Outcomes Measurement & Tracking, 2003. BreathRight: The Diversified Process, 2001. Treating Asthma Today, American Medical Association Annual Symposium on Asthma, 2000.

PROFESSIONAL EXPERIENCE

Your Professional Experience section is the meat of your resume—the "backbone," as we discussed before. It's what gives your resume substance, meaning, and depth. It is also the section that will take you the longest to write. If you've had the same position for 10 years, how can you consolidate all that you have done into one short section? If, on the opposite end of the spectrum, you have had your current position for only 11 months, how can you make it seem substantial and noteworthy? And, if your experience is somewhere in between, what do you include, how, where, and why?

These are not easy questions to answer. In fact, the most truthful response to each question is, "it depends." It depends on you, your experience, your achievements and successes, and your current career objectives.

Here are seven samples of Professional Experience sections. Review how each individual's unique background is organized and emphasized, and consider your own background when using one of these as the template or foundation for developing your Professional Experience section.

Achievement Format

Emphasizes each position, overall scope of responsibility, and resulting achievements.

PROFESSIONAL EXPERIENCE

Multi-Site Operations Manager (1998 to Present)   <u>VETERANS ADMINISTRATION</u>, Washington, D.C.

Recruited to lead the revitalization and growth of Veterans healthcare service options by integrating eight autonomous facilities into a network that includes eight hospitals, 30+ community clinics, and several medical-school affiliations in six states. Work in cooperation with hospital administrators, financial executives, government agencies, legislators, and policymakers to propel innovative managed-care programs to service 1+ million veterans annually. Direct a management team of 15 with overall responsibility for 7000+ corporate, medical, and support staff.

Achievements:

- ✓ Integrated all database systems and standard operating procedures throughout the network, and reduced laboratory costs by $15 million annually.

- ✓ Saved over $6 million by reducing contract staff, standardizing commodities, and facilitating group equipment purchases.

- ✓ Cut administrative overhead nearly 13% in three years; redirected $65+ million to patient care.

- ✓ Championed development of the most sophisticated telemedicine system in the country and opened 25 community-based clinics. Generated nearly $50 million in revenues, exceeding targets 25% despite double-digit increases in medical-care costs.

- ✓ Achieved national distinction among 22 Veterans Administration networks by being the first of only two networks to gain NCQA accreditation.

Challenge, Action, and Results (CAR) Format

Emphasizes the challenges of each position, the actions you took, and the results you delivered.

Professional Experience

Vocational Rehabilitation Counselor (2001 to Present)

JACOBS PSYCHIATRIC INSTITUTE, York, PA

Challenge: **Consumers entered treatment because of highly stressful jobs.**

     Action: **Arranged Family Medical Leave and disability benefits with employers, and negotiated accommodations under the Americans with Disabilities Act (ADA) for transfer to a less stressful position.**

     Results: **Consumers were able to leave treatment and enter a less stressful environment. Achieved/maintained a less-than-5% relapse rate.**

Challenge: **Consumers with erratic work records and/or criminal history had problems finding employment and explaining work gaps.**

     Action: **Worked with state agencies to identify employers who were willing to hire such people and provided job coaching during the first months of employment.**

     Results: **Achieved/maintained a less-than-15% relapse rate.**

Challenge: **Consumers did not have appropriate clothes for interviewing and working.**

     Action: **Organized "dress for success" clothing store, collected used professional clothes from hospital employees and the greater York business community, and provided several free outfits to each consumer active in a job search.**

     Results: **Consumers were able to present a professional image during interviews and at work.**

Functional Format

Emphasizes the functional areas of responsibility within the job and associated achievements.

EXPERIENCE AND ACHIEVEMENTS

LOURDES HOSPITAL, Framingham, Massachusetts

■ **Director of Nursing—Women & Family Services**   1999 to Present

Provide vision, strategic direction, and leadership for 5 nursing departments, 120 staff members in Labor and Delivery, Mother-Baby, Neonatal ICU, Pediatrics, and Perinatal Education. Manage $16M annual operating budget and $1M capital budget. Exceeded all financial, service delivery, and quality goals for 5 consecutive years.

- **New Hospital Design/Development**—Key member of 5-person project team leading the design and development of a new hospital. Responsible for vision and long-range planning including budgeting, financial and staffing projections, occupancy projections, physical design and space layout, and introduction of innovative care protocols. Incorporated Disney Onstage model to create a family-centered and developmentally supportive environment.

- **Healthcare Innovation**—First in the country to design and construct neonatal suites to accommodate critically ill infants and parents. Unit allows individualized infant care, developmentally supportive care, and consideration for family needs and circumstances in the NICU.

- **New Nursing Management Model**—Blended 5 separate departments into one and cross-trained 120 nursing staff to care for different types of patients. Ranked above the 85th percentile on the Jackson Patient Satisfaction Survey for 18 consecutive quarters.

- **International Nursing Training**—Traveled worldwide to teach leading-edge nursing management systems in impoverished nations. Coordinated development of Neonatal Resuscitation Program in Tajikistan, primary nursing care programs in Kiev and Armenia, a fetal monitoring curriculum in Mexico, and an HIV prevention program in the Ukraine.

Career-Track Format

Emphasizes fast-track promotion, overall scope of responsibility, and notable achievements.

CAREER HISTORY

CHARLOTTE EMERGENCY MEDICAL SERVICES, Dayton, OH   1989 to Present

EMT Paramedic/Operations Supervisor (1998 to Present)
Paramedic Crew Chief/Relief Supervisor (1996 to 1998)
Crew Chief (1992 to 1996)
Paramedic (1989 to 1992)

Promoted through a series of increasingly responsible assignments to current position directing field operations and coordinating emergency personnel and resources in a 542-square-mile region with 650,000 residents. Manage interagency disaster control involving multiple-casualty incidents, entrapment, rescue, and triage.

Scope of responsibility is diverse and includes all staffing functions (60 employees), employee services (benefits and compensation), budgeting, media affairs, and fleet repair and maintenance (36 vehicles).

- ▶ **Directed** staff and resources that responded to more than 2000 emergency calls in 2002, 1850 in 2001, and 2200+ in 2000. Maintained a better-than-90% survival rate in situations where the injured were still alive when emergency crews arrived on the scene.

- ▶ **Developed** system for monitoring daily attendance and reduced absenteeism by 20%.

- ▶ **Chaired** 3-person management team that established guidelines for newly created Charlotte-Dade *Advanced Local Emergency Response Team* (ALERT), the nation's first unit providing emergency service response to a terrorist incident involving a weapon of mass destruction.

- ▶ **Co-chaired** Benefits and Compensation Committee that consolidated benefits providers for 200+ employees from 8 to 3 vendors while improving services. Helped design 401(k) plan.

- ▶ **Awarded** Certificate of Recognition from the International Association of Bomb Technicians and Investigators for sharing expertise and providing contributions to the program.

- ▶ **Received** the American Ambulance Association (AAA) "Star of Life" award in 1999 for leadership in developing EMT-D training program.

Project Highlights Format

Places emphasis on specific projects, their scope of responsibility, and their associated achievements.

NURSE REVIEWER   **QUALCARE, INC.** *(healthcare accreditation firm)*
(March 2000 to Present)   Yonkers, NY

Field position with multiple long- and short-term assignments. Audit, examine, and verify medical records and monitor practice sites to ensure documentation accuracy and compliance with standard medical practices and criteria. Conduct an average of 15–18 on-site appointments weekly at medical clinics, hospitals, health plans, and physicians' offices. Review 40–70 charts and complete 3–4 practice site reviews daily. Recent projects include:

- **BlueKey Health Plan.** Performed HEDIS effectiveness of care audits, Medicaid audits, and Healthy Start Initiative and follow-up visit tracking. Practice compliance audits involved medical record reviews for specific disease conditions and/or routine care, including diabetes food, eye, and blood work status; asthma management; immunizations; OB-GYN well visits; and OB care. ***Results: Achieved/maintained a better-than-90% audit accuracy rating.***

- **Americaid.** Conducted medical record documentation reviews and practice site reviews for medical standards and credentialing. ***Results: Facilitated a double-digit increase in the accuracy, thoroughness, and regulatory compliance of all medical documentation.***

- **American Medical Accreditation Program (AMAP)**—Iowa foundation for medical care information system. Performed environment-of-care data collection for the New Jersey Medical Society. Performed medical record review and site assessment to determine clinical performance based on requisite standards and criteria. ***Results: Established nationwide model for environment-of-care audit reviews.***

Skills-Based Format

Puts initial focus on specific skills rather than where and when they were used. Helpful in bringing less-current skill sets to the forefront and avoiding emphasis on employment gaps.

Clinical Laboratory Scientist
Marquette General Health System, Marquette, MI   2000 to Present

Member of the largest laboratory in the Upper Peninsula, serving as the main reference facility for other laboratories and clinics in the Upper Peninsula, Northern Michigan, and Northern Wisconsin. Focus on providing clients and patients with superb customer service and the highest quality of comprehensive and state-of-the-art laboratory services. Technical expertise includes:

Molecular Science: Operate the PCR laboratory, process test specimens required for polymerase chain reaction (PCR) procedures, and train lab technicians in all phases of PCR processing.

☑ *Procedures:* Mitochondrial DNA: Sequenced MtDNA and extracted MtDNS from hair, blood, and other samples ... HCV Genotyping and MTB Genotyping

☑ *Test & Equipment:* Perkin Elmer Genescan 310 Analyzer ... 9600 & 2400 Thermocyclers ... Bio-Rad GS Gene Linker ... Singularity RFLP Analyzer Test (Proscan) ... Amplicor HIV Detection Kit ... UCLA HIV Detection Procedure ... Amplicor Chlamydia Detection Kit ... Cobas ... Perkin Elmer AmpFL STR Profiler Unit ... Promega Gene Print STR System ... Print Light Chemiluminescent Detection System ... MTB Detection by Restriction Enzyme Analysis ... 7700 Sequence Detection System.

Core Lab: Performed routine medical laboratory procedures prior to promotion to Molecular Laboratory position.

☑ *Tests & Equipment:* Urines ... Coag (MLA) ... Hematology (Coulter S+4, Technicon H-1) ... Chemistry (SMA-24, Hitachi, Astra, ACA) ... Drug Screens (Syva, Tecan) ... Blood Bank.

☑ *Microbiology:* Read Plates ... Bactec 260 ... Bactec 860 ... Read Viral Cell Cultures ... Baxter Walk-Away ... Mycology ... Mycobacteriology.

Experience Format

Briefly emphasizes specific highlights of each position. This format is best used in conjunction with a detailed Career Summary.

EXPERIENCE SUMMARY

2001 to Present

INFUSION CARE ASSOCIATES—Seattle, Washington
Nurse Liaison

- Promoted to implement new patient management system, coordinating the flow of information from the discharge nurse at area hospitals to ease the transition from hospital to home health settings.

- Orchestrate the delivery of medications and equipment to the discharge area; internally convey medical information between the pharmacy, office manager, nurse manager, and case managers as necessary.

- Teach patients and home care givers in medical pump or intravenous techniques, troubleshooting, and maintenance.

1998 to 2001

HOME RESPECT HEALTH—Redmond, Washington
Infusion RN

- Initially assigned to home healthcare with responsibility for new mom/ new baby visits, wound care, lab draws, TPN, and in-home chemotherapy. Progressed to infusion care within one year.

- Managed a portfolio of patients, providing them with training in various infusion issues including medication pump usage, troubleshooting, maintenance, and sanitation.

- Ensured that physicians' primary orders were carried out; acted as the first-tier support for medical issues.

1994 to 1998

CARE CENTERS—Sherwood, Washington
Infusion RN

- Completed six-week orientation in infusion protocols for working with central venous lines and line management. Certified in administering chemotherapy, antibiotics, TPN, and pain management.

- Provided patient care from post-op through an average of three days in home settings.

- Consistently praised in evaluations for patient care, reliability, and communication skills.

EDUCATION, CREDENTIALS, AND CERTIFICATIONS

Your Education section should include college, certifications, credentials, licenses, registrations, and continuing education. If you're preparing a CV, you'll want to be sure to include *all* of this information. If you're preparing a resume, you might include it all, or you might just summarize certain items if your list is particularly long. The following sample formats demonstrate how you can do this.

If any of your educational credentials are particularly notable, be sure to highlight them prominently in your Education section or bring them to the top of the resume in your Career Summary (as demonstrated by the Headline format in the preceding section).

Here are six sample Education sections that illustrate a variety of ways to organize and format this information.

Medical Education Format

Medical Education

Medical College of New York	**Doctor of Medicine** (1992)
University of New York	**Master of Public Health** (1987)
University of New York	**Bachelor of Arts** (1985)

Certifications

Board Certified, American Board of Family Practice
Certified Medical Review Officer
Certified Independent Medical Examiner
Certified Ergonomics Specialist
Diploma, American Academy of Pain Management

Licensure

Doctor of Medicine (MD)—Pennsylvania

Executive Education Format

EDUCATION

Executive Development Program	STANFORD UNIVERSITY
Executive Development Program	UNIVERSITY OF CALIFORNIA AT LOS ANGELES
Master of Business Administration (MBA) Degree	UNIVERSITY OF CALIFORNIA AT LOS ANGELES
Bachelor of Science Degree	UNIVERSITY OF CALIFORNIA AT IRVINE

Academic Credentials Format

Education

B.S.N., **Management Science,** Southern Illinois University, 2002

L.P.N., Sanford-Brown College, 1998

ACLS & BCLS Certified, 1998 to Present

Recent Continuing Professional Education

- Improving Quality of Care, Illinois Nursing Association, 2003
- Leading-Edge Case Management Methodologies for Senior Nursing Staff, Purdue University, 2002
- Quality Control in the Operating Room, OR Nurses Association–Illinois State Chapter, 2002
- Advances in Oncological Care, American Nurses Association, 2001

Technical Certifications

- **Certified in Cardiovascular-Interventional Radiology,** AART, 2002
- **Certified in Radiology,** AART, 2000
- **Certified in Peripheral Angiography,** Kettering School of Medicine, 2000
- **Certified in Cardiac Angiography,** Kettering School of Medicine, 2000

Non-Degree Format

TRAINING & EDUCATION

——**UNIVERSITY OF WISCONSIN,** Milwaukee, Wisconsin
BS Candidate—Healthcare Administration *(Senior Class Status)*—2000 to 2002

——**EDMONTON UNIVERSITY,** Reno, Nevada
Dual Majors in Management & Healthcare Administration—1997 to 1999

——**Graduate,** 100+ hours of continuing professional education through the University of Illinois, University of Michigan, and University of Wisconsin. Topics include Healthcare Administration, JCAHO Regulations & Reporting, Patient Care Management, Hospice Programming, and Claims Administration.

No-College Format

PROFESSIONAL DEVELOPMENT	
Communication Skills for the Manager	CONWAY COMMUNITY COLLEGE
Recordkeeping & Administration	CONWAY COMMUNITY COLLEGE
Healthcare Reporting	LEXIS JUNIOR COLLEGE
Basic Laboratory Procedures	CONWAY COMMUNITY COLLEGE

THE "EXTRAS"

The primary focus of your resume is on information (most likely, your professional experience and academic credentials) that is directly related to your career goals. However, you also should include things that will distinguish you from other candidates and clearly demonstrate your value to a prospective employer. And, not too surprisingly, it is often the "extras" that get the interviews.

Following is a list of the other categories you might or might not include in your resume depending on your particular experience and your current career objectives. Review the information. If it's pertinent to you, use the samples for formatting your own data. Remember, however, that if something is truly impressive, you might want to include it in your Career Summary at the beginning of your resume in order to draw even more attention to it. If you do this, it's not necessary to repeat the information at the end of your resume.

Honors and Awards

If you have won honors and awards, you can either include them in a separate section on your resume or integrate them into the Education or Professional Experience section, whichever is most appropriate. If you choose to include them in a separate section, consider this format:

▶ **Nurse Manager of the Year,** Biomax Medical Center, Ames, Iowa, 2002

▶ **Nurse Trainer of the Year,** Biomax Medical Center, Ames, Iowa, 2000

▶ **YMCA Distinguished Leader Award,** Ames, Iowa, 1999

▶ **Mayor's Civic Contribution Award,** Moline, Iowa, 1998

▶ **Summa Cum Laude Graduate,** University of Iowa Nursing School, 1989

Public Speaking

Experts are the ones who are invited to give public presentations at conferences, seminars, workshops, training programs, symposia, and other events. So if you have public speaking experience, others must consider you an expert. Be sure to include this very complimentary information in your resume. Here's one way to present it:

➤ Keynote Speaker, **"Hand-Arm Syndrome,"** Utah Self-Insurer's Association (May 2002)

➤ Keynote Speaker, **"The Therapist's Role in Disability Resolution,"** Mecklenburg Rehab Systems (January 2002)

➤ Panel Presenter, **"Health & Safety Effects for Shift Workers,"** Dermark Safety Leadership Committee (February 2001)

➤ Keynote Speaker, **"Guide to Disability Resolution,"** Knox Power WC Claims Reserve Conference (June 2000)

➤ Speaker, **"How to Overcome Chronic Pain Syndrome,"** Englewood Medical Association Annual Conference (May 1999)

Research and Publications

Research and publications, particularly in the medical field, are almost essential. When you review the qualifications of most top-level medical researchers, professors, and practitioners, almost all are published and have significant research projects to their names. As such, this is an essential component for any resume or CV in the health care industry. If you're a medical practitioner, it might be that your articles have been published in scholarly annals or that you've authored abstracts or conference proceedings. If you're a health care administrator, perhaps you've authored health care policy training manuals or articles for the American Management Association. If you're a nurse, maybe you've written journal articles or nursing procedures.

Regardless of the specific type of project or document, research and publications further validate your knowledge, qualifications, and credibility. Here's an example:

PUBLICATIONS

— *Ovarian Cancer with Minimal Residual Disease at Assessment Laparotomies Treated with Intraperitoneal Therapies in Southwest Oncology Group Study S8372.* Johnson, R., Lester, P., Cote, M., Robertson, D. <u>Southwest Oncology Group</u>, 2002.

— *Results from a Randomized Phase III Study Comparing Combined Treatment with Histamine Dihydrochloride Plus Interleukin-2 Versus Interleukin-2 Alone in Patients with Metastic Melanoma.* Arnold, R., Smith, R., Smith, T., McCoy, L., Salmin, A. <u>Journal of Clinical Oncology</u>, 20(6): 1431-1456, March 2002.

— *Liposome-Encapsulated Doxorubicin Compared with Conventional Doxorubicin in a Randomized Multicenter Trial As First-Line Therapy of Metastic Breast Carcinoma.* Harris, L., Mitchell, D., Logan, R., Meyerson, S. <u>Cancer</u>, 94(1), 25–36, July 2001.

RESEARCH PROJECTS

— Principal Investigator, *"A Randomized, Double-Blind, Placebo-Controlled, Parallel-Group, Dose-Finding Study, Conducted Under In-House Blinding Conditions to Examine the Safety, Tolerability, and Efficacy of MK-08690 for the Prevention of Acute and Delayed Chemotherapy-Induced Emesis Associated with High-Dose Cisplatin."* Protocol No. 040-00. Merck & Co., Inc.

— Principal Investigator, *"Phase III Randomized Study of RFS 2000 (9-Nitro-Camtothecin, 9-NC) Versus Gemcitabine HCI in Chemonaive Pancreatic Cancer in Patients."* Protocol No. RFS 2000-02. SuperGen, Inc.

— Research Study Team Member, *"A Double-Blind Investigation of the Physiological and Psychological Impact of Double-Dose Thorazine Administration in Dually Diagnosed Schizophrenics."* Protocol No. 89-392. SuperGen, Inc.

Technology Equipment and Instrumentation

If you are an administrator of a health care facility, a nurse, a medical assistant, or have held other types of hands-on care provider positions, chances are likely that you'll just include a brief statement in your Career Summary that communicates that you are PC proficient. For example:

PC proficient with Microsoft Word, Access, Excel, and PowerPoint.

If you're employed in a technology-related position in the health care field, however, you'll want to include a separate section with this information (if it's relevant to your current career objectives). You'll also have to consider placement of this section in your resume. If the positions for which you are applying require strong technical skills, we recommend that you insert this section immediately after your Career Summary (or as a part of it). If, on the other hand, your technical skills are more of a plus than a specific requirement, the preferred placement is after your Education section.

Here's an example of one way to format your technology qualifications:

Proficient in the use of:	• A Scans • Slit Lamp • Visual Fields • Tonometry	• Lasers • Lensometry • Topography • Keratometer
Proficient in the diagnosis of:	• Chalazion Surgery • Conjunctivitis • Macular Degeneration • Strabismus	• Glaucoma Treatments • Retinography of Prematurity • NLD Obstruction • Blepharoplasty

Teaching and Training Experience

Many health care professionals also teach or train at colleges, universities, medical schools, and other organizations and institutions, in addition to training that they might offer "on the job." If this is applicable to you, you will want to include that experience on your resume. Here's a format you might use to present the information:

Teaching & Training Experience

▶ **Professor,** Medical School, Morgan State University, 1998 to Present. Teach Advanced Biology, Cell Biology, and Genetics to first- and second-year medical students.

▶ **Adjunct Professor,** Medical School, Clark State University, 1994 to 1999. Taught Advanced Diagnostic Procedures to third-year medical students.

▶ **Medical Trainer,** Clarkson Community Hospital, 2002 to Present. Teach Patient and Management Strategies to medical students from five area medical colleges rotating through the hospital.

▶ **Guest Lecturer,** Health Administration Department, Duke University, 1999 to 2001. Provided semi-annual, day-long lecture series on the integration of patient-centric procedures into a large city medical center.

▶ **Part-Time Lecturer,** Maryland State University, 1997 to 1999. Taught "Principles of Healthcare Administration" to second-year college students.

Committees and Task Forces

Many health care professionals serve on committees, task forces, and other special project teams either as part of, or in addition to, their full-time responsibilities. Again, this type of information further strengthens your credibility, qualifications, and perceived value to a prospective employer. To present this information, consider a format such as the following:

Professional Activities

- ❑ **Computer Advisory Committee, Meridian Health Systems,** 2001 to 2002 *(recommended technological advances, negotiated with vendors, and strategically planned computer network implementation)*

- ❑ **Executive Committee, Meridian Health Systems,** 1998 to 2002 *(member of 8-person senior executive committee directing all operations of 343-bed community hospital)*

- ❑ **Surgical Advisor, Qualcare PPO,** 1997 to 1998 *(top advisor to team of 45 surgeons through a 3-state PPO network)*

- ❑ **Capital Budget Committee, Meridian Medical Center,** 1997 to 1998 *(guided planning and allocation of $250+ million annual operating budget)*

- ❑ **Operating Room Committee Chairman, Meridian Medical Center,** 1994 to 1998 *(managed human and technological resources for six operating suites and over 2000 patients annually)*

Professional Affiliations

If you are a member of any medical, educational, professional, or leadership associations, be sure to include that information on your resume. It communicates a message of professionalism, a desire to stay current with the industry, and a strong professional network. If you have held leadership positions within these organizations, that's even more impressive. Here's an example:

Professional Affiliations

NEW JERSEY INDUSTRY FOR WORKERS' COMPENSATION REFORM
- Committee Chairperson (2001 to Present)
- Committee Co-Chairperson (1999 to 2001)
- Member (1997 to Present)

AMERICAN COLLEGE OF OCCUPATIONAL & ENVIRONMENTAL MEDICINE
- Training Committee Chairperson (2000 to 2002)
- Member (1998 to Present)

AMERICAN ACADEMY OF DISABILITY EVALUATING PHYSICIANS
- Peer Review Committee Chairperson (1999 to 2000)
- Fund Raising Committee Member (1997 to 1999)
- Member (1990 to Present)

AMERICAN ACADEMY OF FAMILY PRACTITIONERS
- Member (1990 to Present)

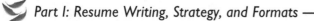

Civic Affiliations

Civic affiliations are fine to include if they

- are with a notable organization,

- demonstrate leadership experience, or

- might be of interest to a prospective employer.

However, things such as treasurer of your local condo association and singer with your church choir are not generally of value in marketing your qualifications. Here's an example of what to include:

> ✓ **Volunteer Chairperson**, United Way of America—Detroit Chapter, 1998 to Present
>
> ✓ **President**, Lambert Valley Conservation District, 1997 to Present
>
> ✓ **Treasurer**, Habitat for Humanity—Detroit Chapter, 1996 to 1997

Personal Information

We do not recommend that you include such personal information as birth date, marital status, number of children, and related data. However, in some instances, personal information is appropriate. If this information will give you a competitive advantage or answer unspoken questions about your background, by all means include it. Here's an example:

> — Born in Argentina. U.S. Permanent Residency Status since 1987.
> — Fluent in English, Spanish, and Portuguese.
> — Competitive Triathlete. Top-5 finish, 1987 Midwest Triathlon and 1992 Des Moines Triathlon.

Note in this example that the job seeker is multilingual. This is a particularly critical selling point. Although it's listed under Personal Information in this example, we recommend that you more appropriately highlight it in your Career Summary.

Consolidating the Extras

Sometimes you have so many extra categories at the end of your resume, each with only a handful of lines, that spacing becomes a problem. You certainly don't want to have to make your resume a page longer to accommodate five lines, nor do you want the "extras" to overwhelm the primary sections of your resume. Yet you believe the information is important and should be included. Or perhaps you have a few small bits of information that you think are important but don't merit an entire section. In these situations, consider consolidating the information using one of the following formats. You'll save space, avoid over-emphasizing individual items, and present a professional, distinguished appearance.

PROFESSIONAL PROFILE	
CERTIFICATIONS	**Certificate of Clinical Competence,** American Speech-Language-Hearing Assoc. **Certificate of Continuing Education** in Elementary Education (Certified K–8)
HONORS & AWARDS	**ACE Award for Excellence in Continuing Education,** 2003 **Clinician of the Year,** Central Michigan University, 2000 **Graduate Fellowship Award,** Central Michigan University, 1999
AFFILIATIONS	American Speech-Language-Hearing Association (ASHA) Michigan Speech-Language-Hearing Association (MSHA) Michigan Education Association (MEA) International Association of Orofacial Myologists (IAOM)
PUBLIC SPEAKING	Speaker, ASHA National Conference, Chicago, 2001 Workshop Presenter, ASHA National Conference, San Diego, 1999 Panelist, MEA State Conference, Duluth, 1998
TECHNOLOGY QUALIFICATIONS	Microsoft Word, Microsoft Access, WordPerfect, Fast Forward
LANGUAGES	Fluent in English, Spanish, and French

Writing Tips, Techniques, and Important Lessons

At this point, you've done a lot of reading, probably taken some notes, high-lighted samples that appeal to you, and are ready to plunge into writing your resume. To make this task as easy as possible, we've compiled some "insider" techniques that we've used in our professional resume-writing practices. We learned these techniques the hard way through years of experience! We know they work; and they will make the writing process easier, faster, and more enjoyable for you.

GET IT DOWN—THEN POLISH AND PERFECT IT

Don't be too concerned with making your resume "perfect" the first time around. It's far better to move fairly swiftly through the process, getting the basic information organized and on paper (or on screen), instead of agonizing about the perfect phrase or ideal formatting. After you complete a draft, we think you'll be surprised at how close to "final" it is, and you'll be able to edit, tighten, and improve formatting fairly quickly.

WRITE YOUR RESUME FROM THE BOTTOM UP

Here's the system:

- **Start with the easy things**—Education, Affiliations, Honors and Awards, Public Speaking, Publications, Research Projects, and any other extras you want to include. These items require little thought—they're generally just a listing—and can be completed in just a few minutes.

- **Write short job descriptions for your older positions, the ones you held years ago.** Be very brief and focus on highlights such as rapid promotion, achievements, innovations, professional honors, or employment with well-respected, well-known health care institutions or practices.

After you complete this, look at how much you've written in a short period of time! Then you can move on to the next step:

- **Write the job descriptions for your most recent positions.** This will take a bit longer than the other sections you have written. Remember to focus on the overall scope of your responsibility, major projects and initiatives, and significant achievements. Tell your reader what you did and how well you did it. You can use any of the formats recommended earlier in this chapter, or you can create something that is unique to you and your career.

Now, see how far along you are? Your resume is 90 percent complete, with only one small section left to do.

- **Write your career summary.** Before you start writing, remember your objective for this section. The summary should not simply rehash your previous experience. Rather, it is designed to highlight the skills and qualifications you have that are most closely related to your current career objective(s). The summary is intended to capture the reader's attention and "sell" your expertise.

That's it. You're done. We guarantee that the process of writing your resume will be much, much easier if you follow the "bottom-up" strategy. Now, on to the next tip.

INCLUDE NOTABLE OR PROMINENT "EXTRA" STUFF IN YOUR CAREER SUMMARY

Remember the "extra-credit sections" that are normally at the bottom of your resume? If this information is particularly significant or prominent—you increased quality of care rankings, developed a new medical procedure, resolved longstanding regulatory issues, pioneered a new biomedical technology, or reduced hospital operating costs—you might want to include it at the top of the resume in your Career Summary. Remember, the summary section is written to distinguish you from the crowd of other qualified candidates. As such, if you've accomplished anything that clearly demonstrates your knowledge, expertise, and credibility, consider moving it to your Career Summary for added attention. Refer to the sample career summaries earlier in the chapter for examples.

USE RESUME SAMPLES TO GET IDEAS FOR CONTENT, FORMAT, AND ORGANIZATION

This book is just one of many resources where you can review the resumes of other health care professionals to help you in defining your resume strategy, writing the text, and selecting the "right" resume format to showcase your talents. What's more, these books are published precisely for that reason. You don't have to struggle alone. Rather, use all the available resources at your disposal.

Be forewarned, however, that it's unlikely you will find a resume that fits your life and career to a "t." It's more likely that you will use "some of this sample" and "some of that sample" to create a resume that is uniquely "you."

SHOULD YOU INCLUDE DATES?

Unless you are over age 50, we recommend that you date your work experience and your education. Without dates, your resume becomes vague and difficult for the typical hiring manager or recruiter to interpret. What's more, it often communicates the message that you are trying to hide something. Maybe you haven't worked in two years, maybe you were fired from each of your last three positions, or maybe you never graduated from college. Being vague and creating a resume that is difficult to read will, inevitably, lead to uncertainty and a quick toss into the "not-interested" pile of candidates. By including the dates of your education and your experience, you create a clean and concise picture that the reader can easily follow to track your career progression.

An Individual Decision

If you are over age 50, dating your early positions must be an individual decision. On one hand, you do not want to "date" yourself out of consideration by including dates from the 1960s and early 1970s. On the other hand, it might be that those positions are worth including for any one of a number of reasons. Further, if you omit those early dates, you might feel as though you are misrepresenting yourself (or lying) to a prospective employer.

> **NOTE:** If you are preparing a CV, be sure to include all of your employment experience. This section, which details how to shorten and summarize your older work experience, does not apply to you. CVs are comprehensive and must include all of your experience.

Here is a strategy to overcome those concerns while still including your early experience: Create a separate category titled "Previous Professional Experience" in which you summarize your earliest employment. You can tailor this statement to emphasize just what is most important about that experience.

If you want to focus on the reputation of your past employers, include a statement such as this:

- Previous experience includes nursing positions with Sloan Kettering, The Johns Hopkins Hospital, and the New York University School of Medicine Hospital.

If you want to focus on the rapid progression of your career, consider this example:

- Promoted rapidly through a series of increasingly responsible radiology and radiology lab management positions with HealthTrend, Inc.

If you want to focus on your early career achievements, include a statement such as this:

> • Earned six promotions in three years with Memorial Community Hospital based on outstanding performance in health care administration, new program development, project management, staff training, and physician relations.

By including any one of the above paragraphs under the heading "Previous Professional Experience," you are clearly communicating to your reader that your employment history dates further back than the dates you have indicated on your resume. In turn, you are being 100 percent above-board and not misrepresenting yourself or your career. What's more, you're focusing on the success, achievement, and prominence of your earliest assignments.

Should You Include Dates in the Education Section?

If you are preparing a resume and are over age 50, we generally do not recommend that you date your education or college degrees. Simply include the degree and the university with no date. Why exclude yourself from consideration by immediately presenting the fact that you earned your college degree in 1958, 1962, or 1966—about the time the hiring manager was probably born? Remember, the goal of your resume is to share the highlights of your career and open doors for interviews. It is *not* to give your entire life story. As such, it is not mandatory to date your college degree.

However, if you use this strategy, be aware that the reader is likely to assume that there is *some* gap between when your education ended and your work experience started. Therefore, if you choose to begin your chronological work history with your first job out of college, omitting your graduation date could actually backfire, because the reader will likely assume that you have experience that predates your first job. In this case, it's best either to *include your graduation date* or *omit dates of earliest experience*, using the summary strategy discussed previously.

> **NOTE:** Again, as in the preceding section, if you are writing a CV, this does not apply to you! It is essential to compile a complete list of education, experience, and dates on your CV.

ALWAYS SEND A COVER LETTER WHEN YOU FORWARD YOUR RESUME

Sending a cover letter every time you send a resume is expected and is appropriate job search etiquette. When you prepare a resume, you are writing a document that you can use for every position you apply for, assuming that the requirements for all of those positions will be similar. The cover letter, then, is the tool that allows you to customize your presentation to each hospital, health care practice, company, or recruiter, addressing their specific hiring requirements. It is also the appropriate place to include any specific information that has been requested such as salary history or salary requirements (see the following section for more on this).

NEVER INCLUDE SALARY HISTORY OR SALARY REQUIREMENTS ON YOUR RESUME

Your resume is *not* the correct forum for a salary discussion. First of all, you should never provide salary information unless a company has requested that information, and then only if you choose to comply. Studies show that if employers are interested in you, they will look at your application with or without salary information. Therefore, you might choose not to respond to this request, thereby avoiding pricing yourself out of the job or locking yourself into a lower salary than the job is worth.

When contacting recruiters, however, we recommend that you do provide salary information, but again, only in your cover letter. With recruiters you want to "put all of your cards on the table" and help them make an appropriate placement by providing information about your current salary and salary objectives. For example, you might say

> Be advised that my current compensation is $65,000 annually and that I am interested in a nursing management position starting at a minimum of $80,000 per year.

Or, if you would prefer to be a little less specific, you might write

> My annual compensation over the past three years has averaged $50,000+.

ALWAYS REMEMBER THAT YOU ARE SELLING

As we have discussed over and over throughout this book, resume writing is sales. Understand and appreciate the value you bring to a prospective employer, and then communicate that value by focusing on your achievements. Companies don't want to hire just anyone; they want to hire "the" someone who will make a difference. Show them that you are that candidate.

CHAPTER **3**

Printed, Scannable, Electronic, and Web Resumes

After you've worked so tirelessly to write a winning resume, your next challenge is the resume's design, layout, and presentation. It's not enough for it to read well; your resume must also have just the right look for the right audience. And, just as with everything else in a job search, no specific answers exist. You must make a few decisions about what your final resume presentation will look like.

The Four Types of Resumes

In today's employment market, job seekers use four types of resume presentations:

- Printed
- Scannable
- Electronic (e-mail attachments and ASCII text files)
- Web

The following sections give details on when you would need each type, as well as how to prepare these types of resumes.

THE PRINTED RESUME

We know the printed resume as the "traditional resume," the one that you mail to a recruiter, take to an interview, and forward by mail or fax in response to an advertisement. When preparing a printed resume, you want to create a sharp, professional, and visually attractive presentation. Remember, that piece of paper conveys the very first impression of you to a potential employer, and that first impression goes a long, long way. Never be fooled into thinking that just because you have the best qualifications in your industry, the visual presentation of your resume does not matter. It does, a great deal.

THE SCANNABLE RESUME

The scannable resume can be referred to as the "plain-Jane" or "plain-vanilla" resume. All of the things that you would normally do to make your printed resume look attractive—bold print, italics, multiple columns, sharp-looking type-style, and more—are stripped away in a scannable resume. You want to present a document that can be easily read and interpreted by scanning technology.

Although the technology continues to improve, and many scanning systems in fact can read a wide variety of type enhancements, it's sensible to appeal to the "lowest common denominator" when creating your scannable resume. Follow these formatting guidelines:

- Choose a commonly used, easily read font such as Arial or Times New Roman.

- Don't use bold, italic, or underlined type.

- Use a minimum of 11-point type size.

- Position your name, and nothing else, on the top line of the resume.

- Keep text left-justified, with a "ragged" right margin.

- It's okay to use common abbreviations (for instance, scanning software will recognize "B.S." as a Bachelor of Science degree). But, when in doubt, spell it out.

- Eliminate graphics, borders, and horizontal lines.

- Use plain, round bullets or asterisks.

- Avoid columns and tables, although a simple two-column listing can be read without difficulty.

- Spell out symbols such as % and &.

- If you divide words with slashes, add a space before and after the slash to be certain the scanner doesn't misread the letters.

- Print using a laser printer on smooth white paper.

- If your resume is longer than one page, be sure to print on only one side of the paper; put your name, telephone number, and e-mail address on the top of page 2; and don't staple the pages together.

- For best possible results, mail your resume (don't fax it), and send it flat in a 9 × 12 envelope so that you won't have to fold it.

Of course, you can avoid scannability issues completely by sending your resume electronically, so that it will not have to pass through a scanner to enter the company's databank. Read the next section for electronic resume guidelines.

THE ELECTRONIC RESUME

Your electronic resume can take two forms: e-mail attachments and ASCII text files.

E-mail Attachments

When including your resume with an e-mail, simply attach the word-processing file of your printed resume. Because a vast majority of businesses use Microsoft Word, it is the most acceptable format and will present the fewest difficulties when attached.

However, given the tremendous variety in versions of software and operating systems, not to mention printer drivers, it's quite possible that your beautifully formatted resume will look quite different when viewed and printed at the other end. To minimize these glitches, use generous margins (at least 0.75 inch all around). Don't use unusual typefaces, and minimize fancy formatting effects.

Test your resume by e-mailing it to several friends or colleagues, and then having them view and print it on their systems. If you use WordPerfect, Microsoft Works, or another word-processing program, consider saving your resume in a more universally accepted format such as RTF or PDF. Again, try it out on friends before sending it to a potential employer.

ASCII Text Files

You'll find many uses for an ASCII text version of your resume:

- To avoid formatting problems, you can paste the text into the body of an e-mail message rather than send an attachment. Many employers actually prefer this method. Pasting text into an e-mail message lets you send your resume without the possibility of also transmitting a computer virus.

- You can readily copy and paste the text version into online job application and resume blank forms, with no worries that formatting glitches will cause confusion.

- Although it's unattractive, the text version is 100 percent scannable.

To create a text version of your resume, follow these simple steps:

1. Create a new version of your resume using the Save As feature of your word-processing program. Select "text only" or "ASCII" in the Save As option box.

2. Close the new file.

3. Reopen the file, and you'll find that your word processor has automatically reformatted your resume into Courier font, removed all formatting, and left-justified the text.

4. To promote maximum readability when sending your resume electronically, reset the margins to 2 inches left and right, so that you have a narrow column of text rather than a full-page width. (This margin setting will not be retained when you close the file, but in the meantime you can adjust the text formatting for best screen appearance. For instance, if you choose to include a horizontal line [perhaps something like this: +++++++++++++++++++++++++++] to separate sections of the resume, by working with the narrow margins you won't make the mistake of creating a line that extends past the normal screen width. Plus, you won't add hard line breaks that create odd-length lines when seen at normal screen width.)

5. Review the resume and fix any "glitches" such as odd characters that may have been inserted to take the place of "curly" quotes, dashes, accents, or other nonstandard symbols.

6. If necessary, add extra blank lines to improve readability.

7. Consider adding horizontal dividers to break the resume into sections for improved skimmability. You can use any standard typewriter symbols such as *, -, (,), =, +, ^, or #.

To illustrate what you can expect when creating these versions of your resume, on the following pages are some examples of the same resume in traditional printed format, scannable version, and electronic (text) format.

THE WEB RESUME

This newest evolution in resumes combines the visually pleasing quality of the printed resume with the technological ease of the electronic resume. You host your Web resume on your own Web site (with your own URL), to which you refer prospective employers and recruiters. Now, instead of seeing just a "plain-Jane" version of your e-mailed resume, with just one click a viewer can access, download, and print your Web resume—an attractive, nicely formatted presentation of your qualifications.

What's more, because the Web resume is such an efficient and easy-to-manage tool, you can choose to include more information than you would in a printed, scannable, or electronic resume. Consider separate pages for achievements, technology qualifications, equipment skills, honors and awards, management skills, and more, if you believe they would improve your market position. Remember, you're working to sell yourself into your next job!

Web resumes are an outstanding tool for people who are in technologically or visually related health care professions. You can create a virtual multimedia presentation that not only tells someone how talented you are, but also visually and technologically demonstrates it.

A simplified version of the Web resume is an online version of your Microsoft Word resume. Instead of attaching a file to an e-mail to an employer, you can include a link to the online version. This format is not as graphically dynamic as a full-fledged Web resume, but it can be a very useful tool for your job search. For instance, you can offer the simplicity of text in your e-mail, plus the instant availability of a printable, formatted word-processing document for the interested recruiter or hiring manager. For a demonstration of this format, go to www.e-resume-central.com and click on "SEE A SAMPLE."

REBECCA UNDERWOOD SMITH, MSW

18790 Southlake Terrace, Montclair, VA 22026   703.730.1234   rsmith@mentalhealth.com

PROFILE

- ☑ Licensed Clinical Social Worker current in field of **Child and Spouse Abuse**
- ☑ Knowledgeable of community resources and contacts in local area
- ☑ Experienced with military population
- ☑ Fluent in Spanish

EDUCATION AND CREDENTIALS

Master of Social Work, Child and Family, University of Illinois, Chicago
Bachelor of Science, *summa cum laude*, Social Work, University of Virginia, Charlottesville

Licensed Clinical Social Worker, State of Virginia
Member, National Association of Social Workers

PROFESSIONAL EXPERIENCE

Assistant Chief, Social Work Service: QUANTICO MARINE HOSPITAL, Quantico, VA, 1998–Present

Provide outpatient, individual, marital, and family therapy for the Quantico community, including crisis intervention and referral to community agencies. Conduct all phases of screening, intake, treatment, and referral. Assess reports and provide treatment of child and spouse abuse referred through the Family Advocacy Program. Clinically supervise social service assistant. Supervise administration staff of four. Serve as consultant for schools, police, healthcare providers, and military commanders for issues concerning child and spouse abuse. Provide education to soldiers on healthy relationships. Committee member of hospital wellness program, focusing on program development.

- ☑ Hand-selected to work with the Family Advocacy Program.
- ☑ Provide intervention on a prevention basis through outpatient services.
- ☑ Chair weekly staff meeting.

Manager/Coordinator: NEIGHBORHOODS SERVICES, INC., Raleigh, NC, 1994–1998

Managed residential services for disabled individuals in community living program. Developed individual service plans, coordinated healthcare, and fostered integration into community. Supervised and trained staff.

- ☑ Administered North Carolina Home-Based Support Services program.
- ☑ Facilitated admissions into CILA services.

Social Worker: UNITED CEREBRAL PALSY, Chicago, IL, 1991–1994

Provided clinical and case management services for developmentally disabled adults at two Adult Program sites. Counseled on individual, group, and family basis, supervised by ACSW.

- ☑ Provided family counseling during home visits.
- ☑ Planned and coordinated staff professional development and yearly retreat.

Case Manager: UNITED CHARITIES, Chicago, IL, 1987–1991

Collaborated as member of professional team in serving multi-problem families. Conducted initial client assessment for clinical and financial services. Facilitated community information and referral.

- ☑ Developed resource file through in-person and telephone interviews.
- ☑ Represented agency at community networking meetings.

Social Work Intern: MONICA'S INN, Durham, NC, 1986–1987

Counseled women and children domestic violence victims in individual and group modes.

The print version of the resume (resume writer: Bonnie Kurka).

Rebecca Underwood Smith, MSW

18790 Southlake Terrace
Montclair, VA 22026
703-730-1234
rsmith@mentalhealth.com

PROFILE

- Licensed Clinical Social Worker current in field of Child and Spouse Abuse
- Knowledgeable of community resources and contacts in local area
- Experienced with military population
- Fluent in Spanish

EDUCATION and CREDENTIALS

Master of Social Work, Child and Family, University of Illinois, Chicago
Bachelor of Science, summa cum laude, Social Work, University of Virginia, Charlottesville

Licensed Clinical Social Worker, State of Virginia
Member, National Association of Social Workers

PROFESSIONAL EXPERIENCE

Assistant Chief, Social Work Service
QUANTICO MARINE HOSPITAL, Quantico, VA
1998–Present

Provide outpatient, individual, marital, and family therapy for the Quantico community, including crisis intervention and referral to community agencies. Conduct all phases of screening, intake, treatment, and referral. Assess reports and provide treatment of child and spouse abuse referred through the Family Advocacy Program. Clinically supervise social service assistant. Supervise administration staff of four. Serve as consultant for schools, police, healthcare providers, and military commanders for issues concerning child and spouse abuse. Provide education to soldiers on healthy relationships. Committee member of hospital wellness program, focusing on program development.

- Hand-selected to work with the Family Advocacy Program.
- Provide intervention on a prevention basis through outpatient services.
- Chair weekly staff meeting.

The scannable version of the resume.

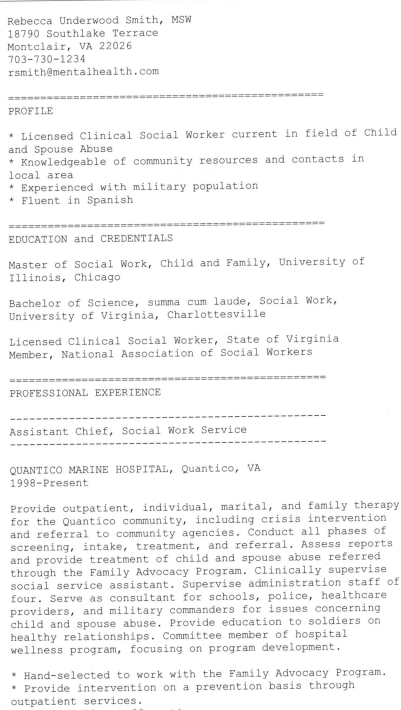

```
Rebecca Underwood Smith, MSW
18790 Southlake Terrace
Montclair, VA 22026
703-730-1234
rsmith@mentalhealth.com


=================================================
PROFILE

* Licensed Clinical Social Worker current in field of Child
and Spouse Abuse
* Knowledgeable of community resources and contacts in
local area
* Experienced with military population
* Fluent in Spanish


=================================================
EDUCATION and CREDENTIALS

Master of Social Work, Child and Family, University of
Illinois, Chicago

Bachelor of Science, summa cum laude, Social Work,
University of Virginia, Charlottesville

Licensed Clinical Social Worker, State of Virginia
Member, National Association of Social Workers


=================================================
PROFESSIONAL EXPERIENCE


-------------------------------------------------
Assistant Chief, Social Work Service
-------------------------------------------------

QUANTICO MARINE HOSPITAL, Quantico, VA
1998-Present

Provide outpatient, individual, marital, and family therapy
for the Quantico community, including crisis intervention
and referral to community agencies. Conduct all phases of
screening, intake, treatment, and referral. Assess reports
and provide treatment of child and spouse abuse referred
through the Family Advocacy Program. Clinically supervise
social service assistant. Supervise administration staff of
four. Serve as consultant for schools, police, healthcare
providers, and military commanders for issues concerning
child and spouse abuse. Provide education to soldiers on
healthy relationships. Committee member of hospital
wellness program, focusing on program development.

* Hand-selected to work with the Family Advocacy Program.
* Provide intervention on a prevention basis through
outpatient services.
* Chair weekly staff meeting.
```

The electronic/text version of the resume.

The Four Resume Types Compared

This chart quickly compares the similarities and differences between the four types of resumes we've discussed in this chapter.

	PRINTED RESUMES	SCANNABLE RESUMES
TYPESTYLE/ FONT	Sharp, conservative, and distinctive (see our recommendations in chapter 1).	Clean, concise, and machine-readable: Times New Roman, Arial, Helvetica.
TYPESTYLE ENHANCEMENTS	**Bold,** *italics,* and <u>underlining</u> for emphasis.	CAPITALIZATION is the only type enhancement you can be certain will transmit.
TYPE SIZE	10-, 11-, or 12-point preferred…larger type sizes (14, 18, 20, 22, and even larger, depending on typestyle) will effectively enhance your name and section headers.	11, 12-point, or larger.
TEXT FORMAT	Use centering and indentations to optimize the visual presentation.	Type all information flush left.
PREFERRED LENGTH	1 to 2 pages; 3 if essential.	1 to 2 pages preferred, although length is not as much of a concern as with printed resumes.
PREFERRED PAPER COLOR	White, ivory, light gray, light blue, or other conservative background.	White or very light with no prints, flecks, or other shading that might affect scannability.
WHITE SPACE	Use appropriately for best readability.	Use generously to maximize scannability.

ELECTRONIC RESUMES	WEB RESUMES
Courier.	Sharp, conservative, and distinctive…attractive onscreen and when printed from an online document.
CAPITALIZATION is the only enhancement available to you.	**Bold,** *italics,* and underlining, and color for emphasis.
12-point.	10-, 11-, or 12-point preferred…larger type sizes (14, 18, 20, 22, even larger, depending on typestyle) will effectively enhance your name and section headers.
Type all information flush left.	Use centering and indentations to optimize the visual presentation.
Length is immaterial; almost definitely, converting your resume to text will make it longer.	Length is immaterial; just be sure your site is well organized so viewers can quickly find the material of greatest interest to them.
N/A.	Paper is not used, but do select your background carefully to maximize readability.
Use white space to break up dense text sections.	Use appropriately for best readability both onscreen and when printed.

Are You Ready to Write Your Resume?

To be sure that you're ready to write your resume, go through the following checklist. Each item is a critical step that you must take in the process of writing and designing your own winning resume.

❑ Clearly define "who you are" and how you want to be perceived.

❑ Document your key skills, qualifications, and knowledge.

❑ Document your notable career achievements and successes.

❑ Identify one or more specific job targets or positions.

❑ Identify specific sub-industries or environments that you are targeting within the health care industry.

❑ Research and compile keywords for your profession, industry, and specific job targets.

❑ Determine which resume format suits you and your career best.

❑ Select an attractive font.

❑ Determine whether you need a print resume, a scannable resume, an electronic resume, a Web resume, or all four.

❑ Secure a private e-mail address.

❑ Review resume samples for up-to-date ideas on resume styles, formats, organization, and language.

PART II

Sample Resumes for Health Care Careers

CHAPTER 4

Resumes for Physicians and Surgeons

- Ob/Gyn Resident

- Osteopath

- Hospital Staff Physician

- Dermatologist

- Family Practice Physician

- Internist/Gastroenterologist

- Surgeon in Private Practice

- Plastic and Reconstructive Surgeon

- Medical Director

- Attending Surgeon/Chief of Surgery

- Physician/Workplace Health Consultant

Increasingly, even physicians and surgeons are using resumes rather than traditional CVs because the resume format allows the inclusion of more descriptive and persuasive information. In some cases, a hybrid resume/CV is an effective compromise.

MEETU CHAUHAN, M.D.

13 Pleasant Ridge
Scarsdale, NY 10583

(914) 725-8350
E-mail: Meetuc@aol.com

OBJECTIVE

Residency in Obstetrics and Gynecology that will utilize comprehensive training, diagnostic strengths, and effective treatment skills and benefit from my broad-based experience in treating people with a diverse range of medical needs.

PROFILE

♦ Dedicated medical professional with strong detail orientation and exceptional follow-through abilities.
♦ Demonstrated ability to effectively prioritize a broad range of responsibilities to consistently meet deadlines.
♦ Strong diagnostic and problem-resolution skills.
♦ Effective interpersonal skills; proven ability to work with individuals on all levels; team player.
♦ Proven ability to work well under pressure.
♦ Solid background in general medicine and surgery.

CERTIFICATION

USMLE Step 1 — achieved score of 86
USMLE Step 2 — *in progress*

RESEARCH

1999 <u>Morbidity and Mortality of In-Patients at R.L. Jalappa Hospital and Research Center for the Year 1998</u> under Dr. Shantharam, Professor and Head of the Department of Community Medicine, R.L. Jalappa Hospital and Research Center

EDUCATION

SRI DEVARAJ URS MEDICAL COLLEGE, Tamaka, Kolar, Karnataka State, India
(Affiliated with **Bangalore University**)
Bachelor of Medicine and Bachelor of Surgery   August 1998

NEW YORK UNIVERSITY, New York, NY
Liberal Arts Major   1991–1992

PROFESSIONAL TRAINING
July 1998–July 1999

R.L. JALAPPA HOSPITAL and RESEARCH CENTER
(Affiliated with Sri Devaraj Urs Medical College)
<u>Clinical Internship Rotations</u>
Obstetrics/Gynecology   July–September 1998
♦ Assisted with Cesarean section and forceps deliveries.
♦ Conducted normal deliveries.
♦ Assisted in hysterectomy procedures and tubal ligation.
♦ Participated in hysterectomies resulting from prolapsed uterus.

Community Medicine   September–December 1998
♦ Devoted 1½ months to research project on campus.
♦ Spent 1½ months in a rural village, in an area endemic for malaria, to treat patients and teach health care.
♦ Conducted clinics and screenings for National Blindness Prevention Program.

Strategy: *Physicians trained outside the U.S. face a tough re-credentialing process when they immigrate. This resume highlights overseas training and experience as added value for a physician seeking a residency.*

Meetu Chauhan   page 2

Internal Medicine   December 1998–February 1999
- ♦ Gained extensive experience caring for patients with asthma, pneumonia, tuberculosis, cholera, leprosy, HIV, and giardia.
- ♦ Supervised administration of medication.
- ♦ Gained ICU experience; monitored myocardial infarction cases.
- ♦ Gained experience performing peritoneal taps and intercostals drainage.

Surgery   March–April 1999
- ♦ Assisted with inguinal hernia repair, appendectomies, and small-bowel obstructions (TB and Typhoid fever).
- ♦ Amputated gangrenous appendages on severe diabetic patients.
- ♦ Treated post-operative complications.
- ♦ Commended by surgeons for exceptional competence. Gained confidence and trust of surgeons.

Pediatrics   May 1999
- ♦ Performed own lab tests to ensure accuracy.
- ♦ Gained experience in the Neonatal ICU.
- ♦ Treated snakebites.
- ♦ Worked with severely malnourished patients, Duchenne's Muscular Dystrophy, rheumatic heart disease, and Kwashiorkor.

Psychiatry   June 1999

Radiology   June 1999

Emergency Room   July 1999
- ♦ Competently handled procedures such as suturing, running IV lines, performing gastric lavage, and administering medications.
- ♦ Treated patients with organo-phosphorous poisoning.
- ♦ Treated patients injured in motor vehicle accidents.

Dentistry   July 1999

ADDITIONAL PROFESSIONAL EXPERIENCE– COMMUNITY MEDICINE
- ♦ Participated in the World Health Organization / Rotary International Pulse Polio Program, December 1995, January 1996, and January 1999.
- ♦ Worked on the National Malaria Control Program, October 1998.
- ♦ Participated in the National Blindness Prevention Program, December 1998.
- ♦ Volunteered in the Community Health Clinic, October 1998–January 1999.
- ♦ Participated in Free Health Camps for the Underprivileged, providing treatment and education in extremely remote areas of the country, September 1998 and February 1999.
- ♦ Volunteered at Meals-on-Wheels in New Rochelle, NY, 1990–1992.

ADDITIONAL   U.S. Permanent Resident

9011 Owasso Court
Clarkston, MI 48347
U.S.A.

PHAM THANH AN, D.O.

Residence: 248.969.9933
Mobile: 248.421.7108
ando@yahoo.com

CREDENTIALS	**Board Certified, National Board of Osteopathic Medicine** ▪ Level I — passed 2002 ▪ Level II — passed 2003 **Pharmacist Licensure:** States of Michigan, Texas, and California
EDUCATION	**Doctor of Osteopathic Medicine** [2003] **TOURO UNIVERSITY COLLEGE OF OSTEOPATHIC MEDICINE** — Vallejo, CA ▪ **Internship: PONTIAC OSTEOPATHIC HOSPITAL** — Pontiac, MI [2003–current] **Doctor of Pharmacy,** Magna Cum Laude [1994] **UNIVERSITY OF TEXAS, SCHOOL OF PHARMACY** — Austin, TX ▪ Earned 95% on boards. **Bachelor of Science, Dietetics and Nutrition** [1990] **CALIFORNIA POLYTECHNIC UNIVERSITY** — San Luis Obispo, CA
PROFESSIONAL EXPERIENCE	**Relief Pharmacist** [1998–2003] **SAFEWAY PHARMACY** and **FIRST HOSPITAL VALLEJO**; Vallejo, CA **Pharmacist in Charge** [1994–1998] **WALGREENS PHARMACY** and **RANDALLS PHARMACY** *(Safeway affiliate)*; Austin, TX **Director of Pharmacy** [1990–1994] **HILLSIDE MEDICAL CENTER**; Austin, TX Oversaw all pharmacy operations, including hiring employees, supervising drug dispensing, counseling patients, providing drug information to other healthcare professionals, performing third-party billing, developing drug formulary, and ensuring quality control; served on drug and therapeutic committee. **Staff Pharmacist** [1990–1994] **BRACKENRIDGE HOSPITAL**; Austin, TX Performed I.V. drug mixing and drug dispensing; provided drug information to other healthcare professionals. **Staff Pharmacist** [1988–1990] **BROWN'S DRUG STORE**; San Luis Obispo, CA Dispensed drugs, provided counseling, and prepared third-party billing.
RESEARCH	**Research Apprentice** **VIETNAMESE MINISTRY OF AGRICULTURE:** "The Use of Chemical Fertilization vs. Compost Manure on Tropical Tuber Farming"
PROFESSIONAL ORGANIZATIONS	**American Osteopathic Association** [1999–current] **Christian Medical and Dental Society** [1996–current] **Student Osteopathic Medical Association** [1999–current] **PAX — Minority Medical Organization** [1997–current] ▪ Secretary; 2000–2001 **National Student Medical Association** [1998–current] ▪ President; 2001 **American Pharmaceutical Association** [1994–current] ▪ President; 1998 ▪ Vice President; 1994–1995

Strategy: *A clean, straightforward CV format works to present the somewhat complicated professional background of this immigrant who had pursued pharmacist credentials before attending a college of osteopathic medicine.*

HONORS & AWARDS	**Merck Pharmacy Academic Scholarship** [1992–1994] UNIVERSITY OF TEXAS, SCHOOL OF PHARMACY **Dean's List** [1991–1994] UNIVERSITY OF TEXAS, SCHOOL OF PHARMACY **Best Student Award, Biological Science** [1980] HANOI MEDICAL UNIVERSITY — Hanoi, Vietnam **President's Academic Award** [1979] HANOI MEDICAL UNIVERSITY — Hanoi, Vietnam
COMMUNITY SERVICE ACTIVITIES	**Volunteer — OSTEOCHAMPS, MICHIGAN STATE COLLEGE OF OSTEOPATHIC MEDICINE (MSCOM)** [2002–current]: Educate 8th–12th graders on benefits of osteopathic medicine; interest them in healthcare industry. Work with approximately 40 students in annual program. **Volunteer — MERCY SHIPS MEDICAL MINISTRIES** [1989–current]: Work with hospitals and drug companies to supply medical equipment and other needs to underprivileged/Third World nations, including Vietnam, Myanmar, Cameroon, and Ecuador. **Speaker — FAITH CHRISTIAN SCHOOL;** Napa, CA [2000–current]: Inform and interest students about careers in the medical profession on Career Day; and educate students on the dangers of street drugs. **Volunteer Pharmacist — UNITED WAY/COMMUNITY PHARMACY** [1999–current]
LANGUAGE FLUENCY	English, Vietnamese, and French

MICHELLE JONES, M.D.

98 Ben Franklin Drive
P.O. Box 219
Cherry Hill, New Jersey 07896   mjones@aol.com

Home: (609) 654–1040
Cell: (609) 654–5809
Home Fax: (609) 654–1755

HEALTH CARE PHYSICIAN

Senior Medical Resident in Internal Medicine with extensive knowledge of community medical diagnostic and patient-care services in various settings, including inpatient and outpatient clinics and government/private hospitals and clinics. Strong understanding of current principles, methods, and procedures for the delivery of medical evaluation, diagnosis, and treatment in women's health care, including rotation in OB-GYN. Outstanding interpersonal and cross-cultural communication skills: fluent in English, Romanian, and French, combined with a basic command of Hungarian.

- ☑ Obstetrics/Gynecology
- ☑ General Surgery
- ☑ Internal Medicine
- ☑ Infectious Diseases
- ☑ Hospital Medical Service
- ☑ Private Practice Experience

- ☑ Pediatrics
- ☑ Outpatient Clinic/Office
- ☑ Emergency Room Experience
- ☑ Rheumatology
- ☑ Urology
- ☑ Nursing Home/Rehab/ Long Term Care

- ☑ Cardiology
- ☑ Orthodontics
- ☑ Neurology
- ☑ Pulmonary
- ☑ Vascular
- ☑ Psychiatry/Behavioral/ Substance Abuse

EDUCATION

Institute of Medicine & Pharmacy — New York

Doctor of Medicine
Class Rank: Top 10%

Institute of Medicine & Pharmacy — New York

Doctor of Medicine
Class Rank: Top 8%

Certifications: Advanced Cardiac Life Support (ACLS)
                     Basic Life Support (BLS)
                     Advanced Trauma Life Support (ATLS)
                     American Board of Internal Medicine (ABIM) — Pending

Professional Licenses: Doctor of Medicine (M.D.) — New Jersey
                         Doctor of Medicine (M.D.) — California — Pending

PROFESSIONAL EXPERIENCE

CLIFTON MEDICAL CENTER — Clifton, New Jersey   Jan 2001–Present
Attending Physician/Staff
Report directly to Chief of Medical Service and Chief of Staff M.D. for 140-bed medical center providing hospital, outpatient clinic, rehabilitation unit, and nursing home services. Scope of responsibilities includes delivering health care, supervising/teaching rounds, teaching clinic, supervising on-call residents, and working with residents on Internal Medicine Residency Program.

- Provide and manage direct patient care, including physical examinations, evaluations, assessments, diagnoses, and treatment.

Strategy: Applying for a position as leading physician in a women's medical practice, Dr. Jones wanted to show leadership as well as medical strengths. An accomplishment-oriented resume format worked well for her.

MICHELLE JONES, M.D.

Professional Experience, Continued

- Train and supervise residents and on-call residents engaged in specialty activities and procedures, including emergency room on-call duties, inpatient area, outpatient clinic, nursing home/rehabilitation and long term care/hospice unit, and off-site outpatient clinics.
- Effectively manage ER, medical floor inpatients, emergencies in ICU/CCU, and all in-house medical residents while on call as attending Medical Officer of the day.
- Frequently function as acting Chief Resident, directing and coordinating the patient-care activities of nursing and support staff.
- Collaborate with residents on Internal Medicine Residency Program.

MEDICINE ASSOCIATES OF BLOOMFIELD — Bloomfield, New Jersey   Jan 1999–Jan 2001
Associate Physician
Reported directly to partner physicians while supervising a staff of four for small private practice. Scope of responsibilities included providing internal medicine, overseeing daily office functions, managing in-hospital patients, and managing patients at several local nursing homes and personal care homes.

- Developed and implemented patient management plans, recorded progress notes, and assisted in provision of continuity of care.
- Managed in-hospital patients at three local hospitals; provided appropriate patient education explaining the necessity, preparation, nature, and anticipated effects of scheduled procedures to the patient.
- Managed patients at several local nursing homes and personal care homes; examined patients, performed comprehensive physical examinations, and compiled patient medical data, including health history and results of physical examination. Prescribed pharmaceuticals, other medications, and treatment regimens as appropriate to assessed medical conditions.

PROFESSIONAL AFFILIATIONS

Member, American Medical Association (AMA)
Member, American Society of Internal Medicine (now called the American College
of Physicians — American Society of Internal Medicine, ACP-ASIM)

PUBLICATIONS

*The Use of a Correction Factor for the Calculation of Suprarenal Outputs as a Function of
Arterial Pressure*, diploma thesis, 1982.

Baucht, J., and Jones, M., "The Use of a Correction Factor for the Calculation of
Suprarenal Outputs as a Function of Arterial Pressure," presented at and published in
the proceedings of The National Symposium of Physiology, New York, August 16–18,
Vol. 1, 2:20–24, 1981.

RESEARCH

Determination by E-testing of sensitivity of gram negative microorganisms to
Levoflaxacin, sponsored by Baxter Pharmaceuticals (submitted for publication).

Measurement of adrenal blood flow in an experiment model.
Advisor: Dr. James Baucht

REFERENCES AVAILABLE UPON REQUEST

TONY G. RAY, M.D.

5712 Roosevelt Way, Seattle, Washington 98177 ~ 206-661-5115 ~ Email: Myderm@aol.com

PROFILE

A transitioning physician with state-of-the-art training in the emerging field of laser surgery and aesthetics, backed with over 20 years of high-intensity emergency and internal medicine.

EDUCATION

Residency: **Southwest Medical Center**   **University of Washington**
               Affiliate: University of Texas   **Health Science Center**
               <u>DALLAS, TEXAS</u>   <u>SEATTLE, WASHINGTON</u>
               PGY-3—Internal Medicine; Chief Medical Resident   *PGY 1-2—Internal Medicine*

Medical   **CMDNJ–Princeton School of Medicine**   **University of Trinidad**
School: 5th Channel Program   **School of Medicine**
               <u>PRINCETON, NEW JERSEY</u>   <u>TRINIDAD, JAMAICA</u>

CERTIFICATIONS

Zyderm / Zyplast I & II   Dermologen Soft Tissue Implantation
Laserscope Lasers: 1064 YAG, 532KTP   ICN-Cool Touch Laser 1320 YAG
ACLS / ATLS

CONTINUING EDUCATION AND TRAINING

Coursework listings are for Aesthetic Dermatology and have been taken through the American Societies for Dermatologic Surgery; Laser Medicine and Surgery; National Procedures Institute; and Academy of Dermatology.

Tissue Augmentation	Acne / Rosacea	Vascular Birthmarks	Sclerotherapy
Chemical Peeling	Laser Hair Removal	Botulinum Toxin	Visage Coblation
Photo Aging / Aging Skin	Cosmetic Surgery	Lasers for Resurfacing	Laser Tissue Interaction
Facial Telangiectasia	Hyperpigmentation	Injectable Fillers	Non-ablative Lasers
IPL System Photofacial	Erbium YAG Training	Tattoo Removal	Laser Leg Vein

DERMATOLOGY AND AESTHETICS

TRUE SKIN DERM AND LASER CENTER—Seattle, Washington
2001 to Present
President / Owner

Accepted the challenge of private practice, capitalizing on two years of study and certification in laser systems and dermatology to provide non-surgical solutions to a variety of cosmetic needs. Sourced an exceptional location in Redmond, Washington, positioning the practice to target Redmond's Silicon Valley income and demographics.

- Sourced vendors for laser equipment (Cool Touch 1320 NdYAG, Aura 532 KTP, Lyra 1064 NdYAG, and Sciton and Erbium YAG laser); analyzed and evaluated cosmeceutical skin-care treatments, selecting Physicians Choice products for quality and cost.
- Created marketing packages providing minimal downtime for laser-based facial rejuvenation, lip augmentation, wrinkles, and leg veins; chemical peels for correction of hyperpigmentation and facial rejuvenation.
- Negotiated lease terms and conditions. Created administrative processes, including physician consent forms. Hired staff.

Of Note:
- Completed the start-up phase, achieving both the first six-month patient-base growth and revenue goals.

Strategy: *Seeking to transition from emergency medicine to dermatology, this physician emphasizes relevant training and his own recent private practice on page 1. Page 2 groups additional medical experience under subheadings for quick review.*

OCCUPATIONAL MEDICINE

MED STOP—Spokane, Washington
1999 to 2001
Medical Director—Gonzaga University
Accepted a reduced-schedule Locum Tenens position in Occupational Medicine to further study in emerging laser technology and aesthetic dermatology. Over a two-year period, completed numerous courses, workshops, and certifications (page one).

NORTHWEST MEDICAL CENTER—Bothell, Washington
1998 to 1999
Medical Director
Treated various job-related injuries.

EMERGENCY MEDICINE

COLUMBIA MEDICAL CENTER OF KENNEWICK—Kennewick, Washington
1995 to 1997
Staff Physician—Emergency Medicine

TRI MED ASSOC. / COLUMBIA BASIN COMMUNITY HOSPITAL—Richland, Washington
1992 to 1994
Staff Physician—Emergency Medicine
Taught students and residents from Columbia Valley Health Science Center in the emergency medical rotation segment, while concurrently managing the duties of an emergency department physician.

HANFORD URGENT CARE CENTER—Pasco, Washington
1989 to 1992
Medical Director
Provided front-line medical response and treatment for industry-based injuries.

PASCO COMMUNITY HOSPITAL—Pasco, Washington
1989 to 1990
Staff Physician—Emergency Medicine

COLUMBIA MEDICAL CENTER EAST—Kennewick, Washington
1981 to 1983
Staff Physician—Emergency Medicine
Assisted with plastic repair in traumatic injury in the emergency department; concurrently performed emergency physician duties.

INTERNAL MEDICINE

During the period below, assisted on plastic surgical cases involving neck and face lifts, liposuction, breast implants / reductions, and reconstructive hand surgery.

RENTON MEMORIAL HOSPITAL—Renton, Washington
1983 to 1988
Internal Medicine

COLUMBIA MEDICAL CENTER WEST—Richland, Washington
1983 to 1988
Chairman / Vice Chairman—Department of Internal Medicine

MADELINE C. McMURRAY, M.D.

14 Deland Park B • Fairport, New York 14450 • 585-425-1569
MadCMcM@msn.com

FAMILY PRACTICE PHYSICIAN

Dynamic Primary Care Physician with outstanding ability to communicate with and educate patients on a broad range of treatment and preventative care issues. Registered Dietitian with strong capacity to integrate nutrition and fitness regimens into overall health-maintenance strategies. Strong interest in geriatric medicine, working with disadvantaged populations, and end-of-life issues.

Board Certified in Family Practice Medicine	*Pediatric Advanced Life Support Certification*
New York State Medical License	*Neonatal Resuscitation Certification*
Privileges — Newark-Wayne Hospital	*Registered Dietitian*
Advanced Cardiac Life Support Certification	*Certified HIV Counselor*

EDUCATION

Medical Doctor   1995
University of Rochester School of Medicine; Rochester, New York

Pre-Professional Certificate in Dietetics   1991
University of Connecticut; Storrs, Connecticut

Bachelor of Science, Nutritional Biochemistry   1989
Dartmouth College; Hanover, New Hampshire
With Distinction

PROFESSIONAL EXPERIENCE

PALMYRA INTERNAL MEDICINE; Palmyra, New York
Family Practice Physician   1998–Present
Accountable for primary care of approximately 1,700 patients, including newborns, children, adolescents, adults, and senior citizens.

- Provide hospital care to general medical and ICU patients in hospital environment.
- Perform routine gynecological and minor surgical procedures in office, as appropriate.
- Conduct home visits of homebound geriatric patients.
- Supervise day-to-day activities of two Nurse Practitioners.

Professional Highlights:

Serve on Medical Records Committee at Newark-Wayne Hospital (Newark, New York).

Function as Acting Practice Manager on an interim basis for periods of up to three months.

Implemented and currently facilitate journal club promoting the concepts of evidence-based medicine.

Supervise first- and second-year medical students during Primary Care Preceptorships in conjunction with University of Rochester School of Medicine Ambulatory Clerkship program.

Evaluate student presentations as part of Family Practice Clerkship in conjunction with U of R School of Medicine, Department of Family Medicine.

Devise and implement systems to facilitate office-based research in medication management for geriatric patients.

Strategy: *A resume format (rather than CV) allowed this doctor to highlight her interest in working with geriatric and disadvantaged patients and her diverse education as both a dietitian and a physician.*

Madeline C. McMurray, M.D.   Résumé — Page Two

MEDICAL TRAINING

ST. MARY'S HOSPITAL HEALTH CENTER; Corning, New York
Chief Resident   1997–1998
- Managed scheduling of 39 Residents to ensure appropriate staffing levels.
- Addressed and mediated issues between Residents and nursing / support staff.
- Fulfilled all patient-care duties associated with medical residency.

Family Practice Resident   1995–1997
- Saw a broad range of in-hospital and clinic patients, with strong Internal Medicine emphasis.

SUNY HEALTH SCIENCE CENTER COLLEGE OF MEDICINE; Binghamton, New York
Instructor, Introduction to Clinical Medicine   1997–1998
Served as member of cross-functional teaching team that provided lectures on basic physiology and common medical conditions, as well as providing first- and second-year medical students with practical experience conducting physical examinations, interviewing and evaluating patients, and making rudimentary diagnoses.

FAMILY HEALTH CENTER; Elmira, New York
Acute Care Physician (Part-Time)   1997–1998
Provided walk-in care to patients for a variety of illnesses and injuries. Served as only physician on duty during weekend shifts.

PROFESSIONAL DEVELOPMENT / AFFILIATIONS

St. Mary's Hospital Health Center Annual Family Practice Refresher Course (2001)
— *Teaching Strategies for Office Teachers; Palliative Care Issues.*

NYS Winter Weekend & Sports Medicine Conferences (1999, 2000)

Scientific Assembly of American Academy of Family Practice (1999)
— *Nutritional Updates for MDs — Patient Use of Herbals; Joint Injection; Occupational Medicine & Disability Evaluations.*

Society for Teachers of Family Medicine Northeast Regional Conference (1999)
— *Teaching Medical Students and Residents.*
— *Analyzing Medical Literature Using Evidence-Based Medicine Principles.*

Family Medicine Residency Journal Club — Strong Memorial Hospital / Highland Hospital

Rochester Office-Based Research Network

American Academy of Family Practitioners
American Medical Association
NYS Academy of Family Physicians

American Dietetic Association
Rochester Business & Professional
    Women's Association (VP of Membership)

COMMUNITY INVOLVEMENT

Volunteer Companion, Lifespan; Rochester, New York
Hospice Volunteer, Visiting Nurse Service; Webster, New York
Troop Leader — Junior Girl Scouts, Girl Scouts of America; Corning / Rochester, New York
Assistant Manager, Soup Kitchen, Center City Churches; Hartford, Connecticut

PETER M. THOMPSON, M.D.

Curriculum Vitae

2036 NW Hoyt Street
Portland, Oregon 97210
petertmd@msn.com

(503) 226-5242 Residence

(503) 226-5243 Fax (Call First)

EXPERTISE

Internal Medicine and Gastroenterology

PROFESSIONAL SUMMARY

Compassionate, capable medical doctor with 20+ years' experience providing outstanding patient care. Excellent diagnostician with strong skills in upper G.I. endoscopy and colonoscopy. Good listener, excellent communicator, diligent in providing counseling in preventive medicine. Strong time-management and record-keeping skills with proven ability to relate well with both peers and employees. Strong ability and willingness to learn new things. Conscientious, dedicated, problem solver.

EDUCATION

Medical	University of Oregon Medical School, Portland, Oregon M.D.	1979
Undergraduate	Oregon State University, Corvallis, Oregon B.S., Pre-Med	1975

MEDICAL TRAINING

Fellowship	University of Oregon Medical School, Portland, Oregon Gastroenterology	1984 to 1985
Residency	University of Oregon Medical School, Portland, Oregon Internal Medicine	1982 to 1984
Internship	Tripler U.S. Army Hospital, Honolulu, Hawaii	1979 to 1980

RECENT PROFESSIONAL DEVELOPMENT COURSEWORK

Medical Knowledge Self Assessment Program 12 (Internal Medicine Study Course), 2002

Medical Grand Rounds, Oregon Health & Science University, Portland, Oregon, 2002

Sommer Memorial Medical Lectures, Portland, Oregon, 2002

LICENSURE AND CERTIFICATION

Passed Special Purpose Examination (SPEX) in General Medicine, 2002

Oregon State Medical License #MD9852432

Board Certified, Internal Medicine

Board Eligible in Gastroenterology

Strategy: *After retirement, this specialist in Internal Medicine and Gastroenterology wanted to go back to work for an HMO. His resume focused on recent coursework and current volunteer experience to show that he had lost neither his knowledge base nor his dedication to the profession.*

PETER M. THOMPSON, M.D.　　　　　　　　　　　　　　　　　Page Two

PROFESSIONAL EXPERIENCE

Private Practitioner, Internal Medicine and Gastroenterology　　　　1990 to 2000
Portland, Oregon

Clinic Practitioner, Internal Medicine and Gastroenterology　　　　1982 to 1990
Rose City Clinic, Portland, Oregon

Medical Officer　　　　　　　　　　　　　　　　　　　　　　　　1980 to 1982
U.S. Army, Fort Lewis, Tacoma, Washington

VOLUNTEER EXPERIENCE

Volunteer Medical Officer　　　　　　　　　　　　　　　　　1995 to Present
Mercy Corps International, Portland, Oregon
Have completed humanitarian projects in Iraq, Afghanistan, and Ethiopia.

Medical Volunteer
American Red Cross, Portland, Oregon　　　　　　　　　　　　　1996 to 2000
Taught variety of medical programs for lay volunteers.

HOSPITAL AFFILIATION

St. Vincent Hospital, Portland, Oregon, 1982 to 2000

Executive Committee Member, five-year term

Other Committee Memberships: Medical, Gastroenterology

PROFESSIONAL AFFILIATIONS

American Society of Internal Medicine

Medical Society of Metropolitan Portland

Oregon Medical Association

RICHARD J. HUNT, M.D., F.A.C.S.

1141 Quiet Valley Road
Lansing, MI 48924

(517) 852-9611
rjhuntmd@earthlink.net

SUMMARY OF QUALIFICATIONS

Physician with 15 years of private practice and hospital staff experience. Proven ability to identify problems and implement practical solutions. Excellent decision-making, planning, and crisis-management skills. Core competencies include

- Cross-functional practice-management expertise
- Knowledge of safety issues and regulations
- Development of effective utilization review programs
- Knowledge of JCAHO regulations, managed care, Medicare, and Medicaid
- Quality-management and peer-review experience in a hospital setting

PROFESSIONAL EXPERIENCE

Private Practitioner—General Surgery
Richard J. Hunt, M.D., Lansing, MI

1987–present

- Developed and maintain a successful practice. Oversee all operations, including strategic planning, staffing, budgetary management, billing, purchasing, safety, and policy development.
- Designed and implemented an OSHA-compliant office exposure control plan.
- Prepared and instituted a small-business compliance plan as recommended by the Center for Medicare and Medicaid Services.

Chairperson of Department of Surgery
Staff Physician
Lansing Medical Center, Lansing, MI

1998–present
1991–present

- Oversee operations of department of surgery, including preparation of on-call schedules, appointment of section heads, and fostering of positive relationships among department members.
- Evaluate performance and credentialing of physicians in department. Review morbidity and mortality data.
- Established a quality-management program that included root-cause analysis of sentinel events.
- Participated in the development of hospital protocol for prevention of wrong-site surgery.
- Planned for and promoted the development of a secondary operating room for procedures requiring local anesthesia. This resulted in more efficient utilization of the main operating room, decreased patient waiting time, and increased staff satisfaction.

Strategy: *For a physician seeking opportunities in practice management, this resume format was highly effective. Both business and medical expertise are highlighted.*

RESUME 7, CONTINUED

Richard J. Hunt, M.D., F.A.C.S. *Page 2*

- Evaluated capital purchases for department and made recommendations to administration.
- Developed staff evaluation criteria for new surgical procedures.
- Participated in preparations for numerous JCAHO reviews.

Staff Physician 1987–1991
Ingham County General Hospital, Lansing, MI

Surgical Resident 1984–1987
Temple University Hospital, Philadelphia, PA

PROFESSIONAL APPOINTMENTS

Lansing Medical Center

Medical Executive Committee   Critical Care Committee
Scientific Review Committee   Quality Assurance Committee
Operating Room Committee   Patient Care Committee
Health Information Committee

Ingham County General Hospital

Operating Room Committee   Utilization Review Committee
Medical Executive Committee   Surgical Case Review Committee
Pharmacy and Dietary Committee

CERTIFICATION AND LICENSURE

Michigan Medical License
National Board of Medical Examiners—Diplomate
American Board of Surgery—Diplomate

EDUCATION

Doctor of Medicine
University of Chicago School of Medicine, Chicago, IL   1984

Bachelor of Science in Biology
University of Illinois at Urbana, Urbana, IL   1980

MIN CHOW, M.D.

4486 Main Street, Apt. 2B • Boston, MA 02133
617-555-8344 • mchow@resumefreedom.com

QUALIFICATIONS SUMMARY

Highly accomplished Graduate of Medical School with excellent medical office administration skills and a deep passion and drive for serving, educating, and contributing to the health and well-being of society.

- Persistent, hard-working physician with extensive experience in providing quality patient care through private practice, free clinics, and charitable foundations.

- Outstanding teacher and educator with experience in teaching, tutoring, and mentoring students and professionals of all ages.

- Well-traveled, artistic, and athletic individual with a passion for improving the community.

- Skilled administrator and office manager. Serve as a positive influence on medical staff.

- Thorough researcher, writer, and presenter with numerous publications and television appearances.

EDUCATIONAL BACKGROUND

Doctor of Medicine — UNIVERSITY OF THE EAST (1990)

PROFESSIONAL EXPERIENCE

PRIVATE PRACTICE / HARVARD MEDICAL CENTER — China / Massachusetts — 1990 to 2003

Plastic and Reconstructive Surgeon / Fellow

Managed the diagnosis and treatment of patients in need of plastic and reconstructive surgery. Coordinated and presented research and scientific papers at medical conferences and on television programs. Published papers and newspaper articles on medicine, longevity, and other health and surgery-related issues. Supervised an office with a staff of 10 people. Developed information campaigns for maternal and child care.

Selected Achievements:

- Only plastic surgeon from China to be sent to study and work with colleagues at Harvard Medical Center.

- Headed a charitable foundation assisting the poor who needed the services of a reconstructive and plastic surgeon but could not afford the cost.

- Organized and managed free clinics throughout China.

- Developed a Web-based communication system linking the members of the Chinese Association of Plastic and Reconstructive Surgery for the purposes of exchanging information; posting meetings; and scheduling exams, conferences, and chats.

PROFESSIONAL ASSOCIATIONS AND CERTIFICATIONS

Member, CHINESE MUTAGEN SOCIETY
Member, CHINESE ASSOCIATION OF PLASTIC AND RECONSTRUCTIVE SURGERY

PUBLICATIONS

"Malignant Granular Cell Tumor," CHINESE ORTHOPEDIC SOCIETY — 1995

Strategy: *This plastic surgeon who had immigrated to the U.S. was in the process of obtaining her credentials in this country. She was looking for a medical office management position in the interim.*

Sam Granahan, MD, FACC

DocSam@hotmail.com
82 Ball Road, Wayne, NJ 07470

973-633-4809 tel
973-633-2656 fax

SUMMARY OF QUALIFICATIONS

Medical Director. 16 years' direct experience in the creative leadership of continuing and long-term healthcare organizations. Clinical abilities complemented by management and administration skills. Demonstrated track record of delivering quality, cost-effective medical care through competencies in strategic analysis, problem solving, decision making, teaching, quality assurance/improvement, audit tool development, and utilization of computer technology.

EDUCATION

Fellowship, Cardiology—Columbia Presbyterian Medical Center, New York, NY — 1981–1983

Residency, Internal Medicine—Columbia Presbyterian Medical Center, New York, NY — 1978–1981

Doctor of Medicine—Cornell University Medical College, New York, NY — 1978

Bachelor of Arts (Summa Cum Laude Honors)—New York University, New York, NY — 1974

BOARD CERTIFICATION & MEDICAL LICENSURE

Board Certified in Cardiovascular Disease — November 1984

Diplomate of the American Board of Internal Medicine — September 1981

New York State Medical License — August 1979

Diplomate of the National Board of Medical Examiners — July 1979

PROFESSIONAL POSITIONS & APPOINTMENTS

Founding Partner, Vice President, and Corporate Medical Director — 1985–Present
Madison Avenue Healthcare Management, New York, NY
Now serving 50 facilities in New York State.

- Selected as Medical Director for Clara Barton Health Center (900-bed facility) with challenge of converting state and federal regulation violations into a sound medical model. Success led to extended services and referrals to perform turnarounds for additional facilities.

- Increased revenues by expanding to provide guidelines and protocols to ensure compliance; medical services through a contingent workforce; an on-call program for night, weekend, and holiday coverage; and administrative/billing services.

- Innovated focused audit tools—for admissions, discharge to hospital, antibiotic usage, and diabetes management—to promote early identification and analysis of specific issues. Worked closely with Quality Improvement staff to develop effective tools and to oversee the program.

- Managed development of computer information systems to coordinate physician schedules and follow-up care.

Strategy: *This resume combines the best elements of a CV and a resume to create a powerful document for this physician/business manager.*

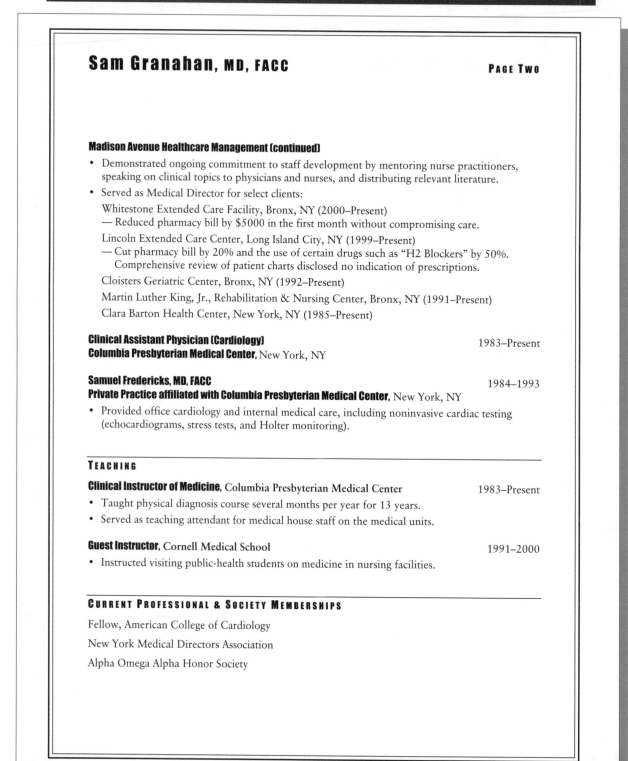

Sam Granahan, MD, FACC

PAGE TWO

Madison Avenue Healthcare Management (continued)

- Demonstrated ongoing commitment to staff development by mentoring nurse practitioners, speaking on clinical topics to physicians and nurses, and distributing relevant literature.
- Served as Medical Director for select clients:

    Whitestone Extended Care Facility, Bronx, NY (2000–Present)
    — Reduced pharmacy bill by $5000 in the first month without compromising care.

    Lincoln Extended Care Center, Long Island City, NY (1999–Present)
    — Cut pharmacy bill by 20% and the use of certain drugs such as "H2 Blockers" by 50%. Comprehensive review of patient charts disclosed no indication of prescriptions.

    Cloisters Geriatric Center, Bronx, NY (1992–Present)

    Martin Luther King, Jr., Rehabilitation & Nursing Center, Bronx, NY (1991–Present)

    Clara Barton Health Center, New York, NY (1985–Present)

Clinical Assistant Physician (Cardiology)   1983–Present
Columbia Presbyterian Medical Center, New York, NY

Samuel Fredericks, MD, FACC   1984–1993
Private Practice affiliated with Columbia Presbyterian Medical Center, New York, NY

- Provided office cardiology and internal medical care, including noninvasive cardiac testing (echocardiograms, stress tests, and Holter monitoring).

TEACHING

Clinical Instructor of Medicine, Columbia Presbyterian Medical Center   1983–Present

- Taught physical diagnosis course several months per year for 13 years.
- Served as teaching attendant for medical house staff on the medical units.

Guest Instructor, Cornell Medical School   1991–2000

- Instructed visiting public-health students on medicine in nursing facilities.

CURRENT PROFESSIONAL & SOCIETY MEMBERSHIPS

Fellow, American College of Cardiology

New York Medical Directors Association

Alpha Omega Alpha Honor Society

JAY GORNITZKY, M.D.

38 Indian Hill Road
Brick, New Jersey 08723

(732) 286-2312
jgmd@aol.com

VISIONARY LEADER SKILLED IN TURNING INSIGHT INTO ACTION

Long and highly successful career reflecting cross-functional management expertise: **policy and procedure setting, operational streamlining, budgeting and cost reduction, negotiations, regulatory reporting and compliance, and equipment standardization.** Provide decisive, proactive guidance within the context of a calm demeanor, utmost professionalism, and commitment to corporate goals and objectives. Technology resource: A+ and Net+ certified.

EXPERIENCE AND ACHIEVEMENTS

Brick Hospital, Division of Meridian Health Care System, Brick, NJ   7/85–Present
Attending Surgeon, 1/90–Present, **Chief of Surgery,** 1/97–12/00;
Surgery Department Vice Chair, 1/93–12/96

Distinguished performance on committees and in leadership positions within this 250-bed acute care, full-service community hospital, currently in the process of adding a Radiation Therapy Department. Key to the formation of the Meridian Health Care System and the Brick Division as writer of Surgery Department bylaws. Manage a general surgical caseload of between 400 and 500 patients annually, encompassing both minor and major operations and featuring both laparoscopic and cancer surgeries.

- As Executive Committee member, drove operating-room efficiency improvements by streamlining O.R. procedures and solidifying block scheduling for more efficient utilization. Captured significant facility revenues by playing a key role in standardizing O.R. equipment. Eliminated the use of a noncompetitively priced equipment vendor and led high-powered vendor negotiations to realize cost savings.

- Orchestrated the transition of Point Pleasant Hospital and Northern Ocean Hospital System operating rooms to the Brick Division of the Meridian Health Care System. Expedited move and guided operating-room personnel through the resulting transition.

- Tapped by Surgery Department Chair to perform prestigious hemorrhagic shock research. Proved ineffectiveness of Narcan, offsetting extensive contrary evidence.

- Gained endorsement of Chief Administrator in handling of medical staff member termination procedure. Gathered evidence, reviewed case, and implemented proctoring prior to disciplinary proceedings.

- Played an active role in Surgery Department meeting JCAHO compliance guidelines for full facility accreditation.

- Provided depositions in a highly publicized case regarding a surgeon attempting to bypass department bylaws.

(Page 1 of 2)

Strategy: *This resume highlights surgical expertise with the medical-management qualifications of this experienced surgeon. It positions him for either a surgical or an administrative role.*

JAY GORNITZKY, M.D.　　　(732) 286-2312　　　jgmd@aol.com　　　**Page 2**

COMMITTEE PARTICIPATION

- **Computer Advisory Committee,** Meridian Health Systems, Brick Division (Recommended technological advances, negotiated with vendors, and strategically planned computer network implementation.)
- **Executive Committee,** Meridian Health Systems, Brick Division
- **Surgical Advisor, Qualcare PPO,** Piscataway, NJ
- **Capital Budget Committee,** Meridian Health Systems, Brick Division
- **Operating Room Committee Chairman,** Meridian Health Systems, Brick Division
- **ICU Committee Chairman,** Meridian Health Systems, Brick Division

PRIVATE PRACTICE

- **Jay Gornitzky, M.D., LLC, Sole Practitioner,** Toms River, NJ (9/01–Present)
- **Point Pleasant School System, School Physician,** Point Pleasant, NJ (9/94–Present)
- **Shore Surgical Group, P.A., Partner,** Brick, NJ (6/90–9/01)

EDUCATION

- **MD, University of Medicine and Dentistry,** Newark, NJ, May 1980, Summa Cum Laude
  Residency: UMDNJ Affiliate Hospitals — General Surgery (1980–1985)
- **BS, Pharmacy, Temple University School of Pharmacy,** Philadelphia, PA, May 1976, Summa Cum Laude
- **Naval Academy,** Annapolis, MD (1969–1970)

CERTIFICATIONS

- **Fellow, American College of Surgeons**
- **Board Certified, American Board of Surgery**
- **A+ Certified**
- **Net+ Certified**

PAPERS

- **Narcan Inhibition of Hepatocyte Gluconeogensis**
  Presented at the Society for Academic Surgery, Syracuse, NY, 1984
- **Protective Effect of Previous Burn in Murine Endotoxemia, Gold Medal Paper**
  Presented at Southeastern Surgical Conference, Nashville, TN, 1984
- **The Detrimental Effect of Ethanol in Experimental Head Trauma, Second Prize**
  Presented at NJACS, 1980
- **Pharmacological Modification of Skin Flap Necrosis, Honorable Mention**
  Presented at NJACS, 1979

PAUL SMITH, M.D., M.P.H.

98 Ben Franklin Drive
Cherry Hill, New Jersey 07896
Pager: (609) 654-2040   psmith@aol.com

Work: (609) 654-1755
Home: (609) 654-1040
Home Fax: (609) 654-5809

QUALIFICATIONS PROFILE

Solo practitioner and independent contractor specializing in workplace health issues related to Workers' Compensation claims. Extensive knowledge of medical diagnostic and patient-care services, providing medical expertise and consultation in various settings, including industrial/manufacturing, healthcare facilities, law firms, and insurance carriers. Strong understanding of current principles, methods, and procedures for the delivery of medical evaluation, diagnosis, and treatment.

☑ Diabetes
☑ Professional Writing
☑ Disability Resolution
☑ Workplace Substance Abuse
☑ Psychological Aspects of Disability
☑ Excellent Management & Organizational Skills

☑ Public Speaking
☑ Effects of Shift Work
☑ Chronic Pain Syndromes
☑ Hand-Arm Vibration Syndrome
☑ Workers' Compensation Management
☑ Outstanding Communication/Interpersonal Skills

EDUCATION

Medical College of New Jersey — New Jersey   **Doctor of Medicine** (1992)

New York University — New York   **Master's in Public Health** (1987)

New York University — New York   **Bachelor of Arts** (1985)

Tufts University — Massachusetts   **Special Studies in Public Health** (1986)

Certifications:
Board Certified, American Board of Family Practice
Certified Medical Review Officer
Certified Independent Medical Examiner
Certified Ergonomics Specialist
Diploma, American Academy of Pain Management

Professional Licenses: Doctor of Medicine (M.D.) — New Jersey

PROFESSIONAL EXPERIENCE

PAUL SMITH, M.D., M.P.H., PC — Clifton, New Jersey   2001–PRESENT
Physician/Principal
Solo practitioner and independent contractor providing workplace health consulting and medical expertise to healthcare facilities, law firms, and insurance carriers in relation to injuries or conditions that occur in the workplace.

- Established and maintained excellent client relationships, providing medical expertise and consultation on a regular basis to Durimax Steel, Celco Power, Vatts Steel, and other independent local clients.
- Successfully led and negotiated contract terms as Medical Director to Clifton Rehabilitation Systems, a statewide physical therapy chain.

Strategy: *This resume was written as a marketing piece to expand the practice of a workplace-health physician. In addition to medical expertise, it shows his ability to help companies reduce worker time off and increase employee productivity.*

PAUL SMITH, M.D., M.P.H.

Professional Experience Continued

- Independently performed IME (Independent Medical Evaluation) reports on injured workers to determine whether injuries had occurred; included conducting medical accident investigations for work relatedness, identifying cause, and providing recommendations for treatment or referral.
- Formulated strategies to reduce Workers' Compensation claims costs for Durimax Steel by 68% over a 3-year period; initiated a return-to-work program and early reporting and treatment of workplace injuries.
- Instrumental in initiating, writing, and administering a workplace drug policy for Durimax Steel, and gaining union support; company's previous experience introducing such policies received strong opposition from its union.
- Provided on-site training in disability case management to company nurses, reducing company costs in lost-time disability.
- Identified new and innovative approaches to enhance the effectiveness of Durimax Steel's Safety Program; integrated medical awareness with safety procedures, initiated a medical accident investigation protocol, and participated as the company's physician in Safety Committee meetings.
- Spearheaded efforts to reduce mistrust between union and management by providing fair and objective management of Workers' Compensation injuries.

BLOOMFIELD OCCUPATIONAL HEALTH SERVICES — Bloomfield, New Jersey   1998–2001
Occupational Medicine Physician/Medical Director
Reported directly to Vice President of Outpatient Services while supervising a staff of 5 for exclusive occupational medical services clinic. Scope of responsibilities included office management, creating office policy, marketing practice, evaluating and treating patients, and overseeing all medical decision-making.

- Created and built a financially viable occupational medicine practice within 3 years without hospital marketing support, increasing corporate client base from zero to over 200 clients.
- Pioneered initiative to create a drug testing/MRO consulting service, providing evaluation, diagnosis, and treatment for over 400 clients without hospital marketing support.
- Initiated efforts to improve operations by creating a practice-based billing system satisfying client needs, resulting in increased profit margins through rapid return on accounts.
- Enhanced marketability by designing and conducting staff training programs in customer-service practices.
- Enhanced the practice's presence within the local community through national certification, increasing client base and marketability; received certification as a Medical Review Officer and as an Independent Medical Evaluator.
- Established reputation as a credible medical consultant within the corporate sector; managed company Workers' Compensation claims, minimizing client financial responsibility and resolving problematic cases swiftly and efficiently.

CLIFTON HEALTHCARE SERVICES — Clifton, New Jersey   1997–1998
Occupational Medicine Physician
Reported directly to Vice President of Ambulatory Care, evaluating and treating injured workers for leading healthcare facility offering Occupational Medicine Services.

- Established reputation as a credible occupational medical consultant within the corporate sector; managed company Workers' Compensation claims, minimizing client financial responsibility and expediting resolution of problematic cases.
- Enhanced reputation by performing on-site visits to client facilities, maintaining strong client relationships, and creating loyal accounts; accurately determined causality for injuries and provided ergonomic and other safety recommendations to prevent similar accidents.

PAUL SMITH, M.D., M.P.H.

Professional Experience Continued

MERCY HOSPITAL OF ENGLEWOOD — Englewood Cliffs, New Jersey   1995–1996
Family Practitioner
Reported directly to Chairman of Department for Englewood Cliffs Clinic at Mercy Hospital, providing primary healthcare services through the evaluation and treatment of patients.

- Developed on-site healthcare presentations at a local halfway house for women with drug-related offenses, educating them on the health effects of addiction to themselves and their children.
- Orchestrated the implementation of the Welfare Disability Examinations initiative, enabling individuals previously labeled as "disabled" to return to work.
- Collaborated with case workers on patient disability cases, performing evaluations to enable able-bodied individuals to return to work.

TRAINING

New Jersey Self Insurers Association Fall Workshop • Musculoskeletal Disorders & Ergonomics • Allergies at Work • Understanding HIPAA • Drug Diversion & Abuse • Risk Management Essentials for Physicians • Medical Review Officer Drug & Alcohol Testing • Principles of Workers' Compensation & Disability Case Management • Conflict Resolution

PRESENTATIONS

"Hand-Arm Syndrome" — New Jersey Self-Insurers Association, New Jersey (Oct 2002)

"The Therapist's Role in Disability Resolution" — Clifton Rehab Systems, New Jersey (Oct 2002)

"Health & Safety Effects for Shift-Workers" — Durimax Safety Leadership Committee, New Jersey (Sept 2002)

"Guide to Disability Resolution" — Celco Power WC Claims Reserves Meeting, New Jersey (Mar 2002)

"Employer's Guide: Return to Work Strategies" — Clifton Services Committee, New Jersey (Mar 2001)

"How to Overcome Chronic Pain Syndrome" — Englewood Claims Association, New Jersey (Jan 2001)

PROFESSIONAL AFFILIATIONS

Chairperson, Industry for Workers' Compensation Reform, New Jersey
Member, American College of Occupational & Environmental Medicine
Member, American Academy of Disability Evaluating Physicians
Member, American Academy of Family Practitioners

REFERENCES AVAILABLE UPON REQUEST

CHAPTER 5

Resumes for Nursing Careers

- Licensed Practical Nurse (LPN)

- Registered Nurse (RN)

- Charge Nurse

- Cardio-Thoracic Surgical Nurse

- Flight Nurse

- Nurse-Midwife

- Nurse Anesthetist

- Licensed Massage Therapist/RN

- Nurse Manager/Case Manager

- Director of Nursing

- Nurse Practitioner

- Legal Nurse Consultant

The term "nursing" covers a wide variety of careers. Most involve direct patient care, which can range from hands-on nursing-home care to high-tech surgical procedures. This chapter also includes resumes for nurse managers, those who manage nursing staff and nursing departments.

Sarah K. Markell, LPN

11539 Sunset Drive, # 8 ◆ Hyattstown, MD 20871   (301) 420-8693 ◆ skm20871@aol.com

Professional Overview

- Dedicated and well-qualified healthcare professional with **hospital, nursing home, home healthcare,** and **doctor's office** experience.
- Excel in working independently, professionally managing caseloads, and setting priorities.
- A dependable and knowledgeable professional whose attention to detail in documentation and chart maintenance led to an award for *Outstanding Contributions to Patient Education.*
- Highly adaptive, flexible style; efficiently and competently work with diverse patient populations.
- Demonstrate a solid understanding of regulatory compliance and an ability to skillfully navigate the Medicare and Medicaid systems.
- Skill strengths include:

Diabetic education	Child psychiatric outpatient
Geriatric care & administration	Pediatric care
Post surgical & wound care	Phlebotomy

Credentials: Maryland # LP34047; Commonwealth of Virginia LP # 0002042663
Certifications: IV Therapy, Intensive Coronary Care, CPR

Highlights of Professional Experience

Hospital ICU, ER, and Med-Surgical Unit

- Secured a position as a Nurse Tech at an 80-bed facility while completing nursing school.
- Acquired cross-functional training in acute care, orthopedics, and surgery.
- Assisted with direct delivery of patient care and self-management education in a pre/post-op environment.
- Instrumental in setting the standards for 12-hour shift scheduling, initiating the program in cooperation with another LPN.
- Selected to complete Intensive Coronary Care certification to support two ICUs.

Private Physician's Office

- Instrumental in helping a doctor of internal medicine build a private practice from 10 to more than 3,000 patients in the first two years of practice.
- Demonstrated outstanding organization and time-management skills in tending more than 40 patients daily.
- Independently completed all initial assessments; charted medical stats, symptoms, and medications; instructed patients in health self-management; called in prescription orders.
- Administered a compassionate level of patient care, directly contributing to ongoing patient referrals and sustained growth of the practice.

Nursing Home and Rehabilitation Facilities

- Delivered comprehensive geriatric nursing care to patients at a 240-bed residential facility. Began employment as a full-time GNA; transitioned to part-time while pursuing LPN certification.
- Supervised a team of four to six GNAs assigned to a unit of a 180-bed geriatric facility; coordinated daily schedule; managed orientation and staff assignments.
- Mastered, through on-the-job training, the care of comatose/near comatose ventilator-dependent patients in a 100-bed rehabilitation facility.

Strategy: The functional style was used very effectively in this resume, allowing this nurse to present her hospital experience first even though she is currently working as a home health nurse. (She wants to go back to the hospital setting.)

Sarah K. Markell, LPN

(301) 420-8693

Page 2

Home Healthcare / Private Duty Nursing

- Held the unique distinction of being the only LPN in the home-care division of a rural hospital to deliver in-home medical services to recent discharges. Visited up to eight patients daily, managing nursing care plans and serving as a liaison between the patient and hospital medical staff. Performed venipunctures, IV therapy, enteral feeding, and decubitus care; made recommendations for discharge plans.
- Provided intensive minute-by-minute private-duty nursing to an adolescent ALD (adrenoleukodystrophy) patient. Performed seizure precautions and procedures; administered PEG feedings and intense physical therapy.
- Currently providing overnight private-duty nursing for an 18-month-old with multiple birth complications. Monitor respiratory status; administer gastrostomy tube feeding; serve as a liaison between the parents and the medical community.

Employment History

Home Health Nurse, Professional Nursing Services, Catonsville, MD   2001–present

LPN, Dr. Margaret Price, Charleston, WV   1999–2001

Private Duty Nurse, Lorenzo Gonzales, Fairfax, VA   1995

LPN, Woodbine Rehabilitation Center, Alexandria, VA   1995

Nurse Supervisor, Life Care Center, Middleton, VA   1994–1995

LPN / Home Health Nurse, Baker Memorial Hospital, Luray, VA   1989–1994

LPN / GNA, Clearview Nursing Home, Luray, VA   1984–1993

Education

Licensed Practical Nursing Certification, Jackson Technical School, Charlottesville, VA

Graduate, Luray High School, Luray, VA

MICHELLE R. BROWN, LPN

428 Walden Avenue • Syracuse, New York 13135 • (315) 555-8328

LICENSED PRACTICAL NURSE
Patient Care and Education / Supervision / Nursing Recruitment / Quality Improvement

Professional Profile:

Over 10 years' experience providing knowledgeable, compassionate, and professional care to patients of all ages and medical conditions. Gained specialized experience working with patients who have sustained traumatic brain injuries and spinal-cord injuries. Provided professional and high-quality patient care in a high-stress, rapidly changing environment while always addressing the patients' health needs, personal concerns, and safety. Identified opportunities to instruct patients and caregivers to promote wellness and healthful follow-up care. Supervised healthcare staff and enhanced productivity and efficiency. Demonstrated skills in public speaking.

Summary:
- Assisted in problem-solving related to staffing, supplies, and resident care.
- Ensured that resident care standards were maintained and the rights of residents and preferences in care and treatment were respected.
- Gained experience in a variety of medical units, including Traumatic Brain Injury and Spinal Cord Rehabilitation, Orthopedics, Internal Medicine, Family Medicine, Telemetry, Ambulatory Surgery, OT / PT / Speech Therapy, and Hemodialysis and Peritoneal Dialysis.
- Instructed patients and family members in safety issues, infection control, wound and injury care, disease and pain management, nutrition, and general wellness.
- Performed diagnostic testing and utilized a variety of test equipment.
- Conveyed a friendly, caring, and positive attitude to patients and their caregivers.
- Served as Team Leader with responsibility for delegating patient-care assignments, documenting treatment and progress, communicating with physicians and other healthcare professionals, and overseeing medication administration.
- Managed such office duties as scheduling, filing, faxing, data entry, typing, answering telephones, and communicating with vendors and insurance companies.
- Utilized computer skills in Microsoft Word, Access, and Excel; and Meditech to update patient information and prepare billing.
- Drew blood and performed extensive laboratory work.
- Demonstrated ability to interact well with people of all ages and backgrounds.

Education:

Cazenovia College, Cazenovia, New York
Associate in Applied Science — Nursing   2001
Graduated with Distinction   3.38 GPA

Syracuse Vocational Technical Center, Syracuse, New York
Licensed Practical Nurse   1991

Professional development training in:

Hemodialysis and Peritoneal Dialysis	Orthopedics and Telemetry	EKG Testing
Venipuncture and IV Insertion	Isolation Techniques	Infection Control
Splint Application and Removal	CVP Flushing, Care, and Use	PCA Pumps
Safe Drug Administration	Computerized Medicine Cart	PICC Lines

Strategy: *An extensive professional profile leads off this resume for an experienced LPN who is seeking a supervisory position. She recently went back to school and earned a nursing degree.*

Michelle R. Brown

Page Two

Licensure:

New York State Licensed Practical Nurse, #135847-1

Clinical Experience:

Fillmore Medical Center — Medical / Surgical and Psychiatric
Children's Hospital — Pediatrics
Sisters of Charity — Oncology
Lancaster Hospital — Medical / Surgical, Maternity, and Geriatrics
Syracuse General — Medical / Surgical

Work Experience:

Aurora Senior Healthcare, Syracuse, New York   2002–Present
LPN Supervisor
Monitor and supervise the personal-care services provided by 12 Resident Assistants. Oversee the administration of medications and treatments and manage the storage and distribution of controlled-substance medications. Ensure a safe and healthful work environment and make certain that quality standards are maintained. Promote the policy and procedures of Aurora Senior Healthcare. Identify and report unusual symptoms, daily needs, and progress of residents. Maintain accurate documentation in case notes, medication administration records, change-of-shift reports, and treatment records.
➢ *Received Nursing Department Achievement Award.*

Fillmore Medical Center, Syracuse, New York   1991–2001
Senior Licensed Practical Nurse
Provided the full range of nursing care. Collected patient data, both objective and subjective, and entered information into kardex/ppc. Prepared progress notes and updated charts. Administered medication orally; topically; and by pump, catheter, tube, and PICC line. Treated patients with chest, oral, nasal, and tracheal tubes. Assisted with burn treatments, wound care, suture and staple care, and decubitus ulcer care. Handled narcotics and controlled substances with responsibility for keys and documentation. Provided pre- and post-op care and pain-management therapy.
➢ *Received Certificate of Merit from the Department of Rehabilitation Medicine.*
➢ *Collaborated with therapists to rearrange patients' schedules to ensure proper morning care and nutrition.*
➢ *Assisted in the creation of therapeutic pass questionnaire to document problems during home visits.*
➢ *Received Certificate of Recognition for outstanding work with brain-injury and spinal-cord-injury patients.*
➢ *Served on Quality Improvement Committee.*

Sisters of Charity, Syracuse, New York   1987–1989
Certified Nursing Assistant

Garden Terrace Nursing Home, Syracuse, New York   1986–1987
Certified Nursing Assistant

CATHERINE POTTER, RN

789 McDonald Avenue, Brooklyn, NY 11218
(718) 855-1467 / (917) 555-1122
cpotterrn@aol.com

Energetic professional with six years' experience in **Medical Surgical / Cardiac / Telemetry / Geriatrics**. Contribute to the delivery of first-rate nursing care in a team environment. Administer prescribed care plans with compassion and sensitivity to patients' needs. Maintain composure in critical situations.

LICENSURE / CERTIFICATIONS

N.Y.S. EDUCATION DEPARTMENT, NEW YORK, NY

Registered Professional Nurse (2001–2004)	Licensed Practical Nurse (1995–2004)

MEDTECH, New York, NY

Advanced Life Support (2001–2003)	ABG Analysis (2002)	Blood Gas Certification (2002)	Basic / Intermediate EKG Analysis (2002)	EKG Certification (2002)

MEMORIAL SLOAN-KETTERING CANCER CENTER, New York, NY

Certificate 16.2 Contact Hours, Education Design 1, Cancer Chemotherapy (2002–2004)

PERIVASCULAR NURSE CONSULTANTS, NEW YORK, NY

Certified: PICC Lines, 11.7 contact hours — IV, Venipuncture — 10.0 contact hours

CORAZON MEDTREN, BROOKLYN, NY

CPR / Infant CPR	First Aid	Fire Safety	Infectious Disease Control	Child Abuse	HIV/Aids

PROFESSIONAL EXPERIENCE

Registered Nurse Supervisor: COBBLE HILL NURSING CENTER, Brooklyn, NY (2002–Present)
Assigned to 55-bed geriatric unit to develop and supervise care-plan delivery by Licensed Practical Nurses and Personal Care Aides. Direct evening interdisciplinary team attending 350 patients. Monitor vital signs and assess patient status. Perform clinical duties in accordance with center guidelines. Guarantee safe, efficient admissions, transfer, and discharge of patients. Coordinate resident transfers to hospitals as ordered by physicians.

Licensed Practical Nurse: COLUMBIA PRESBYTERIAN, NEW YORK, NY (1996–2001)
Attended to medical-surgical patients in 48-bed unit of elite McKeen Pavilion. Medical specialties included cardiac with oncology, telemetry, neurosurgical, neurology, GYN, GU, and ENT.

- Noted for exceptional care delivery, frequently receiving written acknowledgements from patients and families.
- Paved the way for future Brooklyn Adult Licensed Practical Nursing Program graduate hires.

EDUCATION

HELENE FULD COLLEGE OF NURSING, NEW YORK, NY
AAS: Registered Nurse (2001)
GPA 3.93; Dean's List; Class President; Susan Ullman Award: Academic Excellence and Clinical Honors

BOARD OF EDUCATION, BROOKLYN ADULT LICENSED PRACTICAL NURSING PROGRAM, Brooklyn, NY
Licensed Practical Nurse (1995)
Dean's List; Class President; Humanitarian Award

Strategy: *This cleverly designed resume resembles a hospital form and concisely portrays the extensive training, credentials, and experience of this new-graduate RPN with several years of LPN experience.*

ELAINE MARSHALL

(813) 555-1234   4004 Carroll Wood Circle, Tampa, Florida 33625   emarshall@yahoo.com

Registered Nurse
U.S. Air Force, 1993–Present — U.S. Army, 1989–1992

Level III Clinical Nurse, 10/02–Present

Plan and implement nursing care for acute and critically ill patients. Provide immediate post-anesthesia recovery for postoperative patients. Orient and train new personnel. Supervise two Medical Technicians. Serve as Trauma Unit Nurse specializing in liver and kidney transplant in Level 1 Trauma Center.

Triage Telephone Nurse, 01/01–01/02

Facilitated referrals for 140 primary-care providers, specialists, and community resources. Documented patient and nurse interaction and issued advice per established unit protocols. Acted as Triage Nurse in the Emergency Department. Identified patient classification range from emergency to non-urgent. Worked as the Team Coordinator. Formulated and planned care for patient's optimal health, ranging from physiological to psychosocial.

Nurse Manager, 04/00–01/01

Supervised three Telephone Triage Nurses and ten Appointment Clerks. Planned, organized, and directed activities to enhance accessibility and ensure quality patient care for over 90,000 enrolled beneficiaries, including retirees and families.

Staff Nurse, 12/93–07/98

Provided care to critically ill patients requiring complex computerized cardiac hemodynamic monitoring and mechanical ventilation. Supervised five Nurses and three Medical Technicians.

Education & Training

M.S., Community Health Administration and Wellness Promotion: Chicago College of Health Science, Chicago, IL, 2001
B.S., Nursing: Salve Regina College, Newport, RI, 1989
Licensed Vocational Nurse, Salve Regina College, Newport, RI, 1987

RECENT TRAINING:

Telephone Nursing Triage	2002	Trauma Nursing Core Course, Emergency Nurse	1997
Advanced Cardiovascular Life Support	2002	Nursing Service Fundamentals	1995
Basic Life Support	2002	Senior Leadership Training	1995
Pediatric Advanced Life Support	2002	Indoctrination for Medical Services Officers	1993
Nursing Service Management	1997	Casualty Care	1991
Aerospace Medicine School of Flight Nursing	1997	Critical Care Nursing	1991

ANNUAL TRAINING:

Code Procedures	Age-Specific Care
Medical Ethics	Standards of Conduct
Patient Rights	Mentoring for Supervisors
Management of Abused Patients	Putting Prevention into Practice
Infection Control	Anthrax Training
Staff Rights	Family Advocacy
Cultural Diversity	Fire Safety
Sexual Harassment	Electrical Safety
Suicide Awareness	Security Awareness
Anti-Terrorism Measures	

Strategy: *Highlighting extensive experience gained from her military career, this resume helped a nurse transition to civilian employment.*

Benita P. King

(636) 939-1111   19524 St. Charles Drive, St. Charles, Missouri 63301   bpking@juno.com

Qualifications

- **Registered nurse** with **10 years'** experience in a major university hospital.
- Leader and problem-solver with reputation for composure and quick thinking during crises.
- Exceptional planning, prioritizing, and goal-setting abilities to achieve best patient outcome.
- Ability to create and implement more efficient methods of operations; conceptually and technically inclined.
- Educator who assimilates complex information and simplifies the delivery.
- Computer knowledge: Windows, Word, and Excel.

Professional Experience

STAFF NURSE/CHARGE NURSE

As Charge Nurse:
- Supervised up to seven-person staff: RNs, CNAs, and LPNs; accountable for patient assignment, unit operations, and overall patient care.
- Initiated CNAs regarding unit protocol and procedures.
- Scheduled unit staffing bi-monthly.
- Troubleshot problems with patients or staff, analyzing needs and generating referrals to appropriate resources.
- Maintained calm, caring environment throughout shift.

As Staff Nurse:
- Performed assessments; provided intravenous therapy, enteral and parenteral nutrition, and complex wound care; monitored various drainage devices; performed tracheal suctioning and thoracentesis assistance.
- Educated patients on procedures, healthy lifestyle — a holistic approach — and preventive measures for maintaining best outcomes.
- Collaborated daily with physicians and health care team to achieve optimum patient care.

Notable Accomplishments:
- Improved overall unit efficiency (time management) 30% by enhancing and supplementing existing tools:
  - Revamped Cardex patient-information system; simplified a complicated form, creating a "check-off" system that produced time savings during daily nurse updates.
  - Participated in computer charting trials and equipment trials.
    - Co-developed a charting-by-exception checklist to reduce paperwork required for nurse assessments.
    - Selected as a Super User for computer charting.
- Learned operation of orthopedic and CPM machines; self-trained to set up traction in three months (standard learning curve is up to a year or longer); often called on to advise colleagues on mechanical problem resolution.

Continued...

Strategy: *In addition to documenting professional experience and credentials, page 1 of this nurse's resume includes a Notable Accomplishments section that will help her stand out from the crowd.*

Benita P. King

Page Two

Work History

St. Louis University Research Hospital, St. Louis, Missouri   1993 to 2003
Class I Trauma Center/Research & Teaching hospital; 625 beds.

CNII — STAFF NURSE/CHARGE NURSE: NEUROLOGY, RENAL AND TRANSPLANT (1998 TO 2003)
37-bed unit; patient population included neurology, renal, and pre- and post-operative kidney and liver transplants.

CNI — STAFF NURSE: ORTHOPEDIC AND NEUROLOGY (1994 TO 1998)
Patient population included orthopedic surgery patients and a diversity of neurology patients, including those with Parkinson's Disease and Multiple Sclerosis.

LPN — ORTHOPEDIC AND NEUROLOGY (1993 to 1994)

Education

Associate of Science in Nursing, 1992
St. Louis Community College, St. Louis, Missouri

Certificate, **Licensed Practical Nurse,** 1991
St. Louis Area Vocational-Technical School, St. Louis, Missouri
- **Outstanding LPN Nursing Student**
- Member, **National Honor Society**

Licensure

Missouri License: 123456

Affiliations

Member, **National Association of Orthopedic Nurses**
State Parliamentarian, Health Organization Students of America, Area Vocational-Technical School

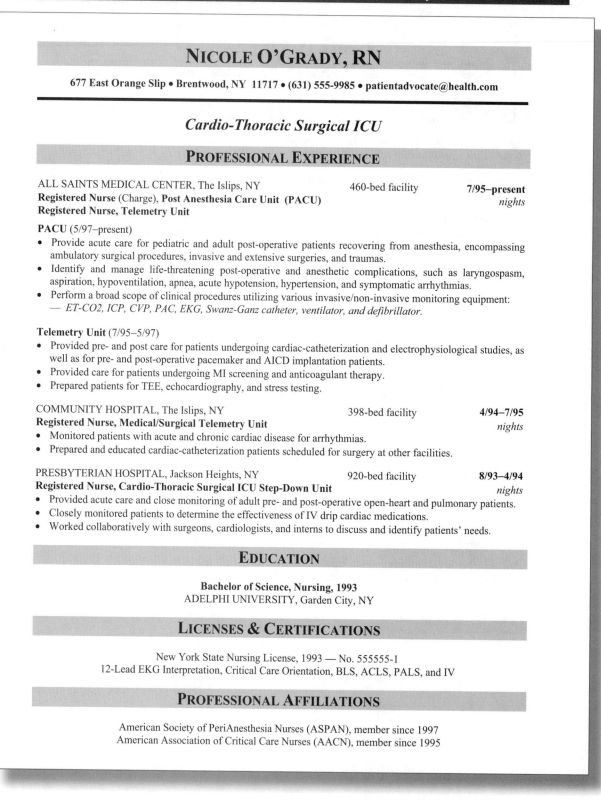

NICOLE O'GRADY, RN

677 East Orange Slip • Brentwood, NY 11717 • (631) 555-9985 • patientadvocate@health.com

Cardio-Thoracic Surgical ICU

PROFESSIONAL EXPERIENCE

ALL SAINTS MEDICAL CENTER, The Islips, NY	460-bed facility	**7/95–present**
Registered Nurse (Charge), **Post Anesthesia Care Unit (PACU)**		*nights*
Registered Nurse, Telemetry Unit		

PACU (5/97–present)

- Provide acute care for pediatric and adult post-operative patients recovering from anesthesia, encompassing ambulatory surgical procedures, invasive and extensive surgeries, and traumas.
- Identify and manage life-threatening post-operative and anesthetic complications, such as laryngospasm, aspiration, hypoventilation, apnea, acute hypotension, hypertension, and symptomatic arrhythmias.
- Perform a broad scope of clinical procedures utilizing various invasive/non-invasive monitoring equipment:
  — *ET-CO2, ICP, CVP, PAC, EKG, Swanz-Ganz catheter, ventilator, and defibrillator.*

Telemetry Unit (7/95–5/97)

- Provided pre- and post care for patients undergoing cardiac-catheterization and electrophysiological studies, as well as for pre- and post-operative pacemaker and AICD implantation patients.
- Provided care for patients undergoing MI screening and anticoagulant therapy.
- Prepared patients for TEE, echocardiography, and stress testing.

COMMUNITY HOSPITAL, The Islips, NY	398-bed facility	**4/94–7/95**
Registered Nurse, Medical/Surgical Telemetry Unit		*nights*

- Monitored patients with acute and chronic cardiac disease for arrhythmias.
- Prepared and educated cardiac-catheterization patients scheduled for surgery at other facilities.

PRESBYTERIAN HOSPITAL, Jackson Heights, NY	920-bed facility	**8/93–4/94**
Registered Nurse, Cardio-Thoracic Surgical ICU Step-Down Unit		*nights*

- Provided acute care and close monitoring of adult pre- and post-operative open-heart and pulmonary patients.
- Closely monitored patients to determine the effectiveness of IV drip cardiac medications.
- Worked collaboratively with surgeons, cardiologists, and interns to discuss and identify patients' needs.

EDUCATION

Bachelor of Science, Nursing, 1993
ADELPHI UNIVERSITY, Garden City, NY

LICENSES & CERTIFICATIONS

New York State Nursing License, 1993 — No. 555555-1
12-Lead EKG Interpretation, Critical Care Orientation, BLS, ACLS, PALS, and IV

PROFESSIONAL AFFILIATIONS

American Society of PeriAnesthesia Nurses (ASPAN), member since 1997
American Association of Critical Care Nurses (AACN), member since 1995

Strategy: *A chronological format was used to show career progression for this acute-care nurse who was seeking employment at a larger hospital.*

STEVEN NIGHTINGALE, RN, BSN

777 Larkspur Lane, Wellington, WA 99999
phone: (777) 771-7771 — pager: (777) 771-0177

Compassionate, dedicated, experienced nursing professional seeking position as **FLIGHT NURSE.** Thrive on challenge; work hard and passionately. Bright, articulate, and expressive, with a timely sense of humor. Respected and well-liked team member. Willing to relocate.

QUALIFICATIONS

- Nursing Licenses: Washington, California, Colorado
- 5+ years' experience in Critical Care, Emergency, and Special Care areas
- Nearly 2 years' patient transport experience
- Designated ICU Nurse for U.S. Naval Reserves
- Strategic thinker, able to synthesize information quickly
- Strong analytical, problem-solving, decision-making, and time-management skills

CAREER HISTORY

PACU Nurse	7/2001–present
Providence Hospital, Everett, WA	
Lieutenant, United States Navy Reserve	12/2001–present
Naval Air Station, Whidbey Island, WA	
Critical Care Transport Nurse	
Cascade Ambulance Service, Ferndale, WA	12/2001–present
Staff RN, ICU/Cardiovascular/Emergency/Special Procedures	
St. Joseph Hospital, Bellingham, WA	12/99–present
Travel Contract, Post-Anesthesia Unit	
Virginia Mason Medical Center, Seattle, WA	10/99–12/99
Travel Contract, Emergency Services	
Yosemite Medical Clinic, Yosemite, CA	6/98–10/99
Travel Contract, Post-Anesthesia Care Unit	
St. Agnes Medical Center, Fresno, CA	4/98–6/98
Travel Contract, Post-Anesthesia Care Unit	
Fresno Community Medical Center, Fresno, CA	1/98–4/98
Agency Nurse, ICU, PACU, and ER for 5 metro-area hospitals	
Health Care Staffing, Denver, CO	1/97–12/97
Staff RN, Intensive Care Unit	
Columbia Medical Care Center of Aurora, Aurora, CO	1/96–12/96

EDUCATION

B.S., Nursing, Creighton University, 1992
B.A., Humanities, Colorado State University, 1989

ACCREDITATIONS

Nursing Licenses—Washington, California, Colorado

Member, American Nurses Association; Washington State Nurses Association

Member Air and Surface Transport Nurses Association

Certifications—Advanced Cardiac Life Support, Pediatric Advanced Life Support, Trauma Nurse Core Course

"...excels in providing care for critically ill and injured patients in the unstable environment of a moving ambulance... outstanding job of providing care to our advanced life support patients ...receives complimentary feedback from physicians...EMT partners look forward to working with him...." AWC, CAS

"...work ethic is outstanding...a pleasant person...willing and rapid learner...." JT, M.D.

"...a winning personality...very calm, level-headed...performs well under pressure... well respected among his peers...strong leadership abilities... able to communicate clearly and concisely...." MW, LT, USAR

"...independent and knowledgeable and enjoys educating colleagues and patients alike...." SLK, CAPT, NC, USNR

Strategy: *A highlight of this resume for a flight nurse is the right column of testimonials.*

PAMELA MURPHY

238 Waterton Avenue • Troy, NY 12180
Home: 518-274-4565 • Mobile: 518-274-0022 • pmrmurphy2@aol.com

NURSE-MIDWIFE

"20 Years of Experience Dedicated to the Care of Women and Newborns"

Experienced Nurse-Midwife with licensure in NY, CT, and the U.S. Virgin Islands
15 years as Clinical Nurse in Labor and Delivery at Yale–New Haven Hospital
5 years as Gynecological Teaching Associate at Yale School of Medicine
Massage Therapist with training in pregnancy and infant massage
Qualified to first-assist physicians with cesarean births

Skilled in providing culturally competent care for ethnically diverse populations
Maintain calm, reassuring demeanor in high-risk and trauma situations
Proficient with, and appreciative of, varied styles of practice
Value safe, positive, and respectful care for all women
Conversant in Spanish

PROFESSIONAL EXPERIENCE

Nurse-Midwife   2002–Present
Oncelet Healthcare Center, Troy, NY

- Deliver full scope of midwifery care in private office setting and in association with Samaritan Hospital.
- Provide in-hospital night-shift coverage: Offer triage and backup evaluation for community physicians, serve as technical resource for nursing staff, provide breastfeeding assistance to new mothers.
- First-assist physicians with cesarean births.

Staff Midwife   2001–2002
Governor Juan Francisco Luis Hospital and Medical Center, Christiansted, St. Croix; U.S.V.I.

- Provided midwifery and nursing care of high-risk antepartum, intrapartum, and postpartum women from ethnically diverse populations, including women from surrounding islands.
- Documented, and communicated to appropriate team members, patient condition, treatment, progress, and other pertinent information relative to maternal/fetal/newborn status.
- Performed triage of pregnant women presenting through the emergency room.

Clinical Nurse, Labor and Birth   1986–2001
Childbirth Educator   1986–1996
Yale–New Haven Hospital, New Haven, CT

- Delivered expert nursing care to childbearing women from local communities referred for high-risk care at this university teaching hospital emphasizing evidence-based practice and customer satisfaction.
- Served as preceptor and mentor to nursing, midwifery, medical, and other allied-health students.
- Provided skilled nursing assistance in operating room and recovery room care of obstetric patients.
- Designed and implemented educational programs for pregnant women and their families.
- Guest lecturer for other educators on the benefits of massage for pregnancy, labor, and birth.

Strategy: *An extensive background in Ob/Gyn nursing strengthens the qualifications for this nursing professional who had only two years of experience in her target role of midwife.*

PAMELA MURPHY—Resume   Page 2

PROFESSIONAL EXPERIENCE (cont'd)

Lecturer/Gynecological Teaching Associates   1995–2001
Yale School of Medicine, New Haven, CT

Certified Licensed Massage Therapist (private practice)   1995–2001
Guilford Center for Alternative Healing, Guilford, CT

Labor and Delivery Nurse   1985–1986
St. Margaret's Hospital for Women, Dorchester, MA

Neonatal Intensive Care Nurse   1981–1983
Hartford Hospital, Hartford, CT

EDUCATION

Master of Science in Nursing, Midwifery Program   2001
State University of New York at Stony Brook

Bachelor of Science in Nursing   1981
University of Connecticut at Storrs

CLINICAL ROTATIONS

Danbury Hospital Women's Center, Danbury, CT (3/1999–9/1999)
Delivered well-woman, antepartum, and postpartum care.

Loyola-Yale Schools of Nursing National Health Care Project, Corozol District, Belize (3/2000)
Provided preventative health care to high-risk women and children. Designed workshops on pregnancy complications and delivered them to traditional birth attendants.

Northern Navajo Medical Center, Shiprock, NM (10/2000–12/2000)
Provided culturally competent nurse-midwifery care of Navajo women and their families during labor and birth. Performed triage, antenatal testing, induction of labor, and treatment of women with pregnancy complications.

Yale–New Haven Hospital Women's Center, New Haven, CT (1999–2001)
Led group Prenatal Care sessions and provided guidance on comfort measures in pregnancy and labor.

CERTIFICATES, LICENSURE, AND TRAINING

Certified by the American College of Nurse-Midwives since 2001

RN and Midwifery licensure held in New York, Connecticut, and the U.S. Virgin Islands
Licensed Massage Therapist in New York and Connecticut

Certificate, New York Massage Therapist Program, Connecticut Center for Massage Therapy; Newington, CT
Certificate, Sexual Assault Nurse Examiner (SANE) course, Quinnipiac University; Hamden, CT
Certificate (in progress), First Assist for Nurse-Midwives

Current in newborn resuscitation and CPR

BRIDGETTE COGSWELL, CRNA

3035 Quemby Street • Houston, Texas 77005 • 713.555.5484 • bridgrn@hotmail.com

NURSE ANESTHETIST/CRITICAL CARE/NURSING MANAGEMENT

➢ Outstanding clinician; detail-oriented, organized, vigilant, and accurate working under pressure in fast-paced environment; adept at managing multiple and diverse tasks simultaneously.

➢ Care for patients from pre-op through surgery and to post-op unit; respond quickly and with expert judgment in emergency situations; ensure quality of care meets or exceeds established standards.

➢ Dynamic communication skills with peers, patients, operating-room team, and physicians, while keeping the needs of patients foremost in mind. Readily establish rapport with individuals of various ages and cultures.

➢ Exceptional leadership, negotiation, organizational, and planning abilities. Self-motivated to work independently and unsupervised; equally effective as a team member; able to motivate others.

➢ Identify and solve problems using available resources; flexible to changing priorities.

PROFESSIONAL EXPERIENCE

New Castle Anesthesia Associates — Houston, Texas   *1999 – Present*
STAFF NURSE ANESTHETIST
• Collaborate with anesthesiologists in providing comprehensive anesthesia care to patients.

• Manage patients receiving regional anesthesia care (spinals, epidurals, and various blocks). Conduct follow-up visits after surgical procedures to evaluate anesthetic results.

Gaston Anesthesia Associates — Dallas, Texas   *1996 – 1999*
STAFF NURSE ANESTHETIST
• Managed patients and provided comprehensive, clinical anesthesia care for an MD/CRNA anesthesia service group.

• Managed patients receiving regional anesthesia.

U.S. Army Hospital — Madrid, Spain   *1990 – 1993*
HEAD NURSE
• Supervised professional and paraprofessional staff in Inpatient Ward and Outpatient Clinic, serving 5,000 patients per month.

• Managed daily administrative operations.

• Selected to serve as Director of Department of Nursing Quality Improvement Committee.

Multinational Force and Observers — Cairo, Egypt   *1988 – 1990*
COMMUNITY HEALTH NURSE
• Provided instruction in basic medical principles, CPR, and preventive medicine to 2,000 personnel from 11 nations.

• Supervised 15 paraprofessionals in basic nursing care. Administered community-health nursing programs; wrote and published a Cairo First Aid Manual; conducted a breast cancer prevention program.

Strategy: *In this resume, special emphasis is placed on the nurse's multiple certifications. A chronological format showcases her career progression.*

Bridgette Cogswell, 713.555.5484, bridgrn@hotmail.com, *Page 2*

U.S. Army Hospital — Madison, Wisconsin   *1986 – 1988*
INTENSIVE CARE UNIT — CLINICAL STAFF NURSE
- Assessed, planned, implemented, evaluated, and documented nursing care within current nursing standards for patients on a 5-bed multiple service ICU/CCU. Interpreted complex cardiac and hemodynamic monitoring data. Made independent decisions within protocol limitations.
- Acted as shift leader with direct supervision of one LPN. Performed duties of Head Nurse as required and Evening/Night/Weekend Supervisor as assigned.
- Provided paraprofessional in-service training and assisted with orientation of newly assigned personnel.

Aurora Medical Center — Kenosha, Wisconsin   *1984 – 1985*
CLINICAL STAFF NURSE
- Provided critical-care nursing services in 400-bed medical center. Implemented advanced cardiac life support. Functioned as charge nurse on rotating shifts.
- Served as member of in-service education committee and acted as unit education coordinator.

Medcentral Health Systems — Mansfield, Ohio   *1984*
GRADUATE STAFF NURSE, medical floor

LICENSES / CERTIFICATION

- ✓ Certification in Nursing Anesthesia, American Association of Nurse Anesthetists
- ✓ Registered Nurse, State of Texas
- ✓ Registered Nurse, Certificate of Authority, State of Ohio
- ✓ Registered Professional Nurse, State of Ohio
- ✓ Registered Nurse/ARNP License/Certification, State of Wisconsin
- ✓ Advanced Cardiac Life Support, American Heart Association

PROFESSIONAL AFFILIATION

American Association of Nurse Anesthetists

EDUCATION / CONTINUING EDUCATION

MS, 1996, Health Sciences, Ohio State University — Columbus, Ohio
Nursing Anesthesia Specialty, 1995, Medical City Dallas Hospital — Dallas, Texas
MBA, 1988, University of Wisconsin — Madison, Wisconsin
Executive Management Course, 1990, U.S. Army — Denver, Colorado
Middle Management Course, 1989, U.S. Army — Grand Forks, North Dakota
Advanced Trauma Life Support, 1989, U.S. Army — Grand Forks, North Dakota
Intensive Care Nursing Course, 1985, U.S. Army — Plattsburgh, New York
BS, Nursing, 1983, University of Akron — Akron, Ohio

Judith J. Jablonski

2231 West John Way ◆ Peoria, AZ 85621 ◆ 602-555-3456 ◆ jjj@juno.com

LICENSED MASSAGE THERAPIST / REGISTERED NURSE
*Seeking to integrate conventional and alternative modalities
for the enhancement of client health and wellness.*

Professional Summary

Highly skilled, quality-driven, and conscientious career professional with 22 years' experience as a massage therapist and 3 years as a registered nurse. Excellent communication skills in one-on-one situations, conducting workshops, or speaking before community organizations. Consummate team player with proven ability to motivate, supervise, and coordinate staff in providing quality patient care.

Strengths & Skills

- Oncology/Bone Marrow Transplants
- Organization/Time Management
- Assessment Skills
- High Ethical Standards/Professional Integrity

- Personnel Training/Supervision
- JCAHO Certification/Documentation
- Exceptional Bedside Manner
- Strong Interpersonal Skills/Educator to Patient, Family, Peer Group

Education & Certifications

Associate Degree in Nursing, Maricopa Community College, Peoria, AZ, 1997
Certified in Massage Therapy, Institute for Holistic Studies, Santa Barbara, CA, 1979
Certified in the Safe Handling and Delivery of Chemotherapy

Licensure

Licensed Massage Therapist, Peoria, AZ, 1980
Registered Nurse, State of Arizona, 1998

Professional Experience

Natural Health Clinic, Peoria, AZ   1980–Present
Co-Owner & Licensed Massage Therapist
- Developed and increased an extensive private practice, managing a personal client base, increasing staff to 3 massage therapists, and building a solid network of referring physicians. Recognized for exceptional customer service and care of clients.
- Integrate addition of massage therapy to help alleviate and/or minimize the associated side effects experienced by cancer patients undergoing conventional treatments.
- Increase community awareness of the benefits of massage therapy; conduct numerous workshops and public-speaking engagements on eating disorders, sexual assault, diet, nutrition, and exercise in correlation with massage therapy.

Strategy: *This nurse/massage therapist wanted to use both of her skill sets in her next position. Therefore, both are equally emphasized in her resume.*

Judith J. Jablonski PAGE 2

- Member of Board of Examiners that re-wrote and revised the ordinances and licensing examination governing massage therapy. This 2-year project resulted in improving the quality of local practitioners. Many of those changes remain in effect to date.
- Trained and experienced in forms of bodywork including Swedish, Shiatsu, Hawaiian, Trager, Deep Tissue, Foot Reflexology, and Craniosacral Therapy.

University Medical Center, Tempe, AZ   1998–Present
Registered Nurse, Oncology/Bone Marrow Transplant
- One of 15 new graduates selected for training in a specialized cancer unit focused on the preparation and care of patients undergoing bone-marrow transplants and other procedures associated with leukemias and lymphomas.
- Supervise patient-care technicians and train newly staffed nurses in unit procedures and routines of a 33-bed unit.
- Maintain excellent documentation on all patients, ensuring total compliance with the requirements mandated by Medicare, Joint Commission Accreditation Hospital Organizations (JCAHO), and various payers.
- Member of the Donor Network Approach, Cost Containment Committee, and UMC Palliative Care Task Force.

Professional Affiliations
Purple Mountain Institute, Vice President, 2000–Present
American Massage Therapy Association, 1992–Present

Awards
Mayor's Copper Letter — recognition of outstanding volunteer service to the City of Peoria

KELVIN M. PARKER

3444 River Lane • Sunset Beach, Hawaii 96712
(808) 555-0988 • kmparker@email.net

NURSE MANAGER • CASE MANAGER • DIRECTOR OF NURSING
Offering 20+ Years' Experience in Both Inpatient and Outpatient Settings

Background includes managing nurse staffs in medical facilities of 36 to 530 beds, including personnel selection, training and development, and dismissal. Maximize quality of care through needs identification and resource optimization. Work well as team member and with people from other cultures and ethnic backgrounds. Working knowledge of nurse association and Teamster contracts.

Expertise in Patient, Nurse, and Physician Relations; Project Management; Team Development; and Conflict Resolution.

- **Computer skills** include WordPerfect, e-mail, Internet, and various hospital documentation and order-entry systems.
- BLS Certified (expires 10/04); RN Licensure Hawaii #999N; ACLS Certification pending.

EMPLOYMENT HISTORY

PAN PACIFIC REHABILITATION HOSPITAL—Honolulu, Hawaii   2002–Present

Nurse Manager
95-bed acute-care rehabilitation services facility. Serve as call-in administrative officer. Accountable for house-wide supervisory coverage, including nurse staffing.

ISLAND MEDICAL CENTER—Honolulu, Hawaii   1988–2002

Nurse Manager
530-bed medical center. Charged with hospital-wide managerial coverage. Handled staff hiring, dismissal, and counseling; continuing education and development; creation and administration of $1.5 million multi-unit budget; capital improvements; contract negotiations; and grievance reconciliation. Served as Nursing Administrative Coordinator.

- Directed 24-hour coverage for 32-bed neurology, 24-bed orthopedic, and 21-bed pediatric medical/surgical units.
- Identified need and developed 4-bed step-down telemetry neurovascular unit for stroke patients.
- Implemented cost-effective chronic ventilator program, opening up beds in critical-care unit.
- Administered sick-child daycare program. Handled marketing and community outreach.
- Member of Information Services Committee. Took active role in evaluation, selection, and realization of progressive hospital-wide technology.
- Selected by physicians to receive **Nursing Leadership Award** for 1999.

Strategy: *Seeking to move from Hawaii to the U.S. mainland, this nurse manager needed a resume that clearly identified his expertise and achievements. The first paragraph under each position describes facility size and arena of care.*

KELVIN M. PARKER

Page 2 of 2

JONES HOSPITAL—Seattle, Washington   1980–1988

Nurse Manager
36-bed surgical unit. Accountable for 24-hour coverage. Established 4 post-ICU beds.

HOSPITAL OF THE NORTHWEST—Vancouver, Washington   1978–1980

Charge Nurse
42-bed hospital. Provided shift coverage for OB, ER, CCU, and medical/surgical units as
night charge nurse.

THE MONUMENT HOSPITAL—Portland, Oregon   1977–1978

Staff Nurse
27-bed hospital. Performed routine nurse duties. Assisted Nurse Practitioner in
outpatient clinic.

PROFESSIONAL ACTIVITIES/COMMUNITY INVOLVEMENT

Co-chair, American Association of Neuroscience Nurses (AANN)—Local Chapter
Active Member, American Organization of Nurse Executives (AONE)

Co-chair, "Think First" Spinal Cord and Head Injury Prevention Program
Yearly Supervisor of Health Care, Hawaii Special Olympics
Yearly Participant, Honolulu Health Fair

EDUCATION

B.S., Nursing, Walla Walla College—Walla Walla, Washington

•   •   •

Shannon Ellis

DIRECTOR OF NURSING
INNOVATIVE MANAGEMENT / INTERDISCIPLINARY RELATIONS/ LONG-RANGE PLANNING
INTERNATIONAL CURRICULUM DEVELOPMENT

PROFILE	A successful leader and visionary who combines business insight with compassion to meet the challenges facing today's healthcare organizations. Expertise in developing and implementing innovative and sophisticated healthcare departments that meet and exceed financial and service goals, as well as exceeding patient expectations. Strong background in developing international healthcare programs. Passionate about healthcare education.
CORE COMPETENCIES	• Vision and Strategic Planning • Group Facilitation • Program and Policy Development • Contract Negotiations • Organizational Development • Conflict Resolution • Resource Allocation • Interdisciplinary Communications • Fiscal Management • Regulatory Compliance
EDUCATION	1994 M.S. University of Colorado School of Nursing, Denver, CO 1983 B.S. University of Colorado School of Nursing, Denver, CO
CERTIFICATIONS	Regional Trainer for Neonatal Resuscitation Program Colorado Registered Nurse License
PROFESSIONAL DEVELOPMENT	AWONN Conference, Boston, MA, 2002, and Seattle, WA, 2000 NAWHP Conference, Fort Lauderdale, FL, 2001 Disney Institute of Quality Service for Hospitals, Walt Disney World, Orlando, FL, 2002
PUBLICATIONS	2000 "The Tajikistan Experience," Central Lines Publication, Vol. 16, Number 5, p. 42 1996 "NRP—The Tajikistan Experience," Poster Presentation, American Academy of Pediatrics Annual Meeting, Boston, MA
AWARDS AND HONORS	2001 Unit ranked above 85th percentile on the Jackson Patient Satisfaction Survey 5 consecutive quarters 1991 Clinical Nurse Excellence Award, Boulder Community Hospital

PROFESSIONAL HISTORY AT COMMUNITY HOSPITAL, LOUISVILLE, CO	Director, Women and Family Services	1995–Present
	Consultant, AIHA, Prevention of Maternal-to-Child HIV Transmission	2001–Present
	Consultant, USAID/AIHA, Primary Healthcare Nursing Curriculum	2000–Present
	Consultant, AIHA, Boulder Dushanbe International Partnership Project	1995–2001
	Director, Nursery/Pediatrics	1993–1995
	Clinical Teaching Associate, University of Colorado	1990–1993
	Director, Nursery	1991–1993
	Nurse Educator, Nursery/Pediatrics	1989–1991
	Staff Nurse/Charge Nurse, NICU	1983–1989

SELECTED EXAMPLES OF QUALIFICATIONS IN ACTION	**DIRECTOR OF WOMEN AND FAMILY SERVICES** Provide vision, strategic direction, and leadership for 5 departments, 120 staff members: Labor and Delivery, Mother-Baby, Neonatal ICU, Pediatrics, and Perinatal Education. ✓ Managed $16M annual operating budget and $1M ongoing capital budget. Surpassed all hospital financial goals and all established department financial goals 5 consecutive years. Exceeded service-delivery goals and physician/employee satisfaction goals 5 consecutive years. Strengthened relationships with physicians and staff by establishing ongoing communications.

123 Montview Lane • Louisville, CO 80027 • 303.555.1234 • shellis@hotmail.com

Strategy: *This combination CV/resume highlights responsibilities, accomplishments, and unique qualifications in a concise format.*

Shannon Ellis

DESIGN AND DEVELOPMENT OF NEW HOSPITAL

✓ Key member of five-year project team to design and develop new hospital. Responsible for vision and long-range planning, including budget planning, projecting census, and bed occupancy. Designed entire inpatient area using innovative care concepts incorporating the Disney Onstage Offstage model, family-centered, and developmentally supportive care.

INNOVATIVE MANAGEMENT

✓ First in country to design and construct neonatal suites to accommodate critically ill infants and parents. The unit allows individualized infant care, developmentally supportive care, and consideration for family needs and circumstances in the NICU.

✓ Developed and implemented new management model that blended 5 separate departments into one (Women's and Family Services Department). Cross-trained 120 staff to care for different types of patients. As a result, staff could easily respond to demands in different service areas and offer care continuity to patients, thereby enhancing physician, staff, and patient satisfaction. Replaced the Postpartum-Well Nursery with Mother-Baby Couplet Care. Patients commented favorably on the change and ranked the unit above the 85th percentile on the Jackson Patient Satisfaction Survey 5 consecutive quarters.

SELECTED EXAMPLES OF QUALIFICATIONS IN ACTION CONTINUED

INTERNATIONAL CURRICULUM

✓ Coordinated the Neonatal Resuscitation Program (NRP) training and certification with City Medical Center in Dushanbe, Tajikistan. Led a team of 5 healthcare providers to Dushanbe to train and certify physicians and nurses. Developed critical-thinking and problem-solving skills/techniques in students to compensate for the primitive conditions (no heat or hot water).

✓ Performed situational evaluation and developed road-show curriculum and primary healthcare nursing modules used to educate 40–60 nurses throughout the former Soviet Union, including Kiev, Ukraine; Ashgabat, Turkmenistan; and Yerevan, Armenia, on patient care and primary healthcare nursing techniques.

✓ Developed and presented fetal-monitoring curriculum offered in Boulder's newest sister city, Manté, Mexico. Provided on-site training to physicians and nurses using donated fetal monitoring equipment to reduce the negative patient outcomes of mothers and infants in Manté.

✓ Currently involved as a consultant in the prevention of Mother-to-Child HIV Transmission in Odessa, Ukraine. Participated in initial assessments of HIV care model for mothers and infants. Working with the University of Colorado and Denver Children's Hospital to modify and enhance the current model and develop training materials.

MEMBERSHIPS

Pending Appointment as Executive Board Member, Colorado Perinatal Care Council
Member of National Association of Neonatal Nurses
Member of Association of Women's Health, Obstetrical, and Neonatal Nurses
Member of Rotary International

Sarah Smith, RNC

2502 Lakefront Drive NE, Albuquerque, NM 87125

(505) 892-2333 Residence   sarahsmithrnc@hotmail.com   (505) 892-3565 Cell

Women's Healthcare Nurse Practitioner

Professional Summary

Dedicated women's healthcare nurse with 20+ years' experience providing positive, high-quality nursing care. RNC in Inpatient Obstetrics; have worked all four areas: Labor and Delivery, Nursery, Postpartum, and Recovery. Experience includes caring for high-risk antepartum and postpartum clients and gynecological surgical patients. As IBCLC, have high level of expertise in lactation consulting. Hard working, dependable.

Key Accomplishments

♦ **Achieved 99% success rate** in assisting any mother/infant couple to breastfeed in 5–10 minutes while offering breastfeeding expertise during underserved shifts at St. Vincent's Hospital.

♦ **Increased profits** of Good Samaritan Hospital by **$17,000 per year** when acknowledged in 1995 for submitting idea to the Value Improvement Program (VIP). Idea eliminated a system inefficiency.

♦ **Achieved 4.0 GPA** in completing Women's Healthcare Nurse Practitioner certificate program while working 12-hour shifts as PRN.

♦ **Mentored new graduates** in all aspects of women's healthcare, including sharing expertise with patient breastfeeding challenges.

Education

Women's Healthcare Nurse Practitioner Certificate, Colorado State University, Denver, CO, 2000
GPA: 4.0

ADN, RN, Linfield College, McMinnville, OR, 1980
GPA: 3.53 Graduated with Honors

Certifications

Licensed in New Mexico, Registered Nurse
Active RN licenses in California, Colorado, Oregon, and Washington

Women's Healthcare Nurse Practitioner, National Certification Corporation (NCC)

RNC, Inpatient Obstetric Nursing, NCC

IBCLC, Internationally Board Certified Lactation Consultant

NRP, Neonatal Resuscitation Program Provider

CPR, Level C

Strategy: *This resume presents impressive accomplishments front and center, followed by education and certification. Work history is detailed on page 2.*

Sarah Smith, RNC   Page Two

Professional Experience

New Mexico State Hospital, Albuquerque, NM   2000–Present
RNC, Women's Care Unit
Mother/Baby OB/GYN high-risk antepartum unit

St. Vincent's Hospital, Albuquerque, NM   1997–Present
RNC, Family Birth Center
Occasionally float to floor taking care of postpartum or labor patients

Good Samaritan Hospital, Portland, OR   1983–1996
RN, LDPR, Postpartum, and Nursery

St. Vincent's Hospital, Portland, OR   1981–1982
RN, Labor and Delivery

Washington Medical Center, Vancouver, WA   1980–1981
RN, Labor and Delivery, Nursery, and Postpartum

Recent Professional Development

Contraceptive Technology Seminar, San Francisco, CA, 2002

Dialogues in Contraception (Lunelle), National Association of Nurse Practitioners in Women's Health Conference, Albuquerque, NM, 2002

Managing Uterine Fibroids, CliniciansCME.com, 2002

Understanding Chinese Medicine, Caring for an Obsessive-Compulsive Disorder, Management of Coronary Artery Disease, CME Resource, 2002

Inevitable Menopause, Nursing Spectrum Continuing Education, 2002

High-Risk Obstetrics, Health Sciences Center, University Hospital, New Mexico State Hospital, 2002

Professional Associations

National Association of Nurse Practitioners in Women's Health (NPWH)

North American Menopause Society (NAMS)

New Mexico Nurse Practitioner Council (NMNPC)

Computer Skills

MS Windows, Internet, e-mail; familiar with computerized charting

TERRY J. ELLECH
R.N., B.S.N., R.H.I.T., C.L.N.C.

109 E. 39th Street, #129 • Kansas City, Missouri 64131
Wireless: 816-376-4908 • Email: terryellech@yahoo.com

LEGAL NURSE CONSULTANT

Multifaceted healthcare professional with experience as a registered nurse and background within a state professional review organization. Knowledge in the critical analysis of healthcare delivery and standards of patient care with the ability to review, summarize, and interpret medical records; research literature; and identify appropriate expert witnesses. Educated in all facets of medical/legal issues related to litigation process, network of medical and professional resources, screening cases for merit, and interpretation of medical records. Expert in health, illness, injury, and recovery.

License/Certification/Professional Designation

Certified Legal Nurse Consultant (CLNC)—2001
Registered Health Information Technician (RHIT)—Recertified 2002
Registered Professional Nurse—Missouri 1991

PROFESSIONAL EXPERIENCE

MERCY HOSPITAL, Kansas City, MO   1991–Present

UNIT NURSE, Mid-America Brain and Stroke Institute
Administer all aspects of health promotion and maintenance by assessing, planning, implementing, and evaluating patient care to include restoration, rehabilitation, health counseling, and education.

OHIO FOUNDATION FOR MEDICAL CARE, Columbus, OH   1980–1990

RETROSPECTIVE REVIEW COORDINATOR, Acute Care Division
Reviewed specified medical records for appropriate utilization of resources, necessity for admission, quality of care, and the diagnostic and procedural information that determined appropriate DRG assignment, utilizing professional judgment and established polices and procedures.
➢ Peer Reviewer: Internal Validity Department; Systemetrics (Super Pro).
➢ Co-Reviewer: Health Care Financial Administration's (HCFA) Uniform Clinical Data Set project researching the computerization of medical records.
➢ Member: Ambulatory Surgery Criteria Committee, Invasive Procedure Review Criteria Development Committee, Internal Quality Control Committee.

FIELD REPRESENTATIVE, Acute Care Division

MEDICAL RECORD ABSTRACTOR, Long-Term Care Division

Strategy: *Legal nurse consultant is a niche profession that requires expertise in both nursing and the many legal issues related to medical care. This resume highlights recent certification in the field along with a solid nursing background.*

TERRY J. ELLECH
R.N., B.S.N., R.H.I.T., C.L.N.C.

Résumé • Page 2

EDUCATIONAL BACKGROUND

WEBSTER UNIVERSITY   Kansas City, MO
BACHELOR OF SCIENCE—NURSING   1996

DES MOINES AREA COMMUNITY COLLEGE   Ankeny, IA
ASSOCIATE IN APPLIED ARTS—NURSING   1991
Recipient of the Roy J. Carver Foundation Scholarship

Continued Professional Development:
- Medical-Legal Consulting Institute, Inc.: CLNC Certification
- Penn Valley Community College: Associate in Applied Science—Medical Record Technology
- National Stroke Convention, San Antonio, TX

PROFESSIONAL AFFILIATIONS

National Legal Nurse Consulting Institute
American Health Information Management Association
American Nursing Association

CIVIC/COMMUNITY INVOLVEMENT

Uplift (Volunteer—Feeding the Homeless)

CHAPTER 6

Resumes for Allied Health Practitioners

- Emergency Medical Technician
- Paramedic
- Chiropractic Assistant
- Physical Therapist Assistant
- Licensed Acupuncturist and Chinese Herbalist
- Physician's Assistant
- Registered Medical Assistant
- Registered Dietitian
- Respiratory Therapist
- Physical Therapist
- Speech-Language Pathologist
- Occupational Therapist
- Vocational Rehabilitation Counselor
- Clinical Dependency Counselor
- Licensed Professional Counselor
- Psychiatric Clinician
- Forensic Pathologist

Clinical expertise is the focal point of these resumes, which represent a diverse array of health care professions. Whenever possible, quantifiable achievements are included as well.

Clark A. Vincent

9909 LaBrett Blvd. • Salt Lake City, UT 84117
801.555.0169 • VinnyClark@yahoo.com

SUMMARY

Well-rounded and enthusiastic student with a diverse background in medical training and emergency preparation. Adventurous spirit with practical training and experience; focused on a career in medicine.

EDUCATION / TRAINING / CERTIFICATION

UNIVERSITY OF UTAH
Prerequisite courses toward PreMed curriculum, 1998–1999; 2000–current

TAHOE COMMUNITY COLLEGE; Lake Tahoe, Nevada
Certified EMT (licensed in state of Nevada), 1999–2000

FEDERAL FIRE ACADEMY
Certified Firefighter / Certified in Hazardous Materials Awareness, 1999–2000

Licensed Category III (Expert) Mountain Bike Rider
Certified Diver
ALS Certified; IV Certified

EXPERIENCE / EMPLOYMENT

RAYTHEON ARCTIC SERVICES; Antarctica
Firefighter, 2000–2001
Responsible for all firefighting operations including truck and equipment operation and maintenance. Assisted search-and-rescue team with flagged routes and aircraft-rescue fire fighting.
- Trained and taught emergency medical procedures to personnel.
- Tended lines during diving sessions for scientists.

AMERICAN MEDICAL RESPONSE; Salt Lake City, Utah
Emergency Medical Technician (EMT), 2000–current
Respond to emergency calls and 911 ambulance runs. Trained in IV, advanced pharmacology, EKGs, defibrillation, and emergency driving.

AMERICAN MEDICAL CENTER; Vellore, India
Volunteer, Summer 2001
Trained national team on spinal precautions.

FLIGHT FOR LIFE; Salt Lake City, Utah
EMT, 2000
Selected as member of emergency flight/helicopter team.

MOUNTAIN RESEARCH STATION
Laboratory Technician/Assistant, 1999
Assisted in numerous activities for the national center for environmental research projects.

VOLUNTEER ASSOCIATIONS & OTHER INFORMATION

Rocky Mountain Rescue Team; Boulder County
Red Cross Volunteer

Strategy: *This young man was a world traveler who found volunteer opportunities in far-flung areas of the world. His adventures add spice to his resume, which is also rich with relevant credentials.*

IRA NEWMAN

127 Washington Avenue
Spring Valley, NY 10977

(914) 679-7029 (C)
(845) 632-7900 (H)
(917) 349-8847 (P)
iranewman@yahoo.com

PARAMEDIC

PROFILE: Dedicated, intelligent, compassionate EMT professional with extensive experience in EMS and ambulance work. Excellent technical skills. Computer proficient.

EDUCATION AND TRAINING

- **Graduate of Paramedic Course Training,** Rockland Community College, Suffern, NY, 6/02
    - → Awarded National Registry Paramedic Certificate & NY State Paramedic Certificate
    - → Considered by instructor as a "good academic student"
    - → Completed hospital rotations at Hackensack University Medical Center (ER),
      Good Samaritan (OR), Nyack (ICU/NICU), St. Joseph's (Pediatrics), and others
    - → Exceeded hours required with paramedic ride-along rotations in urban & suburban areas

- American Heart Association **A.C.L.S. Provider,** Rockland Community College, 6/01
- American Heart Association **P.A.L.S. Provider,** Rockland Community College, 8/02
- **P.H.T.L.S.** certified by National Association of EMTs, 7/01
- **EMT–D** certified, Yeshiva University, Manhattan, NY, 1995
- New York State **DEC** (Department of Environmental Conservation) Certified Search and Rescue Skills, 8/97
- New York State Notary Public, 1/99

EMS EXPERIENCE

RES MEDICAL TRANSPORT, W. Paterson, NJ   2/02–Present
ACE AMBULANCE SERVICE, Clifton, NJ   10/96–11/98
EMT (part-time)
Provide inter-facility transport between nursing homes and hospitals and deliver emergency services to contracted facilities. Pick up patient, assess patient, and ensure patient stability. Provide first aid, CPR, and emergency oxygen as required. Specialize in NICU and PICU transports. Alternate driving duties.

HADASSAH VOLUNTEER AMBULANCE   Brooklyn, NY, Catskills, NY
Volunteer   96–Present
Work closely with paramedics in providing first aid at scene of accidents and medical emergencies. Help stabilize patients and transport to hospital. Alternate driving responsibilities.

BENSONHURST VOLUNTEER EMS   Bensonhurst, NY
Dispatch Volunteer   94–95

BUSINESS EXPERIENCE

T–Z VENDING   Spring Valley, NY
Owner   96–Present
- Service soda and snack vending machines in Rockland, Bergen, and Passaic counties. Responsible for all buying, locating of sites, contracting, filling, and servicing. Expanded business 15% every year.

Strategy: *Strong education and training credentials are emphasized in this resume for a paramedic seeking a hospital-based position.*

Wendy Smith

1 Via Venus, Embrun, On K0A-5F5
(613) 333-4243   wendysmith@aol.com

CHIROPRACTIC HEALTH ASSISTANT / RECEPTIONIST

Friendly, outgoing individual with experience in a variety of positions such as chiropractic health assistant, reception, and office/secretarial work. Superior communication and computer proficiencies. Positive attitude and adaptability to change.

Highlights of Qualifications

➢ Office management experience with busy chiropractic practice, interacting with more than 300 patients weekly.
➢ Superior knowledge of medical office procedures, transcription, and terminology.
➢ Expertise with MS Office suite, e-mail, and Internet; 50 wpm keyboarding skill.
➢ Proven reliability and a commitment to continuous learning.

Member of Ontario Medical Secretaries Association

PROFESSIONAL EXPERIENCE

Reception / Medical Administrative Skills
- Recorded doctor's initial and comparative examinations on cerpics cards.
- Typed and processed doctor's reports.
- Utilized A&L OHIP Medical Billing to process OHIP on weekly and monthly schedules.
- Prepped patients for X rays (measured and recorded FSAP and lumbar lateral measurements), processed X rays, and prepared envelopes.
- Communicated with insurance health adjudicators and other professionals.

Organizational Skills
- Maintained flow of patients within the waiting room and examination rooms.
- Regulated doctor's appointments through system based on time management.
- Implemented dot system for patient cerpic cards, allowing for more efficient method of recording.
- Organized record keeping of monthly invoices, statement, and OHIP billing.
- Trained and supervised team of four chiropractic assistants for one year.

Interpersonal Communication
- Provided receptionist duties using a needs-based process involving assessing client needs, offering alternatives, and deciding on the best solution.
- Participated effectively as member of small medical group.
- Utilized respect and confidentiality when dealing with staff and clients.

Strategy: *This resume uses a functional style to group and highlight important professional skills. The employment history—with several similar jobs—can then be listed without repetitive listing of job duties.*

Wendy Smith

Page 2

EMPLOYMENT HISTORY

Chiropractic Assistant   1996–2002
West Wonderton Chiropractic Clinic, England

Chiropractic Assistant   1996
Belton Chiropractic Clinic, Belton, ON

Chiropractic Assistant / Receptionist   1995
Varry Chiropractic Clinic, Collingswood, ON

Assistant to School Nurse   1993–1995
Hubbard Avenue School, Oromocto, NB

EDUCATION AND PROFESSIONAL DEVELOPMENT

Diploma in Office Administration — Medical   **1995**
Gracian College, Barton, ON

Level four — Secretarial Education   **1986**
Memorial University, Newfoundland

COMMUNITY INVOLVEMENT

➤ Committee Vice-Chairperson. Participated in decision-making, planning, and children's education for Elizabeth Park Church.
➤ Collaborated with parent volunteers to plan and organize fund-raising activities for the Early Learning Center.

References Upon Request

ANDREW REEVES
833 Hillview Court • Fairfax, VA 22031
(703) 379-9201 • andrewr@email.com

PHYSICAL THERAPIST ASSISTANT

Three years of experience in a team-oriented, outpatient facility specializing in *orthopedics* and *sports therapy*. Accustomed to working with diverse patients, including professional athletes and the elderly. Contributed articles to a sports-related performance and injury-prevention newsletter. Experienced in conducting presentations on clinical practices and current research studies. Graduated with academic and clinical honors.

Licensure:	Physical Therapist Assistant, Virginia
Affiliations:	American Physical Therapy Association (APTA)
	Member Fairfax County Runners Club, Northern Virginia Masters Swim Team
Certifications:	Cardiopulmonary Resuscitation (CPR)/First Aid
	Certified Fitness Instructor (CFI), National Strength Professionals Association (NSPA)

RELEVANT EXPERIENCE

DUNHILL ORTHOPEDICS AND SPORTS THERAPY, Manassas, VA   2000–Present
Physical Therapist Assistant (PTA)

Collaborate with Physical Therapists (PTs) in administering patient treatment plans in this outpatient orthopedic and sports therapy practice.
- Work independently with up to 20 patients per day, recovering from orthopedic and sports injuries.
- Work with five PTs with varied treatment styles and expertise and assist in supervising PTA students.
- Assist PTs in obtaining objective and subjective information and providing patient status for reevaluations and progress notes.
- Document problematic situations and collaborate with PTs to implement appropriate intervention.
- Instruct patients' family members in participating in patient treatment and discharge planning.
- Participate in biweekly Journal Club and in-service presentations among co-workers, including orthopedic surgeons, PTs, and athletic trainers.

POWERHOUSE GYM, Arlington, VA   1999–2001
Personal Trainer

Developed and implemented individual general fitness, weight loss, and sports-specific exercise programs for clients with a broad range of fitness levels and goals.

MONROE PHYSICAL & AQUATIC THERAPY ASSOCIATES, Rockville, MD   1998–2000
Physical Therapy Aide

Assisted patients with correct application of therapeutic exercises in the clinic and in aquatic therapy. Assisted PT in transferring patients in and out of the hydrotherapy pool. Provided immediate standby assistance to patients performing therapeutic exercises in an aquatic environment. Maintained patient records and scheduled and supervised maintenance of clinic modalities and equipment.

CLINICAL AFFILIATIONS

Performed the following eight-week rotations in acute care and outpatient settings:
- *Dunhill Orthopedics and Sports Therapy,* Silver Spring, MD, 2000
- *Johns Hopkins University Hospital,* Baltimore, MD, 1999
- *Steven Onslow* (Private Practice), Wheaton, MD, 1999

EDUCATION

A.A.S., Physical Therapist Assistant, George Mason University, Fairfax, VA, 2000
4.0 GPA • Outstanding Clinical Performance Award, Physical Therapist Assistant Program

Completed coursework and received CEUs covering a variety of techniques and pathologies of the lumbar spine, thoracic and cervical spine, shoulder, and geriatric knee.

Strategy: *In a concise one-page format, this resume showcases a wide range of professional abilities for a Physical Therapist Assistant who is also a Certified Fitness Instructor.*

CATHERINE L. MASON, M.S., L.Ac.

2432-D Knob Oak Lane   E-mail: CLMason@aol.com   Home: (704) 365-3909
Charlotte, NC 28211   Cell: (704) 321-5151

LICENSED ACUPUNCTURIST & CHINESE HERBALIST

Highly motivated medical practitioner with a Master's degree in Traditional Oriental Medicine. Skilled in the application of a variety of modalities, including acupuncture, electrical stimulation, cupping, moxabustion, and *tui-na* massage. Successful experience in treatment of orthopedics (back, neck, and muscular injuries), fibromyalgia, carpal tunnel syndrome, menopause, hypertension, and sleep disorders, among others.

- Published author and invited speaker.
- Diplomate in Acupuncture (Dipl. Ac.) and Diplomate in Chinese Herbal Medicine (Dipl. CH) — National Certification Commission for Acupuncture & Oriental Medicine

EDUCATION:

M.S., Traditional Oriental Medicine, *Summa Cum Laude*, 2000
PACIFIC COLLEGE OF ORIENTAL MEDICINE — San Diego, Calif.

B.S., Biology, 1996
QUEENS COLLEGE — Charlotte, N.C.

MEDICAL INTERNSHIPS/ASSISTANTSHIPS:

September 1999– April 2000	**SAN DIEGO HOSPICE** **Intern**	San Diego, Calif.

Served as member of medical palliative care team for terminally ill patients. Instructed/ educated patients in the benefits of Chinese medicine. Participated in comprehensive patient-care conferences with multi-discipline staff (e.g., chaplain, medical director, physician, social worker, and home-healthcare case managers).

Performed acupuncture (auricular and traditional) using channel, divergent, and *zang-fu* diagnostic theories. Also performed *tui-na* (Chinese medical massage) to reduce stress and decrease pain.

- Successfully treated more than 100 patients through palliative care. Aided in pain control and symptom management for patients.

- Provided treatment of symptoms, such as pain, anxiety (including family members experiencing loss), bowel obstruction, dementia, fever, hiccups (chronic), insomnia, nausea, vomiting, and urticaria (itching).

January 1999– April 2000	**PACIFIC COLLEGE OF ORIENTAL MEDICINE** **Intern**	San Diego, Calif.

Completed a 2,000-clinical-hour internship, encompassing treatment and case management of 360+ patients. Worked under supervision of a licensed acupuncturist.

Performed patient intake (gathering and assimilating patient documentation), diagnostics, design and explication of treatment plans, and recommendations of nutritional changes and exercise modalities.

Formulated and prepared Chinese herbal medicine prescriptions.

Strategy: *To highlight strong credentials while downplaying limited formal work experience, this resume showcases publications, internships, and lecturing experience in a combination resume/CV format.*

Catherine L. Mason, M.S., L.Ac.   page 2

- Provided treatment of numerous diseases, syndromes, and ailments, including AIDS, anxiety, arthritis, asthma, carpal tunnel syndrome, CFS, diabetes, fibromyalgia, hypertension, lupus, otitis media, plantar fascitis, and TMJ. Also treated infertility, insomnia, menopause, menstrual disorders, and sports and orthopedic injuries. Applied various modalities, such as acupuncture, electrical stimulation, cupping, moxabustion therapy, and *tui-na* massage.

- Successfully treated (with dramatic results) patients with ailments such as diabetic neuropathy (patient with numbness in both feet had 50%–60% restoration in 6 months), tendon and muscular contractions of middle finger and lateral side of hand (patient was concert pianist whose abilities were restored after 3 treatments), and chronic neck pain (patient experienced total recovery after 4 applications), among others.

January 1998– December 1998	**PACIFIC COLLEGE OF ORIENTAL MEDICINE** **Clinical Assistant**	San Diego, Calif.

Assisted senior intern in diagnostics, preparation of Chinese herbal formulas, and application of various modalities, such as moxabustion therapy and electrical stimulation of acupuncture points.

RELATED EMPLOYMENT EXPERIENCE:

January 1997– June 1997	**EAST-WEST HEALTH CLINIC** **Clinical Assistant**	San Diego, Calif.

Prepared and applied hot packs, electrical stimulation, and ultrasound modalities. Administered *tui-na* massage and explained treatment plans to patients.

LICENSES & CERTIFICATIONS:

☐ National Certification Committee for Acupuncture & Oriental Medicine (NCCAOM)
 – Dipl. Ac., July 1999
 – Dipl. CH, August 1999
☐ California Acupuncture Board License, June 2000
☐ Clean Needle Technique Certification (CCAOM)
☐ Adult, Child, Infant Cardiopulmonary Resuscitation (CPR) Certification
☐ Emergency Management Certification

PROFESSIONAL AFFILIATION:

☐ Member, California Acupuncture Association

PUBLICATIONS/LECTURES/TUTORIALS:

☐ "Pacific in the Community San Diego Hospice," *Oriental Medicine,* Winter 2000
☐ Presenter of in-service training programs to San Diego Hospice medical staff:
 – "Patient Diagnosis and Development of Acupuncture Treatments"
 – "Seasonal Influences of Disease Occurrences in the Hospice Setting"
 – "Treatment Modalities Used in the Hospice Setting"
☐ Tutorials:
 – Served as Teaching Assistant, Pacific College of Oriental Medicine, "Point Location" (following California State Board Certification)
 – Instructed degree candidates, California State Board Review Class
 – Served as tutor in Chinese Herbology, Oriental Medical Theory, and Point Location
 – Lecturer, "The Four Pillars as Applied in Practice," Oriental Medicine II class

Lawrence A. Timmons

585-334-7305   24 Leonardo Drive, Rochester, New York 14624   latpa@webtv.net

SUMMARY: *Physician's Assistant and Licensed Paramedic. Extensive training and field experience in Advanced Life Support and critical care. Twenty years' experience in active duty and management roles with suburban ambulance service.*

EDUCATION:

May 2002   **Bachelor of Science, Physician's Assistant**
University of Rochester; Rochester, New York
GPA: 3.6 / Dean's List

Clinical Rotations:			
– Critical Care Medicine	– Emergency Medicine	– OB/Gyn	– Psychiatry
– Orthopaedics	– General Surgery	– Cardiology	– Pediatrics
– Internal Medicine	– Family Medicine		

May 1998   **Associate of Applied Science, Liberal Arts,**
Monroe Community College; Rochester, New York

CERTIFICATIONS:

Licensed Physician's Assistant (NYS)—1 yr.   Licensed Paramedic (NYS)—7 yrs.
Pediatric Advanced Life Support—7 yrs.   Advanced Cardiac Life Support—7 yrs.
Advanced Trauma Life Support—3 yrs.

RELEVANT EXPERIENCE:

2002–Present   **Park Ridge Hospital Emergency Department; Rochester, New York**
Physician's Assistant
Treat acute and non-acute patients in emergency department setting.
– Examine and evaluate incoming patients; diagnose and assess treatment options.
– Provide treatment and prescribe medications as necessary and appropriate.
– Admit patients to the hospital for further care as required.
– Suture lacerations and treat orthopedic injuries.
– Address needs of patients ranging from pediatric to geriatric.

1985–2001   **Mendon Volunteer Ambulance Corps; Rochester, New York**
Vice President / General Manager (2000–2001)
Directed day-to-day operations for suburban ambulance service responding to more than 4,500 calls per year. Responsibility for 130 paid and volunteer active-duty members.
– Appointed department heads responsible for Basic Life Support, Advanced Life Support, Logistics, Training, and Safety.
– Managed $450,000 operations budget.
EMT / Paramedic (1985–2001)
– Personally logged more than 5,000 hours of active duty time over 16 years.
– Served as Monroe/Livingston County Paramedic Preceptor for five years.

1994–2000   **Flight Paramedic, Mercy Flight; Canandaigua, New York**
Administered critical care to patients for air medical service covering 11-county region and responding to 500 calls per year.
– Responded to accident scenes in remote locations.
– Provided Advanced Life Support to patients as only care-giver aboard flight.

1993–Present   **Trainer / Guest Lecturer**
University of Buffalo and Monroe Community College Paramedic Training Programs.

Strategy: *This resume leverages prior experience as an EMT to support the current career target of a physician's assistant role in the emergency department.*

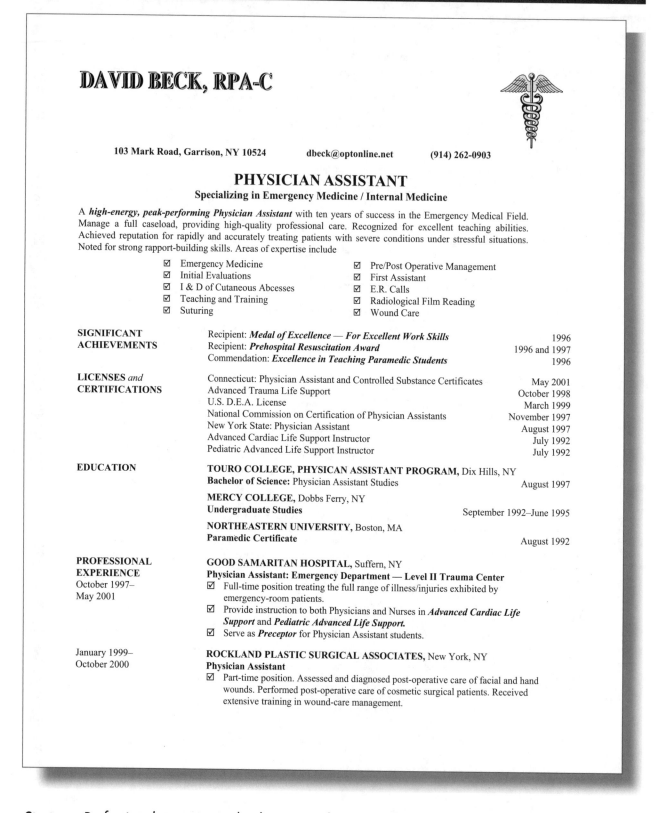

DAVID BECK, RPA-C

103 Mark Road, Garrison, NY 10524　　　dbeck@optonline.net　　　(914) 262-0903

PHYSICIAN ASSISTANT
Specializing in Emergency Medicine / Internal Medicine

A *high-energy, peak-performing Physician Assistant* with ten years of success in the Emergency Medical Field. Manage a full caseload, providing high-quality professional care. Recognized for excellent teaching abilities. Achieved reputation for rapidly and accurately treating patients with severe conditions under stressful situations. Noted for strong rapport-building skills. Areas of expertise include

☑ Emergency Medicine　　　　　　☑ Pre/Post Operative Management
☑ Initial Evaluations　　　　　　　☑ First Assistant
☑ I & D of Cutaneous Abcesses　　☑ E.R. Calls
☑ Teaching and Training　　　　　☑ Radiological Film Reading
☑ Suturing　　　　　　　　　　　☑ Wound Care

SIGNIFICANT ACHIEVEMENTS	Recipient: *Medal of Excellence — For Excellent Work Skills*	1996
	Recipient: *Prehospital Resuscitation Award*	1996 and 1997
	Commendation: *Excellence in Teaching Paramedic Students*	1996
LICENSES *and* **CERTIFICATIONS**	Connecticut: Physician Assistant and Controlled Substance Certificates	May 2001
	Advanced Trauma Life Support	October 1998
	U.S. D.E.A. License	March 1999
	National Commission on Certification of Physician Assistants	November 1997
	New York State: Physician Assistant	August 1997
	Advanced Cardiac Life Support Instructor	July 1992
	Pediatric Advanced Life Support Instructor	July 1992

EDUCATION

TOURO COLLEGE, PHYSICAN ASSISTANT PROGRAM, Dix Hills, NY
Bachelor of Science: Physician Assistant Studies　　　　　　　　　August 1997

MERCY COLLEGE, Dobbs Ferry, NY
Undergraduate Studies　　　　　　　　　　September 1992–June 1995

NORTHEASTERN UNIVERSITY, Boston, MA
Paramedic Certificate　　　　　　　　　　　　　　　　August 1992

PROFESSIONAL EXPERIENCE
October 1997–
May 2001

GOOD SAMARITAN HOSPITAL, Suffern, NY
Physician Assistant: Emergency Department — Level II Trauma Center
☑ Full-time position treating the full range of illness/injuries exhibited by emergency-room patients.
☑ Provide instruction to both Physicians and Nurses in *Advanced Cardiac Life Support* and *Pediatric Advanced Life Support.*
☑ Serve as *Preceptor* for Physician Assistant students.

January 1999–
October 2000

ROCKLAND PLASTIC SURGICAL ASSOCIATES, New York, NY
Physician Assistant
☑ Part-time position. Assessed and diagnosed post-operative care of facial and hand wounds. Performed post-operative care of cosmetic surgical patients. Received extensive training in wound-care management.

Strategy: *Professional expertise is clearly conveyed via a complete listing of all clinical rotations as well as formal experience. A graphic lends interest to the resume.*

RESUME 32, CONTINUED

December 1997– Present	**HUDSON VALLEY HOSPITAL CENTER,** Peekskill, NY **Physician Assistant: Emergency Department—Level II Trauma Center** ☑ Per-diem position.
CLINICAL ROTATIONS August 1996– September 1996	**SURGERY** St. John's Episcopal Hospital, Queens, NY ☑ Extensively trained in wound care, suturing, casting, and splinting techniques.
October 1996	**PSYCHIATRY** St. John's Episcopal Hospital, Queens, NY ☑ *Received excellent commendation* for the handling of psychosocial problems of psychiatric inpatients.
November 1996– December 1996	**OBSTETRICS/GYNECOLOGY** Lenox Hill Hospital, New York, NY ☑ Received vast training in obstetrical and gynecological emergencies.
January 1997	**EMERGENCY MEDICINE** Long Island Jewish Medical Center, Manhasset, NY ☑ Completed extensive training in reading radiological films.
February 1997	**INTERNAL MEDICINE** Westchester County Medical Center, Valhalla, NY ☑ Recertified in Advanced Cardiac Life Support.
April 1997	**PEDIATRICS** Yonkers Community Health Center, Yonkers, NY ☑ Recertified in Pediatric Advanced Life Support
May 1997	**PRIMARY CARE** Yonkers Community Health Center, Yonkers, NY
June 1997	**GERIATRICS** St. John's Episcopal Hospital, Queens, NY
July 1997– August 1997	**CARDIOLOGY** Westchester County Medical Center, Valhalla, NY
TEACHING EXPERIENCE September 1996– Present	**ROCKLAND COMMUNITY COLLEGE,** Suffern, NY **Clinical Instructor** ☑ Lectured on cardiac and respiratory emergencies to paramedic students. Received commendation for excellence in teaching.
PARAMEDIC EXPERIENCE	May 1994–May 1995 **ST. VINCENT'S HOSPITAL,** New York, NY March 1994–January 1999 **ROCKLAND PARAMEDIC SERVICES,** Orangeburg, NY August 1992–March 1994 **LIFESTAR PARAMEDICS,** Amityville, NY
PROFESSIONAL AFFILIATIONS	American Academy of Physician Assistants New York State Society of Physician Assistants Society of Emergency Medicine Physician Assistants

SAMUEL P. THOMAS

1503 North Larrabee Street
Chicago, IL 60610
(312) 915-2323

**REGISTERED MEDICAL
ASSISTANT**

CREDENTIALS
- ❏ Registered Medical Assistant
- ❏ Member, American Association of Medical Assistants
- ❏ Certified in CPR & Basic Life Support; AIDS Certificate
- ❏ Experienced performing laboratory and clinical procedures
- ❏ Proven ability to communicate with patients and healthcare staff
- ❏ Self-motivated and able to anticipate physician needs

EDUCATION
- ❏ **Associate of Science in Medical Assisting** — 1994
  Danville Area Community College, Danville, IL

EXPERIENCE
- ❏ **Medical Assistant,** Fox Valley Family Services, Geneva, IL, 1997–Present
- ❏ **Laboratory Technician,** University Physicians, Clybourn, IL, 1993–1996
  Recognized for outstanding professionalism in patient service.
- ❏ **320-hour Medical Assistant Externship,** Trendale Medical Center, Chicago, IL, 1992

Clinical Procedures

- ❏ Assist physicians in minor office surgeries and procedures.
- ❏ Prepare treatment and examining rooms.
- ❏ Take vital signs and administer injections.
- ❏ Provide patient physicals under supervision.

Laboratory Procedures

- ❏ Utilize laboratory techniques to perform routine tests:
  Strep, CBCs, Blood Sugar, Urinalysis, Pregnancy, Hematology.
- ❏ Utilize knowledge of chemistry to understand and identify reactions involved in testing.
- ❏ Identify minute abnormal details of specimens via microscope.
- ❏ Operate a variety of laboratory instrumentation.
- ❏ Prepare written reports concerning laboratory test results.

Patient Services / Relations

- ❏ Facilitate one-on-one, quality patient care.
- ❏ Write prescriptions for physician approval and signature.
- ❏ Perform call backs to check on patient status.
- ❏ Furnish instructions and information for use of medications.

Administration

- ❏ Handle basic computer functions such as patient data input and billing / insurance using Medisoft Manager.
- ❏ Apply knowledge of ICD-9 and CPT-4 coding to insurance billing.
- ❏ Manage patients' files, charts, and medical records.
- ❏ Answer incoming patient and physician referral calls and schedule appointments.

Strategy: *The chronological-functional format avoids repetition of job duties and allows emphasis on relevant yet diverse areas of training and experience—laboratory procedures, medical assisting, patient relations, and administration.*

RESUME 34: ROLANDE LAPOINTE, CPC, CIPC, CPRW, IJCTC, CCM, CSS, CRW; LEWISTON, ME

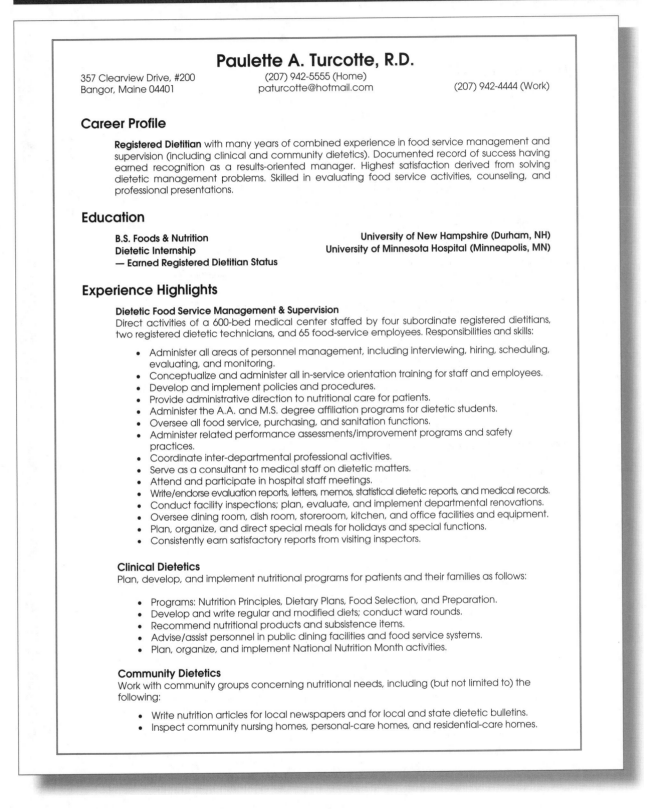

Paulette A. Turcotte, R.D.

357 Clearview Drive, #200
Bangor, Maine 04401

(207) 942-5555 (Home)
paturcotte@hotmail.com

(207) 942-4444 (Work)

Career Profile

Registered Dietitian with many years of combined experience in food service management and supervision (including clinical and community dietetics). Documented record of success having earned recognition as a results-oriented manager. Highest satisfaction derived from solving dietetic management problems. Skilled in evaluating food service activities, counseling, and professional presentations.

Education

B.S. Foods & Nutrition
Dietetic Internship
— Earned Registered Dietitian Status

University of New Hampshire (Durham, NH)
University of Minnesota Hospital (Minneapolis, MN)

Experience Highlights

Dietetic Food Service Management & Supervision
Direct activities of a 600-bed medical center staffed by four subordinate registered dietitians, two registered dietetic technicians, and 65 food-service employees. Responsibilities and skills:

- Administer all areas of personnel management, including interviewing, hiring, scheduling, evaluating, and monitoring.
- Conceptualize and administer all in-service orientation training for staff and employees.
- Develop and implement policies and procedures.
- Provide administrative direction to nutritional care for patients.
- Administer the A.A. and M.S. degree affiliation programs for dietetic students.
- Oversee all food service, purchasing, and sanitation functions.
- Administer related performance assessments/improvement programs and safety practices.
- Coordinate inter-departmental professional activities.
- Serve as a consultant to medical staff on dietetic matters.
- Attend and participate in hospital staff meetings.
- Write/endorse evaluation reports, letters, memos, statistical dietetic reports, and medical records.
- Conduct facility inspections; plan, evaluate, and implement departmental renovations.
- Oversee dining room, dish room, storeroom, kitchen, and office facilities and equipment.
- Plan, organize, and direct special meals for holidays and special functions.
- Consistently earn satisfactory reports from visiting inspectors.

Clinical Dietetics
Plan, develop, and implement nutritional programs for patients and their families as follows:

- Programs: Nutrition Principles, Dietary Plans, Food Selection, and Preparation.
- Develop and write regular and modified diets; conduct ward rounds.
- Recommend nutritional products and subsistence items.
- Advise/assist personnel in public dining facilities and food service systems.
- Plan, organize, and implement National Nutrition Month activities.

Community Dietetics
Work with community groups concerning nutritional needs, including (but not limited to) the following:

- Write nutrition articles for local newspapers and for local and state dietetic bulletins.
- Inspect community nursing homes, personal-care homes, and residential-care homes.

Strategy: Functional headings on page 1 describe extensive experience in the field of dietetics. Page 2 uses a CV format to list details of employment and affiliations.

Employment

Bangor VA Medical Center (Bangor, ME)   **1990–Present**
Assistant Chief, Dietetic Service (1990–1996)
Clinical Nutrition Manager (April 1996–Present) Due to Department Restructuring
- Serve on the VA Homeless Working Group Committee
- Member, Bangor Medical Center Fitness Committee, 1996
- President, Bangor Employee Association, 1996
- Member, Patient Education Committee, 1996
- Member, Station Safety Committee, 1996
- Member, Common Data Base Committee, 1996
  — Assist in Clinical Pathways & Interdisciplinary Computerized Assessment Processing

VA Medical Centers   **1979–1990**
Hampton VA Medical Center (Hampton, VA)   1984–1990
Chief, Clinical Section, Dietetic Service (1985–1990)
Chief, Administrative Section, Dietetic Service (1984–1985)

Des Moines VA Medical Center (Des Moines, IA)   1980–1984
Section Chief, Clinical Section, Dietetic Service

Kansas City VA Medical Center (Kansas City, MO)   1979–1980
Clinical Dietitian, Dietetic Service

U.S. Air Force   **1970–1979**
Ehrling Bergquist USAF Regional Hospital (Offutt AFB, NE)   1976–1979
Administrator, Food Service Management (Captain USAF)

Homestead USAF Regional Hospital (Homestead AFB, FL)   1972–1976
Administrator, Food Service Management

Sheppard USAF Regional Hospital (Sheppard AFB, TX)   1970–1972
Clinical Dietitian

Professional Affiliations

American Cancer Society Board Member	1995–Present
American Heart Association Board Member	1995–Present
President, Tidewater Dietetic Association	1989
Executive Board, Virginia Dietetic Association	1988–1990
Chairman, Federal Women's Program, Des Moines VAMC (Des Moines, IA)	1981
Equal Employment Opportunity, Co-Chairman, Des Moines VAMC (Des Moines, IA)	1980

Volunteer Work

Board Member—United Valley Chapter of the American Red Cross	1990–1995
Augusta Symphony Chorus	1990–1991
Board Member—Habitat for Humanity (1989), Club Member (1991)	1989–1991
Friendship Force, Treasurer (1988), News Editor (1987)	1987–1988
(Organization that promotes world peace)	

Personal Data

Available for work-related travel; willing to relocate.
Traveled extensively utilizing effective communication skills with people of varied cultures.
Served for 9 years as Captain in the USAF; Honorably Discharged.
Separate listing of personal and professional references is available upon request.

ANGELA P. CARDOVA, CRT

1834 Highlands Dr.
Novi, MI 48375

248-555-3729
cardova@msn.com

PROFILE

✓ Over 8 years as Respiratory Therapist.
✓ Adult and pediatric care provider at emergency, critical, and subacute levels. Strong patient-assessment skills.
✓ Additional experience in home-care settings.

HIGHLIGHTS OF CLINICAL SKILLS

✓ Basic respiratory therapy
✓ Ventilator set-up and management (including high-frequency oscillator ventilators)
✓ Nasal CPAP therapy
✓ Arterial blood gas sampling and analysis

✓ Oxygen therapy
✓ Pulmonary function testing
✓ Extubation
✓ Weaning
✓ Protocol-driven therapy

CERTIFICATIONS

✓ Certified Respiratory Therapist/Registry-eligible (NBRC)   ✓ BCLS (American Heart Assoc.)

EMPLOYMENT HISTORY

Respiratory Therapist: MERCY HOSPITAL • Livonia, Michigan   2002–Present
- Set up respiratory and related equipment in homes of recently discharged patients. Equipment includes:
  ✓ Oxygen concentrator   ✓ Nebulizer compressor   ✓ Air compressor
  ✓ Liquid oxygen   ✓ Apnea monitor   ✓ Suction machine
  ✓ Oxygen conserving device   ✓ Ultrasonic nebulizer   ✓ CPAP fitting and set-up
- Perform respiratory assessments.
- Verify health benefits; maintain familiarity with Medicare guidelines.

Polysomnography Technician: OAKDALE HEALTH SYSTEM • Ypsilanti, Michigan   2001–2002
- Prepared for and monitored patients during sleep studies for evaluation of obstructive sleep apnea and other sleeping disorders.

Respiratory Therapist
HALMARK HOME HEALTH CARE CENTERS • Centerline, Michigan   1998–1999
ST. JOSEPH MERCY HOSPITAL • Ann Arbor, Michigan   1995–1998

EDUCATION

AAS in Respiratory Care: GRAND VALLEY STATE UNIVERSITY • Grand Rapids, Michigan   1995
Certified Medical Assistant Program: CLEARY COLLEGE • Ypsilanti, Michigan   1990

ACCOMPLISHMENTS

✓ Collaborated with other students to reactivate Zeta Phi Beta Sorority chapter at Grand Valley State University. Served as Chapter President for one year.

References available on request.

Strategy: *The list of keyword competences at the top provides a sharp focus for this respiratory therapist resume.*

JILLIAN G. SLATTERY

7 Hill Crest Drive
Selkirk, NY 12158

518.653.2748
JillS@hotmail.com

QUALIFICATIONS SUMMARY

Professional **Physical Therapist** with 11 years of rehabilitative care experience in hospitals, geriatric facilities, and private agencies. ❖ Skilled in effective communication with physicians, patients, family members, Medicare, and insurance companies. ❖ Maximized the number of patients served by effectively meeting scheduling and facility limitation challenges. ❖ Recognized by management for thoroughness, efficiency, and sensitivity to patient needs on numerous occasions.

PHYSICAL THERAPY EMPLOYMENT

PHYSICAL THERAPIST, 1993–2003

Albany Veterans Hospital	Albany, NY	1999–2003
Albany Memorial Hospital	Albany, NY	1995–1999
County Nursing Facility	Schenectady, NY	1994–1995
Independent Living Associates	Rochester, NY	1992–1994

❖ Highly effective in diagnosing and preparing treatment plans for patients living with neurological and geriatric orthopedic conditions, resulting in increased independence. Heavily involved with designing discharge plans and follow-up instructions.

❖ Performed prosthetic training with amputee patients. Knowledgeable in E-STEM for wound healing and pain management, and with knee and hip replacement. Experience with technologies and techniques required for effective treatment of cardiac rehabilitation, sports injuries, and cervical and pelvic traction. Used ultrasound, gait belt training equipment, thera-bands, swimming pools, stretching exercises, and hot and cold packs.

❖ Trained PTAs, CNAs, and family members in infection control, injury prevention, and proper rehabilitative care, including wheelchair positioning, proper use of exercise equipment, and how to assist the patient without affecting independence or self-confidence.

EDUCATION & TRAINING

BS — PHYSICAL THERAPY, 1992
Russell Sage College, Troy, NY

❖ Clinical fieldwork conducted in rehabilitation centers and long-term-care facilities operated by the New York State Department of Health.

❖ GPA: 3.47

Extensive list of Certifications and Trainings available for review.

Strategy: Written to quickly show a broad range of experience in the field of physical therapy, this resume combines work experience so as to avoid repetitive job descriptions.

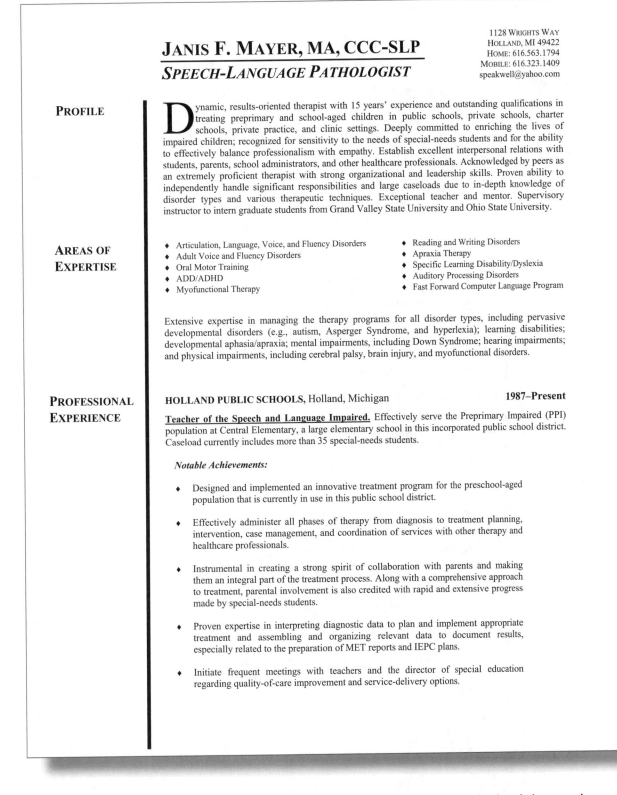

JANIS F. MAYER, MA, CCC-SLP
SPEECH-LANGUAGE PATHOLOGIST

1128 WRIGHTS WAY
HOLLAND, MI 49422
HOME: 616.563.1794
MOBILE: 616.323.1409
speakwell@yahoo.com

PROFILE

Dynamic, results-oriented therapist with 15 years' experience and outstanding qualifications in treating preprimary and school-aged children in public schools, private schools, charter schools, private practice, and clinic settings. Deeply committed to enriching the lives of impaired children; recognized for sensitivity to the needs of special-needs students and for the ability to effectively balance professionalism with empathy. Establish excellent interpersonal relations with students, parents, school administrators, and other healthcare professionals. Acknowledged by peers as an extremely proficient therapist with strong organizational and leadership skills. Proven ability to independently handle significant responsibilities and large caseloads due to in-depth knowledge of disorder types and various therapeutic techniques. Exceptional teacher and mentor. Supervisory instructor to intern graduate students from Grand Valley State University and Ohio State University.

AREAS OF EXPERTISE

- Articulation, Language, Voice, and Fluency Disorders
- Adult Voice and Fluency Disorders
- Oral Motor Training
- ADD/ADHD
- Myofunctional Therapy

- Reading and Writing Disorders
- Apraxia Therapy
- Specific Learning Disability/Dyslexia
- Auditory Processing Disorders
- Fast Forward Computer Language Program

Extensive expertise in managing the therapy programs for all disorder types, including pervasive developmental disorders (e.g., autism, Asperger Syndrome, and hyperlexia); learning disabilities; developmental aphasia/apraxia; mental impairments, including Down Syndrome; hearing impairments; and physical impairments, including cerebral palsy, brain injury, and myofunctional disorders.

PROFESSIONAL EXPERIENCE

HOLLAND PUBLIC SCHOOLS, Holland, Michigan   **1987–Present**

Teacher of the Speech and Language Impaired. Effectively serve the Preprimary Impaired (PPI) population at Central Elementary, a large elementary school in this incorporated public school district. Caseload currently includes more than 35 special-needs students.

Notable Achievements:

- Designed and implemented an innovative treatment program for the preschool-aged population that is currently in use in this public school district.

- Effectively administer all phases of therapy from diagnosis to treatment planning, intervention, case management, and coordination of services with other therapy and healthcare professionals.

- Instrumental in creating a strong spirit of collaboration with parents and making them an integral part of the treatment process. Along with a comprehensive approach to treatment, parental involvement is also credited with rapid and extensive progress made by special-needs students.

- Proven expertise in interpreting diagnostic data to plan and implement appropriate treatment and assembling and organizing relevant data to document results, especially related to the preparation of MET reports and IEPC plans.

- Initiate frequent meetings with teachers and the director of special education regarding quality-of-care improvement and service-delivery options.

Strategy: *This powerful resume begins with an extensive profile that is packed with keywords. It is followed by an Experience section that clearly highlights notable achievements.*

JANIS F. MAYER

Page 2

PROFESSIONAL EXPERIENCE (CONT.)

CENTRAL MICHIGAN SPEECH CENTER, Mount Pleasant, Michigan   **1991–Present**

<u>Speech-Language Pathologist.</u> Part-time private practice providing individual therapy for children and group social skills training. Accomplished therapist emphasizing early intervention in treatment. Research medical cause/etiology for presenting problem, and develop and design therapy plans that are tailored to the individual client. Manage the day-to-day operations of the practice (i.e., appointment scheduling, billing, report writing, etc.). Caseload consists of approximately 20 clients.

Notable Achievements:

- Manage a very successful speech program during the school year that complements therapies performed for the school district. In addition, developed and maintain an innovative summer treatment program for students during summer vacation.

- Foster spirit of collaboration and involvement in treatment process with parents and other family members.

- Successfully incorporate technology into treatment, using a wide range of educational software including the Fast Forward Language/Reading Program.

- Actively consult with medical personnel, teachers, and other speech therapists regarding treatment strategies, when necessary.

- Keenly familiar with Medicaid and insurance billing practices.

- As a result of excellent professional reputation, the practice was featured in a segment broadcast on WWFT channel 8. A piece on the practice was also run in the "Health" section of the *Mount Pleasant Press.*

EDUCATION

Master of Arts, Speech-Language Pathology
CENTRAL MICHIGAN UNIVERSITY, Mount Pleasant, **1986**

Bachelor of Science, Speech Pathology and Audiology
CENTRAL MICHIGAN UNIVERSITY, **1985**

CERTIFICATIONS & AFFILIATIONS

Certificate of Clinical Competence, ASHA

Certificate of Continuing Education in Elementary Education (Certified K–8)

American Speech-Language Hearing Association (ASHA)

Michigan Speech-Language Hearing Association (MSHA)

Michigan Education Association (MEA)

International Association of Orofacial Myologists (IAOM)

AWARDS & HONORS

ACE Award for Continuing Education, ASHA

Clinician of the Year, Central Michigan University

Graduate Fellowship Award, Central Michigan University

Robert Wood Johnson Internship Award, Central Michigan University

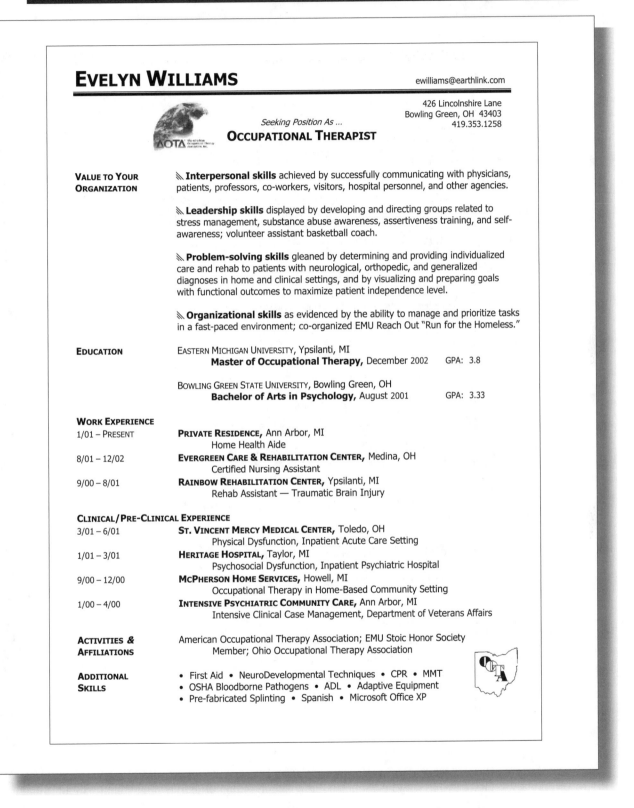

EVELYN WILLIAMS

ewilliams@earthlink.com

426 Lincolnshire Lane
Bowling Green, OH 43403
419.353.1258

Seeking Position As ...
OCCUPATIONAL THERAPIST

VALUE TO YOUR ORGANIZATION

Interpersonal skills achieved by successfully communicating with physicians, patients, professors, co-workers, visitors, hospital personnel, and other agencies.

Leadership skills displayed by developing and directing groups related to stress management, substance abuse awareness, assertiveness training, and self-awareness; volunteer assistant basketball coach.

Problem-solving skills gleaned by determining and providing individualized care and rehab to patients with neurological, orthopedic, and generalized diagnoses in home and clinical settings, and by visualizing and preparing goals with functional outcomes to maximize patient independence level.

Organizational skills as evidenced by the ability to manage and prioritize tasks in a fast-paced environment; co-organized EMU Reach Out "Run for the Homeless."

EDUCATION

EASTERN MICHIGAN UNIVERSITY, Ypsilanti, MI
Master of Occupational Therapy, December 2002   GPA: 3.8

BOWLING GREEN STATE UNIVERSITY, Bowling Green, OH
Bachelor of Arts in Psychology, August 2001   GPA: 3.33

WORK EXPERIENCE

1/01 – PRESENT   **PRIVATE RESIDENCE,** Ann Arbor, MI
Home Health Aide

8/01 – 12/02   **EVERGREEN CARE & REHABILITATION CENTER,** Medina, OH
Certified Nursing Assistant

9/00 – 8/01   **RAINBOW REHABILITATION CENTER,** Ypsilanti, MI
Rehab Assistant — Traumatic Brain Injury

CLINICAL/PRE-CLINICAL EXPERIENCE

3/01 – 6/01   **ST. VINCENT MERCY MEDICAL CENTER,** Toledo, OH
Physical Dysfunction, Inpatient Acute Care Setting

1/01 – 3/01   **HERITAGE HOSPITAL,** Taylor, MI
Psychosocial Dysfunction, Inpatient Psychiatric Hospital

9/00 – 12/00   **McPHERSON HOME SERVICES,** Howell, MI
Occupational Therapy in Home-Based Community Setting

1/00 – 4/00   **INTENSIVE PSYCHIATRIC COMMUNITY CARE,** Ann Arbor, MI
Intensive Clinical Case Management, Department of Veterans Affairs

ACTIVITIES & AFFILIATIONS

American Occupational Therapy Association; EMU Stoic Honor Society Member; Ohio Occupational Therapy Association

ADDITIONAL SKILLS

- First Aid • NeuroDevelopmental Techniques • CPR • MMT
- OSHA Bloodborne Pathogens • ADL • Adaptive Equipment
- Pre-fabricated Splinting • Spanish • Microsoft Office XP

Strategy: *Even a new graduate can emphasize value to an organization, as shown in this resume.*

OTTO K. SPIEGEL

335 Opal Avenue
Avon, Connecticut 06001
860.345.5432
mirrorotto@msn.com

VOCATIONAL REHABILITATION COUNSELOR

Excellent problem-solving and abstract thinking skills, with proven ability to analyze problems, identify possible solutions, and initiate and carry through action plans. Empathetic listener with capability to set firm boundaries. Comfortable working with diverse populations. Trilingual, English/Spanish/German. Computer skills include Word, Excel, PowerPoint, Publisher.

PROFESSIONAL HIGHLIGHTS

Vocational Rehabilitation Counselor   1998–Present
JACOBS PSYCHIATRIC INSTITUTE, Hartford, CT

- ◈ *Challenge:* Consumers entered treatment because of highly stressful jobs.
- ◈ *Action:* Arranged Family Medical Leave and disability benefits with employer, and negotiated accommodation under Americans with Disabilities Act for transfer to a less stressful position; or assisted consumer in finding new, less stressful position with another employer.
- ◈ *Result:* Consumers were able to leave treatment and enter a less stressful environment without relapsing.

- ◈ *Challenge:* Consumers with spotty work records and/or criminal history had problems finding employment and explaining work gaps.
- ◈ *Action:* Worked with state agencies to identify employers who were willing to hire such people; provided job coaching during first months on job. Also, rehearsed with consumers how to explain gaps during interviews.
- ◈ *Result:* Consumers were able to keep jobs and avoid relapsing.

- ◈ *Challenge:* Consumers did not have appropriate clothes for interviewing and working.
- ◈ *Action:* Organized "dress for success" clothing store, collected used professional clothes from hospital employees and greater Hartford community, and provided several free outfits for consumers in job search.
- ◈ *Result:* Consumers were able to present professional image during interview and at work.

- ◈ *Challenge:* Consumers had long history of mental illness and had acquired no job skills.
- ◈ *Action:* Provided work skills training and volunteer experiences to prepare them for the workplace; identified employers who would be willing to hire consumers; provided job coaching during first months on job.
- ◈ *Result:* Some consumers were able to hold part-time jobs while remaining in treatment.

Career Counselor   1994–1998
Tucson Community College, Tucson, AZ

EDUCATION

Arizona State University, Tempe, AZ
M.Ed., Counseling
B.S., Psychology

Strategy: *The Challenge-Action-Result format makes a strong impact and clearly communicates unique career achievements.*

ANDREW J. HOLMES

1293 Oakland Drive
Chicago, Illinois 60612
773-299-1255
Andrew12@net.com

■ CAREER FOCUS

Chemical Dependency Counseling

■ SKILLS ANALYSIS

- Familiar with various phases of treatment, including
  - Inpatient
  - Family
  - Continuing Care
  - Outpatient
  - Social Work
  - Residential

Counseling:
- Knowledgeable concerning group process.
- Facilitate small group; caring, compassionate demeanor.
- Record subjective impressions of individuals.
- Evaluate progress and results of clients' treatment plans.
- Effective as a group team leader/team member.

Communications:
- Display empathetic concern for clients.
- Participate as an active listener.
- Share professional needs with staff.
- Actively involved in community education/resources.
- Member of interdisciplinary team.

Managing:
- Execute the responsibilities as Residential Manager for 15-person, male residential unit at the Wood Oaks Center in Chicago.
- Provide one-to-one counseling and coaching.
- Maintain accurate documentation and records.
- Serve as role model for residents.

■ EXPERIENCE

- Residential Manager, Wood Oaks Center, Chicago, Illinois, 1997–Present
- Chemical Dependency Counselor, Stator Hospital, Peoria, Illinois, 1993–1997

■ EDUCATION

- Chemical Dependency Counseling Certificate, Roe College, Peoria, Illinois, 1992
- Associate of Arts, Illinois Community College, Springfield, Illinois, 1991
- Alcoholics Anonymous — Active Member, 1991–Present

Strategy: *To assist in a transition from management back to counseling, this resume downplays management experience and highlights professional credentials and skills in direct care.*

MAY REINER, M.Ed., L.P.C.

972.522.3221
1100 Elm Drive
McKinney, TX 75069   mr1@ev1.net   Mobile: 214.799.9083

806.798.0414
3722 87th Place
Lubbock, TX 79423

LICENSED PROFESSIONAL COUNSELOR

Over 13 years of experience as a clinician, providing

- *Crisis intervention, therapy, advocacy, and support services for victims of or witnesses to family violence, sexual assault, and other violent crimes.*

- *Therapy services to battered and abused women and their families.*

- *Therapy and support services to abused and traumatized children, adolescents, and their families.*

- *Case management and coordination of referrals for additional mental health and social services needed by clients.*

- *Clinical services as part of multidisciplinary teams.*

Extensive training and experience in providing therapy services in both public and private sectors. Additional areas of therapeutic expertise and experience:

- Depression, anxiety, divorce
- Family relationship issues

- Child and adolescent issues
- Illness and disability issues
- Grief, bereavement, and loss

- School concerns
- Parenting issues

PROFESSIONAL TRAINING AND EDUCATION

Galveston Family Institute, individual and family therapy — one-year doctoral-level practicum supervised by Victor Loos, Ph.D., Clinical Psychologist.

Houston Child Guidance Center, individual and family therapy for children, adolescents, and adults — one-year training supervised by Patrick Brady, Ph.D., Clinical Psychologist.

National Office of Victims Assistance (NOVA), National Community Crisis Response Team Training — Basic and Advanced — 60 hours of training.

Training in play therapy.

Numerous hours of continuing professional education, including training in family violence, child abuse, sexual abuse, trauma, bereavement and loss, and suicide prevention.

M.Ed., Counseling Psychology, University of Houston.

M.A., Programs for the Deaf (Educational Administration and Supervision), California State University, Northridge.

B.S., Deaf Education and Mental Retardation Major, Texas Tech University.

LICENSURE

Texas Licensed Professional Counselor (L.P.C.)

Strategy: *Seeking a transition from school to hospital-based physical therapy, this candidate "hid" her recent school-based experience on page 2 and sold herself on the strong first page.*

MAY REINER, M.Ed., L.P.C.

Mobile: 214.799.9083
Dallas Residence: 972.522.3221
Page Two
mr1@ev1.net
Lubbock Residence: 806.798.0414

CERTIFICATIONS

School Counselor (Texas, all-level)
Mental Retardation (Texas, all-level)
Deaf Education (Texas, all-level)

Professional Mid-Management (Texas)
Special Education Supervisor (Texas, all-level)
Educational Supervisor (Texas, all-level)

SELECTED PROFESSIONAL ACCOMPLISHMENTS

- Experienced therapist with traumatized individuals and families from multicultural backgrounds and across all income levels.

- Leader in the development and implementation of the Houston Independent School District's (HISD) North District Community Guidance Center situated in low-income and high-violence area of Houston.

- Served on multidisciplinary teams with other mental health professionals, including social workers, nurses, psychologists, speech therapists, physical therapists, and consulting physicians.

- Successful program development and implementation — assisted in writing and implementing a million-dollar grant for a violence-prevention program — one of six awarded by Department of Education.

- Designed and developed district-wide plan for the implementation of HISD's Student Assistance Programs for Safe and Drug-Free Schools.

- Developed, designed, and implemented an HISD district-wide program for deaf/multi-handicapped students from 3 to 22 years.

- HISD VIP'S (Volunteers in Public Schools) Outstanding Employee Award.

- Presenter at local, state, and national conferences.

EXPERIENCE

Therapist and Consultant, La Rosa — non-profit community agency serving battered women and families, Houston, TX — 1998–2001

Counselor, North District Community Guidance Center and Alternative School, Houston Independent School District (HISD), Houston, TX — 1995–2001

Counselor Specialist, Student Assistance Program, HISD, Houston, TX — 1991–1995

Group Therapist, Houston International Hospital, Houston, TX — 1989–1990

Assistant Principal, T.H. Rogers School and Grady Special School — gifted and talented and deaf and multi-handicapped students; **Instructional Supervisor,** Regional Program for the Deaf, HISD, Houston, TX — 1975–1989

MEMBERSHIPS AND VOLUNTEER ACTIVITIES

Member: American Counseling Association, Texas Counseling Association, AK Rice Institute.
Volunteer: Family Service Center; Children's Sex Abuse Program; Casa de Esperanza, serving abused and traumatized children; and Big Brothers/Big Sisters of Houston.

Genevieve L. Swanson, MSW, LCSW

12 Leete's Island Road • Branford, CT 06405 • glswanson2@snet.net
203.515.2222 (res.) • 203.314.4444 (cell)

Qualifications Profile — Candidate: Psychiatric Clinician

- **Empathetic, effective, and motivated Mental Health Professional** with proactive, positive approach reinforced by 14 years' clinical experience (including that as a private practitioner).
- Keen understanding of diverse cultural backgrounds; highly responsive to widely varied patient needs and circumstances. Extensive familiarity with assessment techniques, differential diagnoses, and DSM-IV codes; key resource to colleagues and allied health professionals. Collaborative team player. Expert networking, mediation, and conflict-resolution skills. Excellent communication abilities; highly compassionate.

Professional Experience

PSYCHIATRIC INSTITUTE / ST. FRANCIS HOSPITAL • Hartford, CT   Nov. 2002–Present
Senior Psychiatric Clinician

Provide psychiatric clinical assessments and high level of support to Emergency Department's psychiatric unit patients (outpatients as well as those admitted) and walk-in/residential patients of Psychiatric Institute program; approximately 80% of 400 patients seen per month in ED/walk-in facility are admitted.

- Efficiently conduct comprehensive 17-page assessments; 1 of 2 clinicians with disposition privileges.
- Frequently selected to manage highest-profile assessments (well-known public figures/celebrities).
- Supervise/mentor MSW and LCSW candidates, psychiatry residents, and Physician Assistant students.
- Identify critical needs and provide full range of trauma support within Emergency Department; employ highly empathetic approach and quickly build rapport with counseling families.
- Skilled in immediately assessing and appropriately handling potentially dangerous situations; defusing stressful scenarios; and effectively liaising among physicians, patients, families, emergency medical personnel, and law enforcement representatives to assure most appropriate patient treatment/response.
- Facilitate ongoing Crisis Intervention and Critical Incident Stress Debriefing education to staff and community. Member, Disaster Relief Team.
- At own initiative, design assessment and peer-review tools; source and scrutinize best business practices utilized in other facilities to enhance internal application.
- Participate in focus-group discussions, involving family members wherever possible.
- On a contractual basis, conduct utilization reviews with several managed-care companies.

PRIVATE PRACTICE • Branford, CT   Jan. 1999–Jan. 2002
Psychotherapist

- As part-time practitioner, provided individual, group, and marital therapy; brief and long-term modalities.

BEHAVIORAL SERVICES OF CONNECTICUT • East Hartford, CT   Jan. 1999–Nov. 2000
Psychotherapist

- Provided individual and marital therapy in an outpatient setting; primarily supported an adult and geriatric population. Simultaneously conducted utilization review with managed-care companies.
- Initiated outreach to community and family members; identified comprehensive services available.

Strategy: *An effective page-1 resume format that showcases extensive experience and expert qualifications is followed by CV-style content on page 2.*

Genevieve L. Swanson, MSW, LCSW   Page Two

Professional Experience *(continued)*

NETCARE, Inc. • Avon, CT   **Jan. 1997–Jan. 1999**
Utilization / Care Manager
- Scope of responsibility entailed case management, daily utilization review for Connecticare Behavioral Health, and doctor-to-doctor reviews.
- Facilitated and sustained effective network between providers and patients.

YALE–NEW HAVEN HOSPITAL • New Haven, CT   **Jan. 1995–Jan. 1997**
Psychiatric Clinician
- Provided crisis assessment and short-term crisis counseling for Emergency Department, including counseling to physicians following patient deaths.
- By special request, facilitated workshops regarding suicide in public schools.

Education   UNIVERSITY OF MASSACHUSETTS • Amherst, MA
- **Master of Social Work Degree, Clinical Social Work** (1994)
- School of Social Work
- Master's Dissertation: Exploring Human-Animal Bond with Bereavement

UNIVERSITY OF MASSACHUSETTS • Amherst, MA
- **Bachelor of Science Degree, Human Development and Family Relations** (1989)
- School of Family Studies

Continuing Professional Education includes numerous CEUs; select highlights follow:
- **Keeping the Soul Alive** (2002)
- **Cultural Awareness of Beliefs and Practices at the Time of Terminal Illness and Death** (2002)
- **Journey Through Grief** (2002)
- **Ethics and Professional Conduct** (2002)
- **Diversity and Cultural Relations** (2002)
- **Psychopharmacology for Clinicians** (2001)

Certifications
- **L.C.S.W.** — Connecticut (1995–Present)
- **L.C.S.W.** — Massachusetts (2000–Present)

Affiliations
- **National Association of Social Workers** (1995–Present)
- **Nature Conservancy** (1989–Present)
- **Humane Society of the United States** (lifetime member)
- **New Haven Symphony Orchestra** (1990–Present)
- **Branford Alliance for the Arts** (1997–Present)

ALEX AHOKA

3477 Red Wall Street
Cary, North Carolina 27615
(919) 921-5578
aahoka@earthline.com

FORENSIC PATHOLOGIST
Focused on a position with the Arizona Criminal Investigation Bureau
Native American Division – Cherokee Nation

Multi-year, diversified experience in the area of laboratory/field research and analysis. 11+ years of experience in forensic science and laboratory procedures with the North Carolina State Bureau of Investigation, early experience with the Federal Bureau of Investigation. Qualified as an expert in fingerprint, footwear, and tire-track examinations for State and Federal courts. Seeking opportunity as a forensic pathologist where these skills will be valued and utilized:

*	*Crime Scene Processing*	*	*Forensic Impressions Expert*
*	*Trainer – SBI/FBI Level*	*	*Expert: Fingerprints, Footwear, Tire Tracks*
*	*Forensic Latent Print Analysis*	*	*Strong Oral and Written Communications*
*	*Image Enhancement Processes*	*	*Examination/Results Reporting*
*	*Criminal Identification Methods*	*	*Evidence Collection Procedures*
*	*SOP/Policy/Procedure Development*	*	*Instrumentation/Laboratory Equipment*
*	*Laboratory Techniques/Safety*	*	*Technology Implementations*
*	*National/International Travel Experience*	*	*Latent Palm/Fingerprint Identification*
*	*Precise/Accurate Research*	*	*Internal/External Government Liaison*
*	*HAZMAT Environmental Experience*	*	*Expertise in Forensic Science Methodology*
*	*North Carolina Criminal Law Knowledge*	*	*Federal Law Knowledge*

SUMMARY OF QUALIFICATIONS

- *Strong training and background in forensic science, laboratory processes and procedures, crime-scene processing, AFIS searches, and image enhancement. Expert knowledge of latent print examination procedures. Known throughout the industry as a highly detailed analyst who thrives on working with complex and critical cases.*
- *Successfully conducted multiple crime-scene and evidence-collection activities for major field investigations.*
- *Outstanding ability to produce analysis, research, and technical reports. Proven experience conducting forensic analysis of latent prints and communicating findings as an expert witness.*
- *11+ years of proven experience as a scientific researcher; effectively orchestrate independent studies and research to improve forensic analysis techniques and criminal identification methods and procedures.*
- *Capable of developing and conducting training programs and teaching current crime-scene data collection and preservation techniques to new field personnel.*
- *Expert laboratory skills with the ability to oversee, coordinate, and review the work of other latent print analysts and laboratory technicians.*
- *Diversified field research project teamwork in a variety of settings. Able to adapt to any team-focused research atmosphere and assist or research with cross-functional team members.*

CONDUCTED TRAINING FOR MULTIPLE ORGANIZATIONS

- SBI ACADEMY, Salemburg, NC
- NORTH CAROLINA DIVISION OF THE INTERNATIONAL ASSOCIATION FOR IDENTIFICATION
- UNIVERSITY OF TENNESSEE, DEPARTMENT OF FORENSIC SCIENCE, Knoxville, TN
- FORSYTH TECHNICAL COMMUNITY COLLEGE, Winston-Salem, NC
- THE FBI ACADEMY, Quantico, VA
- INTERNATIONAL ASSOCIATION OF IDENTIFICATION TRAINING CONFERENCES

Strategy: *This detail-rich presentation covers the lengthy career of an experienced forensic pathologist. Both key competencies (page 1) and equipment capabilities (page 2) are shown in a chart format.*

ALEX AHOKA

PROFESSIONAL EXPERIENCE

NORTH CAROLINA BUREAU OF INVESTIGATION, Raleigh, NC
Forensic Impression Analyst II, 1987–Present
FEDERAL BUREAU OF INVESTIGATION, Washington, DC
Fingerprint Technologist, 1979–1987

- Conduct detailed, complex, and independent forensic analyses to develop, enhance, search for, and identify latent finger/palm prints.
- Serve as a liaison with representatives of government agencies and provide assistance on technological developments, analytical techniques, and problem resolutions. Sources of contact include
  - SBI Personnel
  - State Law Enforcement Officers
  - Court Officials
  - State Medical Examiner's Office Staff
  - City/County Law Enforcement Officers
  - Federal Court Officials
  - Academic & Scientific Professionals
  - Defense Attorneys & Prosecuting Experts
  - Victims & Witnesses
  - Business Professionals
- Work within deadline-oriented environments where schedules need to be flexible and travel is expected. Proven ability to manage heavy workloads and adapt to ever-changing methodologies and technologies for the collection and analysis of evidence. Able to make effective repairs on proprietary equipment and instrumentation.
- Maintain a current working knowledge of the methods, procedures, and practices used in the investigation of criminal offenses. Ensure that proper procedures are followed to secure and identify crime scenes and related evidence.
- Utilize expert knowledge of North Carolina state laws and how they are applied in the interpretation of investigative cases. Applications involve crime scenes, arrests, the compilation of detailed reports, and effective court testimony.
- Utilize firearms, tools, and equipment that may be involved in the evidence collection and preservation process.
- Integrate knowledge of scientific methodology and laboratory safety practices with the principles, concepts, and theories involved with the forensic examination and analyses of friction ridge detail, shoe track, and impression evidence.
- Analyze and compare critical and often very minute and detailed differences in impressions using high-end instrumentation for complex investigations.
- Assist in the administration of specialized and ongoing technical training curriculum for new forensic analyst team members.
- Conduct and manage complex and often routine chemical procedures. Analyze and report results through methodological interpretation and theoretical problem-solving techniques.
- Communicate and serve as a member of the team. Work effectively with laboratory personnel and other law-enforcement agents.

EQUIPMENT & MATERIAL SKILLS SUMMARY

Laboratory Model Argon Ion Laser	*Dye Laser (599-01)*
Stat Camera/4H5 Cameras/35mm Cameras	*Omniprint 1000, Spectrum 9000, Crimescope*
Spectroline UV	*Ardox UV*
Xenon Arc Lamp	*Forensic Macroscopic Comparator*
Forensic Macroscopic Magnifier	*CU5 & MP4 Polaroid Cameras*
More Hits Computer Software	*Electrostatic Dust Print Lifter*
Precision Calipers	*Automated Fingerprint Identification System*
Personal Computers/Proprietary Applications	*Various Field Equipment*

EDUCATION & CERTIFICATION

NORTH CAROLINA STATE UNIVERSITY, Raleigh, NC
B.S. in Criminal Justice, May 1988

CERTIFIED LAW ENFORCEMENT OFFICER

References Available Upon Request

CHAPTER 7

Resumes for Allied Health Technicians and Technologists

- Laboratory Technologist
- Molecular Laboratory Technician
- Biochemical Clinical Technologist
- Ophthalmology Technician
- Ultrasound Technologist
- Radiologic/Mammography Technologist
- Phlebotomy Technician
- Certified Surgical Technologist
- Hearing Instrument Specialist
- Biomedical Instrument Technician
- Diagnostic Services Supervisor

Specialized knowledge is a key factor for employment as a technician or technologist. Many of the following resumes contain sections that detail specific training, instrumentation, clinical skills, and other competencies to demonstrate mastery of a field of knowledge.

Donna W. Boylen

777 18th Street #4
West Des Moines, IA 50265
Phone: (515) 444-4444
donnatechnician@aol.com

Laboratory Technologist

Laboratory Technologist with four years of combined experience preparing and running chemistry, microbiology, and biotechnology analysis. Meticulous documentation of test results and maintenance of lab notebooks.

Accurate, organized, and detail-oriented professional who follows laboratory's standard operating procedures (SOPs) for specimen collection and handling/processing, as well as test analysis and reporting.

Lab profile includes monitoring and using laboratory equipment (calibration, maintenance, and troubleshooting), initiating inventory-control improvements, and solving problems using independent judgment with minimal supervision.

Cross-functional background in management and training positions supervising 60+ employees, and designing and implementing science and math curriculum for over 40 high school and adult students.

Computer Skills: Windows 95/98/2000; Laboratory Information Management Systems (LIMS); MS Word, PowerPoint, Excel, Access, and Outlook; WordPerfect.

Notable Achievements

- Promoted rapidly within nine months of hire from Laboratory Aide to Laboratory Technologist for City of Urbandale.

- Met the challenge to handle weekend shift alone. In only one month, trained for 11 new analyses and calibration of appropriate equipment.

- Initiated and carried out complete update of obsolete Material Safety Data Sheets (MSDS).

- Achieved 100% accuracy for any unknowns reported to DNR and State of Iowa throughout four-year career.

- Maintained quality assurance/quality control standards of <5% and kept lab accidents at <.5%.

- Graduated as member of first-ever Biotechnology program at DMACC. Helped build Biotechnology Club to become top group on campus.

Work History

Laboratory Technologist, 1999–2002
City of Urbandale Wastewater Treatment Facility, Urbandale, IA

Laboratory Technologist, 1999
Minnesota Valley Testing Lab, Carroll, IA

Research Assistant / Biotechnology Intern, 1998–1999
Pioneer Hi-Bred International, Inc., Johnston, IA

Science Tutor / Volunteer Tutor, Summer 1996 & 1997
DMACC Tutoring Services, Ankeny, IA / Adult Basic Education, Ankeny, IA

Early career in retail sales, volunteer EMT, and audiovisual librarian positions.

Competencies

Chemistry Wet Lab

VA Volatile Acids

Alkalinity

Reagent Water Quality Check

Total Kjeldahl Nitrogen (TKN)

Total Solids/Volatile Solids (TS/VS)

Total Suspended Solids/Volatile Suspended Solids (TSS/VSS)

Set Funnel Grease and Oil

Settable Solids... pH

Dissolved Oxygen (DO)

Winkler Dissolved Oxygen (DO)

Fecal Coliforms

Chemical Oxygen Demand (COD)

CL_2 Residual Chlorine

Biochemical O_2 Demand (BOD)

Carbonaceous Biochemical O_2 Demand (CBOD)

Ammonia-N (NH_3-N)

Education

Des Moines Area Community College (DMACC) Ankeny, IA 1998

Triple Degrees:
Associate of Science, Science
Associate of Science, Biotechnology
Associate of Arts, Liberal Arts

Charter Member
Biotechnology Club
Vice President, 1997–1998

Leadership

MEA Board Member

Lab Safety Committee

WRF Safety Committee

Employee Association Committee

Strategy: *Categories are broken up into easy-to-find sections. Competencies are clearly identified in the left column, and items in the Notable Achievements section help this candidate stand out from the crowd.*

VICTOR P. MASON

500 West College Avenue
Marquette, MI 49855
(906) 228-1367
vicmason@sprintmail.com

MOLECULAR LABORATORY TECHNICIAN

ASCP Registered Medical Laboratory Technician (MLT)
Michigan Lab License #HP11135452

Talented and resourceful professional with both clinical and forensic laboratory expertise. Committed to seeking opportunities to advance knowledge of emerging molecular biology applications. Excel in teamwork, team leader, and trainer capacities. Self-motivated, highly ethical, detail oriented, and organized. Core competencies and test experience include:

- DNA Sequencing Methods
- Genotyping
- Hybridization
- Electrophoresis
- Hazardous Materials
- Hematology

- Quantitative PCR
- Amplification
- Quality Control
- Southern Blotting
- Amplification
- Routine Lab Tests

- Automated Liquid Handling Systems
- Chain of Custody Procedures
- Lab Instrumentation Management
- Fluorescent in Situ Hybridization (FISH)
- Hemostasis
- Nucleic Acid Extraction

EDUCATION & TRAINING

MA, Microbiology—Dept. of Molecular Biosciences—University of Kansas, Wichita, KS—1985
BS, Medical Technology—University of Kansas, Wichita, KS—1983
AS, Medical Laboratory Technology—Wichita Area Technical College, Wichita, KS—1981

PROFESSIONAL EXPERIENCE

CLINICAL LABORATORY SCIENTIST—Marquette General Health System, Marquette, MI—1985–Present

- *Member of the largest laboratory in the Upper Peninsula, serving as the main reference facility for other laboratories and clinics in the Upper Peninsula, Northern Michigan, and Northern Wisconsin.*
- *Focused on providing clients and patients with superb customer service and the highest quality of comprehensive and state-of-the-art laboratory services.*

Molecular Science: Operate the PCR core laboratory, process test specimens required for polymerase chain reaction (PCR)-based procedures, and train laboratory techs in all phases of PCR-based procedures.

- *Procedures:* Performed procedures involving:
  - Mitochondrial DNA: Sequenced MtDNA and extracted MtDNA from hair, blood, and other samples.
  - HCV Genotyping and MTB Genotyping.

- *Tests & Equipment:* … Perkin Elmer Genescan 310 Analyzer … 9600 & 2400 Thermocyclers … Bio-Rad GS Gene Linker … Singularity RFLP Analyzer Test (Proscan) … Amplicor HIV Detection Kit … UCLA HIV Detection Procedure … Amplicor Chlamydia Detection Kit … Cobas … Perkin Elmer AmpFL STR Profiler Unit … Profiler + Cofiler … PM + DQalpha 1 … Promega Gene Print STR System … AmpliFLP D1S80 Kit … Silver Staining of Vertical Gels … Print Light Chemiluminescent Detection System … MTB Detection by Restriction Enzyme Analysis … 7700 Sequence Detection System.

Core Lab: Performed routine medical laboratory procedures prior to molecular laboratory promotion.

- *Tests & Equipment:* … Urines … Coag (MLA) … Hematology (Coulter S+4, Technicon H-1) … Chemistry (SMA-24, Hitachi, Astra, ACA) … Drug Screens (Syva, Tecan) … Blood Bank.

- *Microbiology:* … Read Plates … Bactec 260 … Bactec 860 … Read Viral Cell Cultures … Baxter Walkaway … Mycology … Mycobacteriology.

Strategy: *Lists of tests and equipment are shown in a concise format, with leader dots helping to separate the items. Impressive educational credentials take center stage.*

Karen Mok, Ph.D.

HP: 410.377.1067
WP: 410.614.1019
kmok@netzero.net

320 Ross Bldg./720 Rutland Ave.
Johns Hopkins University School of Medicine
Baltimore, MD 21205

BIOCHEMICAL CLINICAL TECHNOLOGIST
MEDICINAL/ORGANIC

Postdoc Experience in Synthesizing/Evaluating Novel Nicotinic Receptors with PET/SPECT Studies
Industrial Postdoc Experience in Synthesizing Brominated Furanones
Lead Technical Teams in Complex Biochemical Experiments

KEY CLINICAL SKILLS

- Organic Synthesis
- Column Chromatograph
- Cold Chemistry
- Hot Radiochemistry

- Solid Support Synthesis
- Dialysis Technique
- NMR
- IR

- Inorganic Chemistry
- Molecular Modeling
- PET/SPET
- GC/MS

- Radiochemistry
- Enzyme Assay
- HPLC
- UV/VIS

EDUCATION

Ph.D., *Organic Chemistry,* Louisiana State University—2000
B.S., *Biochemical Engineering,* Beijing Institute of Chemical Technology—1990

PROFESSIONAL EXPERIENCE

JOHNS HOPKINS UNIVERSITY SCHOOL OF MEDICINE, Baltimore, MD   2000–Present
Postdoctoral Fellow
Perform nicotinic radioligands synthesis studies based on the 3-pyridyl ether series and epibatidine-based derivatives.

- Label new compounds in development with C-11, H-3, F-18, and I-125/I-123 in "hot" radiochemistry studies.
- Evaluate nicotinic radioligands with mouse-brain biodistribution and PET/SPET imagine studies of baboons and human subjects.

ALBEMARLE CORPORATION, Baton Rouge, LA   1999
Industrial Postdoctoral Researcher
Performed fimbrolides synthesis studies and their analogs that can be tested for efficacy at biofilm removal and economically synthesized for cost-effective use.

LOUISIANA STATE UNIVERSITY, Baton Rouge, LA   1993–1999
Graduate Research Assistant and Graduate Teaching Assistant
Studied solution-phase and solid-phase synthesis of phosphonopeptides as inhibitors of proteases and reaction mechanisms of phosphorus chemistry. Supervised one undergraduate researcher.

- Taught graduate/undergraduate organic laboratory classes for eight semesters to average 14-student classes and one semester of 18 students.

INSTITUTE OF MICROBIOLOGY, CHINESE ACADEMY OF SCIENCES, Beijing, China   1990–1993
Assistant Engineer
Conducted research, development, and production of Clinic Cholesterol Enzyme Kits in pilot plant of Institute of Microbiology. Supervised 9 technicians.

- Increased fermentation efficacy process 14% by scaling from 10-liter to 500-liter reactor.

AWARDS

Outstanding Graduate Student Travel Grant Award, 16th American Peptide Symposium—1999
Louisiana State University "GRADS" Travel Funds Award—1997
Vice President of Chinese Students and Scholars Association Award, Louisiana State University—1994
Outstanding Young Scientist Award, Chinese Academy of Sciences Institute of Microbiology—1992
Valued Employee Award, Institute of Microbiology, Chinese Academy of Sciences—1991

Strategy: *For a new Ph.D., education and education-related research are the central components of this resume. Awards add a positive footnote.*

MEREDITH STEVENSON

1289 Elm Street • Louisville, Kentucky 40257
Meredith@resumefreedom.com • (502) 555-0998

QUALIFICATIONS PROFILE

Energetic, personable professional with over 10 years of experience in healthcare as both **Ophthalmology Technician** and **Medical Technician.**

➢ Excellent customer service skills. Dedicated to providing 110% effort in every endeavor.
➢ Experienced working with populations diverse in culture and age.
➢ Quick and efficient learner. Adapt easily to new tasks and situations.
➢ Detail-oriented with excellent record-keeping, reporting, and tracking skills.
➢ Work well in a fast-paced, constantly changing environment.
➢ Skilled in numerous medical procedures, patient care, diagnostic testing, and surgical assisting.
➢ Computer literate, with skills in using Word and Excel. Type 40 words per minute.

PROFESSIONAL EXPERIENCE

UNITED STATES ARMY   1993 to 2003

Medical Technician (2002 to 2003) — Fort Knox, Kentucky

Oversaw all aspects of patient visits, including booking appointments, assisting patients in filling out medical forms, taking vital signs, checking height and weight, screening patients, and running tests such as EKGs. Prioritized patient care and scheduled procedures. Set up patient exam rooms.
♦ Maintained accurate, updated testing and patient records.

Ophthalmology / Optometry Technician (1995 to 2003) – United Kingdom

Administered direct patient care, medication, and testing (i.e., glaucoma, accommodative ability, muscle balance, near and distance vision, central and peripheral field limits) to individuals ranging in age from infant to geriatric, in need of optometric and ophthalmic services. Served as special surgical assistant to doctors performing various ophthalmic surgeries. Provided screening services to over 4,800 individuals preparing to deploy. Kept detailed records of each test and patient visit.
♦ Received Army Achievement Medal for assisting in multiple sight-saving ophthalmic surgical cases after the Nairobi U.S. Embassy bombing.
♦ Assisted Optometrists in discovering over 100 children with undetected cases of nearsightedness, farsightedness, color blindness, and other eye conditions at various community school screenings.
♦ Successfully trained 3 medics with no previous eye experience to become ophthalmic surgical assistants and technicians.

Ophthalmology / Optometry Technician (1993 to 1995) — Fort Campbell, Kentucky

Assisted in performing various routine diagnostic vision and color vision tests during physical exams. Measured interpupillary distance, bridge size, and temple length for glasses. Adjusted and repaired spectacles as needed. Tracked the order and delivery of all spectacles by computer. Instructed patients in the usage of contact lenses.
♦ Assisted in numerous types of ophthalmic surgeries.

EDUCATIONAL BACKGROUND

Diploma, Eye Technician, U.S. ARMY ACADEMY OF HEALTH SCIENCES (1991)

— **Professional References Available on Request** —

Strategy: *Seeking a position as either an Ophthalmology Technician or a Medical Technician upon separating from the military, this job seeker presented both areas of expertise in her resume. The summary highlights personal attributes that are a plus in her profession.*

Alice Swanson

100 South City Road, Orange, CA 92865
(714) 555-1292 • aswanson@mailmail.net

Ultrasound Technologist

Perform all ultrasound techniques including, but not limited to:

- Carotid & vascular exams
- Prostate scans
- Hystero-sonography
- Amniocentesis

- Liver, thyroid, kidney biopsies
- PICC line
- Paracentesis/thoracentesis
- and other procedures

Employment

4/01–Present	**Ultrasound Technologist: Technician Registry,** Orange, CA Assigned to various Orange County clinics & hospitals.
4/99–9/01	**Ultrasound Technologist: Med-West Medical Corporation** Orange Medical Center, Orange County East Medical Center, Clinic for Women's Health, South County Medical Center.
4/96–8/98	**Aide/Clerk/Trainer, Radiology Dept.:** Mercy Hospital, Orange, CA

Education, Training & Certification

12/01	ARDMS Certification: California State Board
8/98–7/99	Ultrasound Internship: Westport Imaging Center/Brea Medical Center
7/99	Ultrasound Technology Certificate: Coastline Community College
6/99	A.A., General Education (major: Health Sciences): Coastline Community College (GPA 3.6/Dean's Honor List)
8/89–Present	Equipment Training/Upgrades: Siemens, Acuson, Aspen, Diasonics, Toshiba, and ATL 3000
6/96–8/97	Anatomy & Physiology, Cross Sectional Imaging/Survey of Disease: Coastline Community College
6/94	Graduate (Honors Classes): West Orange High School, Orange, CA

Personal Data

Have been commended for excellence in patient care, medical staff liaison, and professional attitude. Seeking employment that will capitalize on existing skills and offer opportunities for continuing training and advancement. References available.

Strategy: *An energetic, contemporary format was used to convey this job seeker's positive attitude and zest for her profession.*

LISA A. MILLS, RT-M, LRT
414 St. John Place
Rochester, New York 14623
585-765-4321
millsla@earthlink.com

RADIOLOGIC TECHNOLOGIST / MAMMOGRAPHY TECHNOLOGIST
Healthcare ♦ Teaching ♦ Consulting / Private Industry

Accomplished healthcare professional with track record of acquiring and applying leading-edge technologies and procedures in clinical settings. Outstanding patient rapport and exceptional patient satisfaction. Superb teamwork skills, plus strong organizational/administrative capabilities. Excellent project management skills, encompassing sourcing and purchasing capital equipment and supplies, collaborating with engineers on facilities-construction issues, and developing written procedures for new clinical techniques.

PROFESSIONAL EXPERIENCE

ROCHESTER GENERAL HOSPITAL; Rochester, New York (1985–Present)

Mammography / Radiologic Technician—Women's Health Center   **1998–Present**
- See up to 30 mammogram patients daily.
- Assist physicians with various procedures, including stereotactic procedures and breast biopsies.
- Educate patients about procedures and train co-workers in new protocols.
- Ensure that quality standards, including Mammography Quality Standards Act (MQSA) inspection requirements, are maintained.

Key Accomplishments:

Chosen to serve on team that pioneered Women's Health Center at Rochester General Hospital, with specific accountability for setup and launch of Mammography Department.
- Conferred with clinical engineers and medical physicists on the physical layout of the department.
- Ensured that facilities met federal and state regulations for quality standards and environmental issues.
- Sourced and evaluated equipment and supplies; made purchase recommendations to decision-makers.
- Wrote manuals and policies for mammography, breast biopsies, and other related procedures.

Played a key role in introducing stereotactic breast biopsy procedures to the department.
- Evaluated equipment and reviewed facilities needs for this new technology.
- Established sterile processes and set up surgical procedures.
- Collaborated with other hospital departments to ensure that all clinical requirements were met.
- Coordinated administrative procedures with outpatient registration and nursing staff to facilitate processing of patients and proper charting/documentation.

Radiologic Technologist   **1985–1998**
Performed general radiography tests and procedures.
- Utilized portable radiography equipment and performed operating-room procedures.
- Conducted gastro-intestinal (GI) tract and vascular tests.
- Performed mammography tests until joining Women's Health Center in 1998.
- Maintained positive and productive rapport with emergency, nursing, and OR departments.

Key Accomplishment:

Pioneered introduction of mammography to RGH in 1986. Acquired specialized training, instructed colleagues in newly learned techniques, and ensured that strict quality standards were maintained. Functioned as in-house mammography specialist, leading to participation in setup of Women's Health Center.

Strategy: *This Radiologic/Mammography Technologist helped pioneer several new technologies, and her contributions are highlighted in the strong Key Accomplishments segments of her resume.*

Lisa A. Mills   Résumé—Page Two

ADDITIONAL EXPERIENCE

FINGER LAKES COMMUNITY COLLEGE; Canandaigua, New York
Adjunct Instructor   **1986–Present**
Train and mentor college students majoring in Radiologic Technology.
- Follow three to four students during extensive clinical rotations.
- Provide hands-on training on various equipment and procedures.
- Conduct competency tests to establish students' speed and accuracy in performing tests.

EAST ROCHESTER UNION FREE SCHOOL DISTRICT; Rochester, New York
Mentor   **1989–1990**
Introduced middle school students to radiography as a potential career choice. Allowed students to observe day-to-day activities and responded to questions about radiography.

EDUCATION

FINGER LAKES COMMUNITY COLLEGE; Canandaigua, New York
Associate of Applied Science, Radiologic Technology   **1984**
GPA: 3.75; Honors Graduate

Associate of Applied Science, Secretarial Science (Medical)   **1982**
GPA: 3.5

PROFESSIONAL DEVELOPMENT

SLOAN-KETTERING CANCER INSTITUTE; New York, New York
—*Breast Radiology, Chemotherapy & Radiation Therapy, Stereotactic Positioning (one-day program)*

Numerous additional continuing education programs and professional conferences.

TECHNICAL PROFICIENCIES

Fisher Stereotactic Table; LoRad Mammography techniques; GE and Phillips radiology equipment. Windows, Microsoft Office, online patient information systems.

LICENSURE

American Registry of Radiologic Technologists (1984–Present).
American Registry of Radiologic Technologists—Mammography (1991–Present).
NYS Department of Health—Diagnostic Radiology (1984–Present).

References Provided on Request

GERALD WHITE
gwhite@hotmail.com

267 North 15th Street
Milwaukee, WI 53202

Pager: (414) 818-9845
Residence: (414) 871-3443

PHLEBOTOMY TECHNICIAN/MEDICAL ASSISTANT PROFILE
Seeking Part-Time/Pool Position (12 to 16 hours weekly)

Highly professional phlebotomy technician with 18 years of combined military and civilian medical experience. Excellent interpersonal communication, client service, and organizational skills—expert working with "difficult" clients including Neonatal, Oncology, and Geriatric. Experienced working in clinical, hospital, and home-health environments. Strong attention to detail with ability to precisely follow procedures and maintain the highest standards of quality and integrity. Demonstrated competencies include

- Health history & vital signs
- Venipuncture, arterial, & capillary collection
- IV therapy & immunizations

- Clinical, hospital, & home settings
- Specimen transport & processing
- ICD coding
- Medical supplies management

PROFESSIONAL EXPERIENCE

Midwest Laboratories, Jesuits Shared Laboratory, Inc.
A division of *All Saints Healthcare Systems*—Milwaukee, WI

June 1999 to Present
Oct. 1995 to Apr. 1996

PATIENT SERVICE CENTER TECHNICIAN (June 1999 to Present)
PHLEBOTOMIST (Oct. 1995 to Apr. 1996)
- Perform a variety of routine and difficult phlebotomy and invasive procedures while maintaining client comfort and confidentiality. Use standard equipment, including vacutainer tubes, tourniquets, syringes, and butterfly needles.
- Ensure proper identification and processing of all specimens.
- Coordinate service-center operations, including opening, closing, patient scheduling, customer service, data entry, and maintenance of proper inventory levels.
- Interact with clients, medical professionals, and laboratory technicians. Communicate information related to specimen-collection requirements, turnaround times, result availability, and reports.
- Float between 10 service centers, recalling and using each center's unique processes.

Med Professionals—Waukesha, WI
A provider of temporary, professional medical services.

Jan. 1995 to Oct. 1995

HOSPITAL PHLEBOTOMIST
- Assigned to Waukegan Memorial Hospital.
- Collected specimens from patients in all hospital areas, including regular intensive care and neonatal intensive care.

Strategy: *This resume captures extensive civilian and military health care experience. Note the sub-heading that indicates a part-time position is being sought.*

GERALD WHITE RÉSUMÉ	Res (414) 871-3443	Pager (414) 818-9845	Page 2 of 2

PROFESSIONAL EXPERIENCE (CONTINUED)

United States Army — Various Locations Domestic & Abroad .... Nov. 1981 to Jan. 1995
Honorably discharged, attained grade of E-6

EMERGENCY MEDICAL SUPERVISOR (1993 to 1995)

- Provided care to 35 residents aboard an Army logistical support vessel. Performed daily "sick call," assessed patients, and provided treatments including minor surgical procedures.
- Recognized for establishing a highly professional, efficient operation with proper accountability.

EMERGENCY TREATMENT TECHNICIAN/SUPERVISOR (1986 to 1993)

- Provided basic emergency treatment for dive-team members. Assisted with operation of hyperbaric chamber.
- Supervised 6-member trauma-treatment team and established field-trauma treatment area.
- Coordinated evacuation of critically ill/injured patients by land or air.
- Supervised 4 medical assistants supporting emergency-room operations. Followed directions of professional staff. Trained and counseled subordinates.
- Supervised preventative-maintenance program for medical equipment and vehicles. Ensured rooms were clean and restocked after patient treatments.

FIELD MEDICAL TECHNICIAN (1983 to 1986)

- Assisted with triage, daily "sick call," and subsequent treatment.

PATIENT CARE SPECIALIST (1981 to 1983)

- Performed nursing duties when a member of National Guard prior to active service.

Military Awards include 1 Commendation and 2 Achievement Medals.

EDUCATION & CERTIFICATIONS

LPN Certificate (Pending Completion of 3 credits)
Milwaukee Technical Institute — Milwaukee, WI

Graduate, Urbana High School — Urbana, IL, 1981

Basic Life Support Instructor Certificate, Army Hospital — Fort Campbell, KY, 1993
Adv. Medical Supervisor Certificate, U.S. Army Health Services Command — San Antonio, TX, 1989
Practical Nursing Certificate, U.S. Army Health Services Command — San Antonio, TX, 1982

ADDITIONAL WORK EXPERIENCE

Midwest Forge — Milwaukee, WI .... Apr. 1996 to June 1999

DENNIS RYDER, CST

265 Charlotte Street · Asheville, NC 28801
(828) 255-5555 · dennisryder@mail.com

Certified Surgical Technologist
Open Heart / Vascular Surgery

RESULTS-DRIVEN medical professional with 15 years' experience in pursuit of higher standard of patient care and outcome. Aggressive in skill development, resulting in expanded leadership, educational, administrative, and fiscal roles. Demonstrated expertise in theory and application of sterile and aseptic techniques, knowledge of human anatomy, surgical procedures, and implementation of tools/technologies.

Recognized Peak Performer:
- Participant in 17 endovascular technology procedures, Phase 3 trials, under Michael Norman, M.D., and Richard Brook, M.D.
- Surgeon-requested assignments include Randall Jones, M.D. (Mitral Homograft); Ronson Doster, M.D. (Stentless Aortic Valve Replacement); Don Viros, M.D. (Ross Pulmonary Transposition); Miles Griff, M.D. (Heart Port minimally invasive surgery); and Marlene Trump, M.D. (Stentless Aortic Valve Replacement, Mitral Homograft).

Proactive Problem Solver:
- Worked with physicians, surgical directors, and nursing staff to initiate aseptic technique issues that raised standards of optimal patient care. Example result: Decreased patient infection rates through changes in sterile techniques.
- Initiated research into ergonomic aspects of OR furniture to prevent neck and back injuries to surgical personnel.
- Initiated review of decontamination/cleaning equipment used in OR and substerile areas, resulting in cleaner environment.

Captured cost reductions while raising patient care standards:
- Pioneered implementation of Cardiovascular First Assistant Certification Program at St. Francis Hospital System, ensuring competent surgical assistants without direct cost to hospital, while providing revenue for hospital system.
- Worked one-on-one with medical-equipment vendors to consolidate surgical supplies, eliminating time and effort concerns.
- Initiated research and provided product information on room stereo sound systems that allowed St. Francis Hospital to optimally use purchasing resources for best quality.

*Multi-tasking and calm under pressure . . . Alert, active listener; attentive to detail . . .
Outstanding manual dexterity, with quick response . . . Interact well with patients and medical staff . . .
Conscientious, orderly; aware of consequence of error . . . Durable*

CLINICAL AND PROFESSIONAL TRAINING

Aggressive in pursuit of lifelong, ongoing skills training. Completed more than 250 hours in clinical training and seminars in all applicable fields (including plastic surgery); the more relevant within the last 5 years are listed below:

Hands-on Training:

- EVT Ancure System
- Ross Pulmonary Transposition
- Heart Port
- Mitral Valve Homograft Surgery
- Stentless Aortic Valve Procedure

- Mid CAB
- Op CAB
- Bi-ventricular Assist Device
- Endovascular Vein Harvesting

Strategy: *Highlights of experience and achievements are captured on page 1, along with training credentials. The experience history on page 2 is brief, to avoid repetition.*

DENNIS RYDER, CST · Page 2

CLINICAL AND PROFESSIONAL TRAINING, continued

Seminars:

- Technology Trends in Cardiovascular Surgery
- Allograft / Homograft Heart Valves
- Cardiac Surgery Updates
- Cardiac Anesthesia: Techniques & Agents
- Microvascular Surgery Reconstruction
- Mitral Heart Valves
- New Research on CNS Control of Autonomic Nervous System in the Surgical Patient

- Women & Heart Disease
- Management of Pediatric Cardiac Anomalies
- Continuous Warm Blood Cardioplegia
- Cardiopulmonary Resuscitation
- Electrocardiogram Interpretation
- Blood Component Therapy in the Operating Room
- Update on New Drugs Currently in Use in the OR
- Preventive Innovations in Cardiovascular Perfusion

HIGHLIGHTS OF PROFESSIONAL EXPERIENCE

St. Francis Health Care System, Asheville, NC — 1995–Present
Certified Surgical Technologist / Cardiovascular Services

Baptist Hospital of Miami, Miami, FL — 1994–1995
Surgical Technologist / Cardiovascular Services & Ortho/Neuro Service

Member of team performing difficult virgin and re-do total joint reconstructions in shoulder, knee, and hip. Recruited by staff to work on Cardiovascular Service.

United States Air Force, Homestead Air Force Base, FL, and Ellsworth AFB, SD — 1989–1994
Surgical Technologist / Assistant In Charge of Surgical Services (General, OB–GYN, Orthopedics)

Given unusual responsibilities for rank. Orchestrated daily responsibilities of surgical staff, assigning personnel to surgical procedures and other related areas (e.g., recovery room, central sterile supply, pre-op nursing area), as well as ensuring readiness of surgical equipment / supplies. Monitored continuing education of employees.

- Used outstanding organizational abilities to expedite surgical instrumentation during procedures (e.g., implemented nondisposable surgical kits for air transport hospital), reducing financial and environmental costs.
- Awarded Good Conduct Medal and Achievement Medal for Meritorious Service. Promoted to rank of Sergeant.

Graduate, Surgical Services Specialist, 1989
School of Health Care Sciences, USAF, Sheppard Air Force Base, TX
A.A. equivalent (320 hours)

Member, Association of Surgical Technologists
Certified PADI Diver

JOSHUA A. LAWSON

221 South Fulton Street
Chillicothe, Ohio 45601

(740) 771-0026
jalawson@adelphia.net

Board Certified Hearing Instrument Specialist
(Licensed in the State of Ohio: #5599 ◆ Board Certification: January 2001—#6895)

PROFESSIONAL OVERVIEW

Skilled **hearing instrument specialist** driven by the desire to provide top-notch healthcare by **educating** the hearing-impaired community, **promoting** their self-esteem, and **improving** their quality of life. Excellent oral and written **communication skills. Clinical strengths:** Evaluation and counseling. **Personal strengths:** Self-management, more than 15 years of successful sales experience, and encouraging a healthy patient/hearing-specialist relationship.

PROFESSIONAL EXPERIENCE

Ohio Hearing Specialists, Chillicothe, Ohio

2001 to Present

Board Certified Hearing Instrument Specialist: Perform evaluations and provide counseling to the adult and geriatric populations. Recommend, program, adjust, and dispense high-tech digital and programmable hearing instruments. Encourage and guide the patient in becoming accustomed to the device and the need to accept responsibility for adjusting the aid to fit their personal, immediate environment. **Technical strengths** include troubleshooting and the resolution of hearing-instrument problems, computer system malfunctions, and other issues. Trained in the use of Miracle Ear's signal testing methods.

Achievements:

◆ In first full year on the job, increased annual sales from $160K to $250K.
◆ Tied in first place for the fewest number of returns. This personal achievement is based on effective counseling methods that improve customer satisfaction and cooperation.
◆ Invented the "Lawson Method" (dubbed as such by a training instructor), which enables a user to easily remember the steps required to conduct the speech-masking test.

Awards:

◆ Customer Satisfaction Award—2001, 2002
◆ Quality Product Award—2001
◆ Binaural Award—2001, 2002
◆ Pride Group Award—2002

Prior Employment:
Owner/Operator, Lawson Carpet Cleaning, Chillicothe, Ohio   1987 to 1999
Customer Accounts Investigator, Tri-State Electric, Chillicothe, Ohio   1984 to 1987
Area Sales & Marketing Representative, Best Cookie Company, Tampa, Florida   1981 to 1984

EDUCATION AND AFFILIATIONS

Courses: Ohio State University, Columbus, Ohio. Business Management, Organizational Behavior, and Physical Science.
Memberships: Ohio Hearing Aid Society (OHAS) and International Hearing Society (IHS).

◆ *References Available upon Request* ◆

Strategy: *Achievements and awards are standout qualifications for this individual, so they become the focal point of his resume. Because he has only a few years of experience in his current field, his prior employment history is included but without detail.*

CAREY MORANT

5 Keats Place
Signal Hill, CA 90806

Email: morry@bigpool.com

Mobile: (360) 544-3344
Business: (360) 511-2210

BIOMEDICAL INSTRUMENT TECHNICIAN

Accomplished biomedical instrumentation expert with 10+ years of progressive and multifaceted experiences in the medical sector. Precision craftsmanship, applied throughout engineering design, production, and repair projects, is further complemented by dedication to high professional standards that set new benchmarks for quality. Advancement to team and departmental management roles has offered opportunities to drive efficiency and productivity improvements for continuous cost containment and customer satisfaction. Considered a solid communicator—a first point of contact for technical and personal troubleshooting; skilled in achieving consensus and restoring calm.

Professional strengths include

- QA protocol design & implementation
- New instrumentation / equipment engineering
- Staff training course development & delivery
- High-precision surgical instrumentation
- Warehousing, stock control & logistics
- Staff supervision & leadership
- Critical problem solving & troubleshooting
- Instrumentation research

- Prototype design & development
- Product evaluations & inspections
- Workplace health & safety operations
- Freight management
- Budget administration
- Resource expenditure authorizations
- Process reengineering
- Productivity/ efficiency improvements

Software knowledge: Excel, Word, PowerPoint, Outlook; BOB2010, BERGER;
in-house invoicing, inventory control, transportation software.

PROFESSIONAL EXPERIENCE

MATHYS AUSTRALIA PTY LTD., Brisbane   1999–2003

Switzerland-based multinational, manufacturing orthopedic instruments and implants, and pneumatic and battery-driven equipment; acknowledged industry-wide for setting benchmarks in products and quality standards.

QLD Orthopedic Coordinator

Reported to: State Business Manager; Staff: 9

Presided over medical instrumentation stocks and equipment, optimizing processes and productivity methods to meet urgent daily delivery orders and provide responsive customer service. Coordinated and sourced equipment locally and interstate for internal and external customers; set and prioritized maintenance schedules; devised and administered strict budgets; and directed all purchasing, logistics, invoicing, and freight management.

Selected Accomplishments:

- Slashed 50% off staff processing times and substantially reduced error rates by redesigning consignment forms for recipient to check orders with supplied items upon delivery.

- Overhauled equipment booking and dispatch processes plagued with inaccurate paper trails, errors, and equipment losses. Revolutionized system by upgrading key processes that assured finely tuned tracking of equipment movements and reduced errors through a series of checks and balances.

- Commended by surgeon for meeting urgent request for equipment while operation was in progress. Located equipment, negotiated with hospital for release, and delivered items personally.

- Virtually eliminated cases of damaged equipment being sent to hospitals, pioneering a series of maintenance sheets that recorded complete details and checklists.

Carey Morant   Page 1   Confidential

Strategy: *Written for a career goal of Biomedical Instrument Technician, this resume also includes leadership skills demonstrated in all prior positions.*

PROFESSIONAL EXPERIENCE
continued

TOOL AND INSTRUMENT ENGINEERING P/L, Gold Coast   1992–1999
Designer, engineer, manufacturer, and modifier of surgical instrumentation including forceps, laparoscopic and ophthalmic instruments, and stainless-steel trolleys.

Senior Biomedical Instrument Technician

Reported to: Managing Director; Staff: 11

Joined company with unique reputation for providing surgical instrument repair services unparalleled in terms of quality—with end results considered vastly better than originals in terms of strength and reliability. Considered an expert in ophthalmic instrument repairs; was placed to work exclusively in this area, engineering new instrumentation and repairing, sharpening, and polishing instruments to finely tuned tolerances. Appointed to a team leadership role; trained and supervised staff in hand-tool usage, workshop machinery, welding, and high-precision designs. Inspected all finished articles for quality, monitored stock levels, invoiced orders, and coordinated transportation logistics.

- Key contributor in senior technical team appointed to design, implement, update, and continually monitor department-wide compliance with critical quality-assurance protocols.

- Successfully developed a series of training sessions and workshops to elevate the technical expertise, qualifications, and customer-service ethic of new recruits and existing employees.

- Spearheaded a series of cost-containment initiatives, including devising several new repair techniques that slashed machinery operation times and reduced excess stock.

- Frequently commended by clients for high standards of work. Ophthalmic Surgery Centre cited in letter of appreciation that they *"wouldn't use anyone else"* because of the team's *"continuous precision workmanship."*

- Developed several new prototypes acclaimed for ingenuity, strength, and precision.

EDUCATION

Infection Control, OH&S, Duty of Care, Manual Handling
ONLEE Clinical Education, Brisbane

Customer Care in Action / Telephone Techniques
TACK Training International, Brisbane

Hundreds of hours devoted to education and professional development. Includes in-house product training courses and bone-reduction and fixation workshops. Hold Senior First Aid Certificate.

Lisa Marie Barkema

1994 Dennler Drive • Alleman, IA 50007
Home: (515) 999-9888 • Work: (515) 294-5888 • lmbarkema@iastate.edu

DIAGNOSTIC SERVICES SUPERVISOR

ASCP CERTIFIED MEDICAL TECHNOLOGY GENERALIST and Interim Diagnostic Services Supervisor with over seven years of experience working independently or as part of a team in both clinic and hospital settings. Innovative, with ability to prioritize, accept and learn new ideas quickly, and adapt easily to changes in technology.

Effective communicator in one-on-one and group situations with staff, management, physicians, nurses, and patients. **Organized and detail oriented** with strong problem-solving skills used to improve efficiency and manage multiple tasks simultaneously. **Excellent phlebotomy skills.**

PROFESSIONAL EXPERIENCE

IOWA STATE UNIVERSITY, THIELEN STUDENT HEALTH CENTER, AMES, IA   1995–PRESENT

Interim Diagnostic Services Supervisor (2002–Present)
Supervise two full- and four part-time medical technologists and X-ray technicians. Participate on 13-member management team. Attend monthly meetings, meet with pathology consultant to discuss problems or changes for department, and ensure regular meetings with Diagnostics Services Department. Continue to carry out full-time duties of Medical Technologist.

- Wrote procedure for QuickView Influenza test.
- Implemented ongoing Quality Improvement projects to meet or exceed quality standards expectations.
- Attended Management Training for First-Time Supervisors, Lab Managers Annual Meeting, and Workers Compensation Presentation.

Medical Technologist (1995–Present)
Manage daily operations of lab, instruct patients in proper laboratory collection procedures, analyze specimens according to lab procedure, process specimens for reference laboratory, and monitor inventory. Conduct and interpret quality control on all instruments and test kits daily; carry out calibration and maintenance procedures on instruments.

- Developed a first-time inventory system and spreadsheet to effectively order and manage supplies.
- Worked as part of three-member team that earned 100% accuracy rating on most recent Proficiency Test.
- Directly involved in bi-annual CLIAA inspections; reviewed, updated, and wrote manual test procedures to meet inspections requirements and maintain certification.
- Developed employee training checklist to shorten length of time needed to train new staff members.
- Helped develop method of study and directly participated in CBC and UA turnaround-time study.
- Wrote detailed laboratory collection/instruction sheets that eliminated patient questions.
- Developed numerous laboratory logs for tracking and maintaining quality control.
- Complimented for excellent phlebotomy skills.

IOWA METHODIST MEDICAL CENTER, DES MOINES, IA   1994–1995

Medical Technologist—Analyzed specimens in all areas of fast-paced laboratory using highly technical instruments. Performed quality control and communicated effectively with nursing and laboratory staff.

TECHNOLGY SKILLS / EQUIPMENT

Coulter Onyx; Cell-dyn 3200; Kodak DT60
Medical Manager Software; Microsoft Excel, Word, and Outlook

EDUCATION & CERTIFICATION

American Society of Clinical Pathologists (ASCP) Certified
BS, **Medical Technology,** University of Nebraska Medical Center, Omaha, NE, 1994
BS, **Natural Sciences,** Midland Lutheran College, Fremont, NE, 1993

Strategy: *After being named to an interim position, Lisa Marie prepared her resume in hopes of earning the position permanently. Technical strengths were highlighted extensively to draw attention from her minimal supervisory experience.*

CHAPTER 8

Resumes for Dental Careers

- Dental Assistant

- Dental Lab Technician

- Advanced Qualified Person (AQP)

- Dental Prosthetics Specialist

- Dentist

As with other specialized areas of health care, dentistry-related resumes focus on specific professional skills and may also include accomplishments in areas such as business operations, patient care, efficiency, and productivity.

DENISE A. WOLFE

7102 Dalewood Court — Nashville, Tennessee 37207 — (615) 860-2922

SUMMARY OF QUALIFICATIONS

- **REGISTERED DENTAL ASSISTANT** with ten years' experience assisting with direct patient care. Special interest in pediatric patient care, with the desire and willingness to learn other areas of dentistry.

- Graduate of Dental Assistant program at Volunteer State Community College. Continuing Dental Education in Coronal Polishing. CPR certified.

- Special expertise in patient management and making patients of all ages feel as relaxed and comfortable as possible, relieving any anxiety or tension they might have. Skilled working with handicapped and other special-needs patients.

- Sound knowledge of clinical procedures and dental/medical terminology.

DENTAL HEALTHCARE EXPERIENCE

DENTAL ASSISTANT ....1997 to 2003
David A. Lambert, D.D.S. — Montgomery, Alabama

- Performed general chairside duties (four-handed dentistry) and assisted with all types of procedures, including extraction, crowns, pulpotomy, and composites. Monitored nitrous oxide and applied topical anesthetics.
- Prepared patients (children, adolescents, young adults, handicapped, special needs) for treatment, making them as comfortable and at ease as possible. Assisted with in-hospital visits and procedures.
- Performed coronal polishing, oral examinations, and charting.
- Sterilized instruments and equipment. Prepared tray setups for procedures.
- Mixed amalgams, cements, and other dental materials. Took and poured impressions.
- Took, processed, and mounted X rays. Used intraoral camera equipment.
- Scheduled and confirmed appointments. Ordered dental supplies and maintained inventory levels.

DENTAL ASSISTANT ....1993 to 1997
Timothy J. Koeppel, D.M.D. — Hendersonville, Tennessee

- Took impressions, poured and trimmed models, and made night guards.
- Took and processed panorex and cephalometric X rays.
- Instructed and encouraged patients to develop good oral-hygiene habits.

EDUCATION AND TRAINING

Coronal Polishing — Continuing Dental Education — 1997
University of Tennessee, Memphis College of Dentistry

Dental Assistant Certificate of Proficiency — 1993
Volunteer State Community College — Gallatin, Tennessee

Certified in CPR through American Heart Association — 1993 to Present

Strategy: *Qualifications, training, and work experience are equally emphasized in this resume for a technician seeking a similar position after relocation.*

Marla Melendez
1215 Kendall Road, Kennet City, Florida 34688 ♦ (727) 833-4320 ♦ mmelendez@aol.com

IMMEDIATE FOCUS
Employment as a Dental Assistant enabling me to perform vital skills that contribute to an organization's success.

EMPLOYMENT HISTORY
2001–Present   The Dental Lab, St. Petersburg, FL
Dental Technician
♦ Perform dental prophylactic treatments, chart conditions of decay and disease, remove sutures and dressings, and develop X-ray films.

1995–2000   Social Service Industries, Balem, Brazil
Endodontist
♦ In a clinical environment, performed root canals and related procedures, managing a caseload of 5 to 6 patients per day.
♦ Examined, diagnosed, and treated diseases of nerve, pulp, and other dental tissues affecting the vitality of teeth. Typically, patients were afflicted with abscess problems or periodontal gum inflammation.
♦ Performed some orthodontic work (braces & retainers), occasional fillings, and bleaching or teeth whitening.
♦ Performed partial or total removal of pulp and filled pulp chamber and canal with endodontic materials.
♦ Total familiarity with state-of-the-art dental instruments, X-ray devices, MRIs, ultrasonic devices, and other diagnostic equipment.

1995–2000   Municipal General Office, Balem, Brazil (Concurrent with above)
General Dentist
♦ Provided dental care for infants and children ranging in age up to 12 years.
♦ Counseled and advised patients or mothers on matters such as mouth cleansing after infant feeding to prevent dental caries.
♦ Treated primary and secondary teeth and performed fillings or extractions as needed.
♦ Provided preventive services through use of fluorides and sealants, as well as instruction on dental care.

1992–1995   Municipal General Hospital, Balem, Brazil
Emergency Dentist
♦ Attended patients who were accident victims or suffered other emergencies; i.e., dislocated teeth requiring dental treatment and suturing. Used acrylics and resins.

1988–1992   Melendez Associates, Private Practice, Balem, Brazil
Dentist
♦ Opened an office shortly after graduating from dentistry school and began a small general dentistry practice. Patients were routinely referred by dental professionals and area businesses.

EDUCATION
♦ **Federal University of Para**, Para, Brazil
Awarded Degree of Surgeon Dentist, 1988 (Equivalent U.S. degree: Doctor of Dental Surgery)
♦ **Brazilian Association of Dentistry**
Studied 2½ years specializing in Root Canal Dentistry.
♦ **Certified in Oral and Maxillofacial Radiology** and its related fields by the Faculty of Dentistry, Osaka, Japan, as a JICA participant; February, 1999.

Strategy: *This resume clearly shows how a dental technician made a smooth and successful transition from state-sponsored health care in Brazil to a for-profit operation in the U.S. She is working as a dental technician while pursuing U.S. certification as a dentist.*

PHILIP JORDAIN

334 Aspen Street ~ Springfield, Massachusetts 01121 ~ 413.789.5432 ~ jordain@mindspring.com

DENTAL LAB TECHNICIAN / LAB MANAGER

Highly qualified dental lab technician with strong problem-solving abilities. Excellent finishing skills, including creating removable dentures, cast partials, and crown and bridge. Comfortable working with patients of all ages and with dentists, displaying strong interpersonal skills. Received outstanding annual evaluations from employer. Detail-oriented without losing the overall picture. Experienced in repairs, relines, and rebases. Trilingual English/Spanish/French; some knowledge of German and Greek.

"I consider Phil to be the foundation for a successful lab operation in Massachusetts. He has done an excellent job . . . excellent one-on-one trainer . . . always willing to do more than asked." —Michael A. George, General Lab Manager, Apex Dental.

PROFESSIONAL HISTORY

Massachusetts Lab Manager, Apex Dental, Syracuse, NY   1991–2002
- Best production report of all regions, according to supervisor.
- Evaluated lab technicians in nine offices throughout Massachusetts.
- Ordered and approved supplies.
- Troubleshot errors and worked with dentists to correct problems.
- Hired and trained technicians in various locations.
- Exhibited strong interpersonal skills working with patients, technicians, and dentists.

Dental Technician, Avery Dental, Enfield, CT   1989–1991
- Worked with cast partials and removables.
- Replaced four finishers and did all the work myself.

EDUCATION

Degussa & Kulzer, Frankfurt am Main, Germany
Six months of special training for dental technology and management

Tanasopulos, Athens, Greece
Ten months studying and practicing thermoplastic partials

New York City College of Technology, Brooklyn, NY
Dental Lab Technology

Strategy: *A powerful testimonial from his supervisor is a highlight of this resume for a dental lab technician. Education in top training programs worldwide is also spotlighted.*

PATRICIA A. TRAVERSE

2328 Elkins Court
Fairborn, OH 45324
937-677-9230
pat@yahoo.com

ADVANCED QUALIFIED PERSON

Highly skilled dental professional with 6 years of experience as ADVANCED QUALIFIED PERSON, and a total of 11 years in providing dental services.

Strengths
- Planning, organizational, and follow-through skills.
- Outgoing and enthusiastic personality; ability to communicate and interact with cross-cultural clientele.
- Strong work ethic and commitment to customer satisfaction.
- Ability to manage simultaneous assignments without loss of productivity.

EDUCATION / CERTIFICATION

Board Certified Advanced Qualified Person, State of Ohio, 1993
Passed exam on first try.

Sinclair Community College, Dayton, OH
Advanced Qualified Person Certification

Certified X-ray Technician, State of Ohio

Certified Dental Assistant, State of Ohio

PROFESSIONAL EXPERIENCE

Advanced Qualified Person for leading Dayton-area dentist.   1998–Present

Perform dental services that include

- Fillings
- X rays
- Impressions
- Crown adjustments
- Packing

Prescott Dental & Denture Center, Dayton, OH   1994–1999

- Advanced Qualified Person adjusting dentures, making temporary crowns and bridge work, filling teeth, taking X rays and impressions, adjusting crowns, and packing teeth.

Strategy: *Because her experience was somewhat limited, emphasis was placed on this individual's strong educational qualifications.*

GUS A. KENTRITAS, C.D.T.

19 Jumping Brook Boulevard • Plainfield, NJ 07061 • 732-431-0984 • gak@aol.com

DENTAL PROSTHETICS SPECIALIST

Laboratory Operations — R&D — Quality Control
Sales and Marketing — Customer Service — Consulting — Training

Well-qualified professional with extensive industry experience and a strong combination of technical and business-development expertise. In-depth knowledge of industry trends, new materials, state-of-the-art equipment / laboratory techniques, and dental office procedures. Involvement in the development and testing of lab techniques and denture designs with leading dental manufacturers, including Jelanko, Unitek, and Dentsply. Successful in collaborating with dental practices to significantly reduce chair time and enhance product quality. Published author.

PROFESSIONAL ACHIEVEMENTS

Laboratory Startup and Management

- Orchestrated the startup of three quality-oriented, state-of-the-art dental laboratories, including facility design, equipment purchasing, policy / procedure development, QC, recruiting, marketing, and client relations.
- Worked closely with dentists to produce full and partial dentures requiring minimal adjustments; reduced chair time by 30–60 minutes per patient.
- Supervised the partial denture department at a U.S. Public Health Service laboratory servicing 34 military installations; directed laboratory operations in the absence of the Director.

Sales and Marketing / Client Relations

- Aggressively promoted laboratory services through telephone and in-person contact and direct mailings.
- Succeeded in building a high rate of repeat and referral business; achieved 90+% retention rate by paying meticulous attention to detail and delivering precision products.
- Frequently provided chairside guidance for dentists to ensure optimal results.

Research and Development / Consulting

- Personally developed products now being patented — a denture apparatus and technique for operatory and dental lab use, and a chemical substance for use in denture fabrication.
- Recruited by dental manufacturing companies throughout the U.S. to provide onsite R&D consulting services.
- Performed product testing at laboratory and provided feedback on a wide range of dental materials and techniques for manufacturers of dental products.

Training

- Conducted presentations for laboratory owners, dentists, and technicians throughout the tri-state area on industry developments, new products, and aesthetics and function of full and partial dentures.
- Trained / updated staff in laboratory operations and use of new equipment, products, and techniques.

AWARDS

Recipient of two awards by the U.S. Assistant Surgeon General for

- Research and Clinical Study on the Swing Lock Partial Denture
- Exceptional Quality Control and Production Results

EMPLOYMENT HISTORY

Owner / Manager, Plainfield Dental Laboratory, Plainfield, NJ	1991–Present
Owner / Manager, Kentritas Dental, Somerville, NJ	1980–1991
Laboratory Supervisor, U.S. Public Health Service, Staten Island, NY	1976–1980

PROFESSIONAL AFFILIATIONS

New Jersey Dental Laboratory Association (NJDLA): former Vice President, Treasurer, Secretary, Newsletter Editor
National Association of Dental Laboratories (NADL)

CREDENTIALS / EDUCATION

Certified Dental Technician
A.S., Dental Laboratory Technology, University of New Jersey, New Brunswick, NJ
Infection Control Certification

Strategy: A functional format was used to showcase many skills and avoid redundancy in detailing his extensive background in dental prosthetics.

LAVERNE G. HILEMAN, D.D.S.

Cell: 708-997-4333
Home: 847-278-7000

455 Hunting Trails Drive
Hoffman Estates, IL 60195

— PERSONAL PROFILE —

Analytical and scientifically disciplined professional seeking an opportunity to utilize demonstrated strengths in a dental-related business environment. Superior technical knowledge, doctor/patient relationship skills, patient education expertise, personnel training abilities, and accuracy in diagnosis.

— EDUCATION —

DOCTOR OF DENTAL SURGERY (D.D.S.), June 2001
University of Illinois—Chicago
License # 099-043650

BACHELOR OF SCIENCE: BIOLOGY
Winona State University—Minnesota
Cum Laude Graduate

— CAREER PATH —

Dentist   2001–Present
Provide on-site dental services to retirement and nursing homes. Set up own dental equipment. Treat patients and train staff on oral care and hygiene for residents between visits.

THE DENTAL CARE COMPANY, Elk Grove, Illinois
Dental Assistant   1993–1997
Responsibilities included infection control measures, chairside assistance, and lab work. Occasionally performed receptionist duties.

DANIEL FOSTER, D.D.S., Woodstock, Illinois
Dental Assistant   1991–1993

— CERTIFICATION —

Midwest Regional Dental Board

— MEMBERSHIPS AND AWARDS —

Recipient of Comprehensive Patient Care Award
Illinois Dental Association

Strategy: *This dentist used this straightforward resume to seek a supplemental part-time position while she builds her practice.*

ROBERT MARTIN, D.D.S.
477 Covington Avenue
Bloomfield, CT 06002

(860) 243-0590

rmartin@yahoo.com

PROFESSIONAL SUMMARY

Recognized internationally as a pioneer in the implementation of leading-edge techniques with a specialization in restorative and periodontal dentistry.

Distinguished career encompasses consulting, teaching, and leadership roles with a major medical center as well as national and state professional associations in the dental field.

SPECIAL AWARDS & LICENSURE

Fellow of the Academy of General Dentistry
Master-candidate of the Academy of General Dentistry
State of Connecticut License in Dentistry

SELECTED ACHIEVEMENTS

- **Grew dental practice to a profitable business through effective business planning, cost controls, consistent service excellence, and referral-based marketing.**
- **Achieved reputation for innovation and expertise in the dental profession as one of the first to implement state-of-the-art nonsurgical periodontal techniques.**
- **Elected President of the Connecticut Academy of General Dentistry and spearheaded the development and implementation of innovative programs that improved profitability.**
- **Honored as "Dentist of the Year" by the American Dental Association for contributions and dedication to the field of dentistry.**
- **Invited to join Connecticut State Board of Dentistry as consultant and provide expertise on program development and consumer relations.**
- **Fostered a motivating work environment and promoted open communications, resulting in high performance and staff retention.**

MANAGEMENT EXPERIENCE

HARTFORD DENTAL GROUP • Hartford, CT
President / Dentist (1970–Present)

Established and built highly successful business providing comprehensive dental services to several thousand patients. Acquired 3 private practices and led office in steady growth. Recruited and managed team of professional and support personnel. Provided ongoing staff training and development, leading to peak productivity, exceptional patient relations, and continual referrals.

CONSULTING & TEACHING EXPERIENCE

CONNECTICUT BOARD OF DENTISTRY • Hartford, CT
Consultant (1984–present)

Selected as consultant to the statewide organization in the design and implementation of educational, consumer relations, and other programs.

Strategy: *Because he was seeking to transition to a consulting role with a dental-products company, this experienced dentist highlighted both dental expertise and business achievements in his resume.*

ROBERT MARTIN, D.D.S. – Page 2

UNIVERSITY OF CONNECTICUT SCHOOL OF DENTISTRY • Hartford, CT
Instructor (1990–present)

Revamped and expanded the curriculum. Teach operative dentistry and other courses in the School of Dentistry.

NEW YORK MEDICAL CENTER • New York, NY
Consultant (1999–present)

Consultant to medical center's pain-management program for patients suffering from TMJ disorder.

EDUCATIONAL CREDENTIALS

Doctor of Dental Science
University of Connecticut School of Dentistry, Hartford, CT
Graduated with high honors

Continuing Education:

Successfully completed over 1,000 hours of continuing education, earning graduate credits in all areas of general dentistry and practice management, including

TM Disorders	Tooth Colored Restorations	Soft Tissue Surgery
Implants	Overlay Dentures	Endodontics Esthetics
Ceramic Restorations	Oral Pathology	Orthodontics
Auxiliary Utilization	Pharmacotherapeutics	Fixed Prosthodontics
Dental Materials	Dental Jurisprudence	Operative Dentistry
Table Clinics	Partial Dentures	Radiology
Treatment Planning	Clinical Diagnosis	Surgical Endodontics
Oral & Maxillofacial Surgery	Removable Prosthetics	Financial Management
Practice Management	Periodontics	Patient Education
	Patient Insurance Programs	

AFFILIATIONS

American Dental Association
Connecticut Dental Association
Academy of General Dentistry
Connecticut Dental Research Group

CHAPTER 9

Resumes for Pharmacists and Pharmacy Technicians

- Pharmacy Technician
- Registered Pharmacist
- Retail Pharmacist
- Clinical Pharmacist
- Director of Pharmacy Services

New pharmacy graduates often use a CV format, as is shown in the first resume of this chapter, whereas experienced pharmacists more often find that the resume style is more effective in conveying business achievements and depth of expertise.

RESUME 62: MICHELE HAFFNER, CPRW, JCTC; GLENDALE, WI

ALEXANDRA KENNEDY
akennedy@students.wisc.edu

<u>Permanent</u>
5001 County Highway SS
Sussex, WI 53022
(262) 897-9787

<u>January to May 2003</u>
2234 Cambridge St., Apt 6
Madison, WI 53502
(608) 278-0539

EDUCATION

DOCTOR OF PHARMACY, *University of Wisconsin School of Pharmacy*   to be conferred May 2003
BACHELOR OF SCIENCE—MEDICAL TECHNOLOGY, *Marquette University*   May 1995

PROFESSIONAL EXPERIENCE

MEDICAL TECHNOLOGIST—MICROBIOLOGY LABORATORY   May 1995 to Present

<u>Midwest Laboratories, Milwaukee, WI</u>
Identify pathogens from cultures, prepare antibiotic sensitivities, compile data for hospital MIC reports, verify accuracy of reports sent to physicians, train student interns and new employees, conduct tours of department for students and medical personnel.

CLINICAL CLERKSHIPS

<u>Neurology</u>   Sep 2002 to Oct 2002
University Hospital and Clinics, Madison, WI

<u>Cardiovascular Medicine</u>   Jun 2002 to Aug 2002
University Hospital and Clinics, Madison, WI

EXTERNSHIPS

<u>Community Pharmacy</u>   Oct 2002 to Dec 2002
Winter's Pharmacy, Milwaukee, WI

<u>Outpatient Clinics</u>   Oct 2002 to Dec 2002
Veterans Administration Medical Center, Milwaukee, WI

PENDING ROTATIONS

<u>Trauma and Life Support</u>   Jan 2003 to Feb 2003
University Hospital and Clinics, Madison, WI

<u>Nutrition</u>   Feb 2003 to Mar 2003
All Saints Hospital and Medical Center, Madison, WI

<u>Infectious Diseases</u>   Mar 2003 to Apr 2003
Park Hospital, Madison, WI

<u>Community/Mail-Order Pharmacy</u>   Apr 2003 to May 2003
University International Pharmacy, Madison, WI

Strategy: *The resume for a soon-to-graduate pharmacist follows the traditional CV format recommended by the American Pharmaceutical Association.*

Alexandra Kennedy
Curriculum Vitae, Page 2
akennedy@students.wisc.edu

PROFESSIONAL ACTIVITIES

HONORS AND AWARDS

University of Wisconsin
Rho Chi Honor Society, recognition for scholastic achievement	2001
Phi Kappa Phi Honor Society	2001
Honor Roll	1999 to 2002

CLINICAL PRESENTATIONS

Anti-Platelet Therapy in CVA Prevention   Oct 2002
Residents
University of Wisconsin Hospital and Clinics, Madison, WI

AIDSVAX: Use in the Prevention and Treatment of HIV   Sep 2002
4th Year Pharmacy Students and Pharmacists in Pharmacy Practicum 771
University Hospital and Clinics, Madison, WI

Vancomycin Resistant Enterococci: Treatment and Prevention   Apr 2002
3rd Year Pharmacy Students and Pharmacists in Pharmacy Practicum 771
University Hospital and Clinics, Madison, WI

PROFESSIONAL AFFILIATIONS

American Pharmaceutical Association   1999 to Present
University of Wisconsin Chapter

American Society of Health-System Pharmacists   2002
University of Wisconsin Chapter

ORGANIZATIONAL ACTIVITIES

Rho Chi Delegate at the APhA Conference   2001 & 2002
University of Wisconsin Chapter

COMMUNITY SERVICE

Medic Clinic—The Salvation Army, Madison, WI   2000 to 2001
Volunteer assistant.

Transitional Care Nursing Home, Madison, WI   2000 to 2001
Volunteer assistant.

Please See Attached Listing of Professional References and Preceptors.

Priscilla K. Balding

3333 Tree Lane
Spokane, WA 99214
(509) 727-7347

Pharmacy — Medical Billing — Medical Office Administration

PROFILE

Team-spirited professional, patient and resourceful. Positive attitude, creative thinker/problem solver—effective in streamlining operations, improving productivity, and reducing costs.

Able to handle multiple responsibilities, set priorities, clearly communicate ideas to others, and respond positively to demanding situations. Recognized for speed, accuracy, quality of work, and outstanding customer service.

QUALIFICATIONS

- Insurance Billing—online and hand-billing experience for all insurances including Medicare and Medicaid—detailed working knowledge of insurance plans, overrides, and billing codes.
- 11 years' pharmacy experience—drug formulary, ingredients, compounding, analyzing prescriptions/inventory management/recordkeeping.
- Outstanding customer service—recipient of numerous "Mystery Shopper" Customer Service Awards.

Added Value:

- 10+ years' experience in hospitality industry—catering, staff management, event planning.

CAREER SUMMARY

Pharmacy Technician Level A, Rite-Aid, Spokane, WA, 1995–Present
Completed training program to become PTLA while working as cashier.

Main source of flow for prescriptions—analyze prescriptions; type prescriptions; count, compound, and dispense drugs. Order drugs and supplies. Provide extensive, caring, and informed Customer Service—established loyal customer base.

Access insurance company computers—set up prescriptions, calculate supply and quantity—utilize knowledge of limitations of different insurance plans. Maintain customer records and profiles on nationally linked proprietary computer system.

Assistant Manager, Wellington Yacht Club, Spokane, WA, 1989–1992
Answered to Board of Directors and General Manager of Catering and Fine Dining establishment.

Supervised up to 30 employees in all aspects of food and beverage area of Club. Assisted chef with menu planning and food-cost control. Instrumental in bringing about modernization of service styles. Initiated systems to improve efficiency and food service.

Food and Beverage/Catering Manager, Holiday Inn, Spokane, WA, 1988–1995 *(now Best Western Lakeway)*

Oversaw staff of 60+ people—purchasing, scheduling, event planning, budgeting. Assisted chef with menu planning. Involved with entire remodel and re-imaging of hotel and lounge—participated in selecting and training staff, initiating new procedures, implementing new computer system.

PROFESSIONAL DEVELOPMENT

Washington State Pharmacy Technician License—current
Pharmacy Training, Rite-Aid
Coursework in Accounting/General Business, City Community College

Strategy: *To cover a lot of ground for an experienced pharmacy technician who is considering other medical-related career options, this resume includes both pharmacy and business-management experience and achievements.*

Curriculum Vitae
of
GEORGE P. WINSTON, R.PH., M.S.
1500 East Robin Way, Chandler, AZ 85226
(480) 732-8700 (H) ▪ (480) 977-4130 (W) ▪ gwinston@cox.net

PROFESSIONAL PROFILE

Registered Pharmacist with more than 19 years of experience in retail and hospital environments. Interface with drug regulatory boards and agencies, manufacturers, and law-enforcement officials to ensure safety and well-being of patients. Major areas of expertise include

- **Pharmacy rules & regulations**
- **Drug recalls**
- **Schedule II procedures & protocols**
- **Patient compliance programs**
- **Employee recruiting & training**
- **Introduction of new products**
- **Emergency procedures**
- **Public presentations**

Registered Pharmacist in Arizona, California, Nevada, and Washington

PROFESSIONAL EXPERIENCE

SAFEWAY, Scottsdale, AZ   1986 to Present

Safeway acquired American Stores, Inc., parent company of Cost-Plus Drugs, in 1998. Promoted to management positions at various pharmacies in California. Transferred to Phoenix in 1996.

Pharmacy Category Manager, Scottsdale, AZ (2001–Present)

Based in corporate drug regional office, procure approximately $4 billion in pharmaceutical products for 2,000 Safeway pharmacies throughout the U.S. Have complete P&L accountability for department. Oversee activities of 7 employees; report to Director of Pharmacy Procurement.

- Interact extensively with drug manufacturers, FDA, and Boards of Pharmacy to initiate and implement disease-state management programs that provide education to consumers nationwide.
- Develop patient compliance programs, using written or verbal communications to remind patients to renew medications for chronic conditions.
- Work in cooperation with FDA, DEA, and Boards of Pharmacy to develop and implement emergency procedures to ensure patients' access to medication in case of national emergencies.
- Interact with DEA to monitor Schedule II narcotics usage and ensure compliance on regulatory documentation regarding legal purchase and proper destruction of outdated drugs.
- Actively engage in proper notification of FDA drug recalls to all pharmacies within company, working in concert with manufacturers to ensure patient safety.
- Use industry knowledge to purchase in cost-saving quantities. Monitor accounts payable, flagging delinquent accounts; oversee purchase of updated and new products; supervise returns for credit.

Regional Pharmacy Manager, Cost-Plus / Xtra Drugs, Anaheim, CA / Phoenix, AZ (1994–2001)

Managed pharmacy operations for 60 pharmacies, including P&L accountability, recruiting and manpower planning, legal pharmacy compliance, standards of operational excellence, budget

Strategy: *Not all resumes are used for a job search. This individual was being considered for a position on the Board of Directors of the Arizona Pharmacy Association.*

GEORGE P. WINSTON, R.PH., M.S.
Page 2

development and execution, pharmacy management training, product pricing, vendor marketing, business acquisition, and new business development.

- Represented company before Board of Pharmacy regarding questions of pharmaceutical practices.
- Coordinated Pharmacy Summer Intern Program.

Regional Pharmacy Trainer, Cost-Plus Drugs, Anaheim, CA (1994)

Reviewed and developed training materials and facilitated training sessions in 10 different disciplines. Motivated and trained new facilitators; participated in hiring new associates. Accountable for operations at 6 training sites. Reported to Vice President of Pharmacy Operations.

Pharmacy Manager, Cost-Plus Drugs, various stores in CA (1987–1994)

Managed 24-hour pharmacy operation, supervising 7 staff pharmacists and 9 technicians dispensing approximately 4,000 prescriptions per week. Accountable for bottom-line profitability of pharmacy. Oversaw staffing, scheduling, payroll, inventory control. Dispensed prescriptions and counseled patients. Served as pricing-tier coordinator for 40+ pharmacies. Provided consultation services for other pharmacies in district.

Staff Pharmacist, Cost-Plus Drugs, various stores in NV (1986–1987)

VETERANS ADMINISTRATION HOSPITAL, Seattle, WA   1983 to 1986

Outpatient Night / Weekend Supervisor (1984–1986)
Graduate Intern (1983–1984)

BLUE CROWN LABORATORIES, Seattle, WA   1979 to 1982

Laboratory Technician

EDUCATION

Master of Business Administration — Anticipated Graduation Date: June 2003
INTERNATIONAL GRADUATE SCHOOL OF MANAGEMENT, Scottsdale, AZ

Master of Science, Pharmaceutical Sciences and Toxicology — 1986
Master's Thesis: *HPLC Determination of Two Calcium Channel Blockers*
Bachelor of Science, Pharmacy — 1983
WASHINGTON STATE UNIVERSITY, Seattle, WA

Adjunct Faculty — University of Arizona College of Pharmacy, Tucson, Arizona — 2000 to Present
Class: *Chain Pharmacy Management*

GEORGE P. WINSTON, R.PH., M.S.

ADDENDUM

PROFESSIONAL DEVELOPMENT

- **NARP Annual Convention,** New York, New York — Workshops covering Patient Compliance, New Models of Biotechnology, and HIPPA Regulations — 2002
- **Success Leadership Seminar,** Phoenix, Arizona — 2001
- **NTL Institute Human Interaction Workshop,** San Diego, California — 1999
- **Management for Inspired Performance,** Safeway — 1998
- **Relationships and Communication Workshop,** Scottsdale, Arizona — 1998
- **Communication Workshop,** Anaheim, California — 1997

MEMBERSHIPS

Phoenix Pharmacist Association — Member, Board of Directors — 1998 to 2000
- Monitored legislative influence on pharmacy issues.
- Monitored Arizona Board of Pharmacy proposed regulatory changes.
- Appeared before Arizona Board of Pharmacy to represent pharmaceutical retail interests.

University of Arizona College of Pharmacy — Member, Advisory Board — 1995 to Present

AWARDS / HONORS

President's Award for Excellence — 1999
Excellence in Operations — 1995
Warehouse Utilization and Excellence in Operations — 1992
Rho Chi Pharmaceutical Honor Society — 1989
Blue Key National Honor Fraternity — 1988

PUBLICATIONS

Journal of Pharmaceutical Sciences

"Isocratic High-Performance Liquid Chromatographic Method for the Determination of Tricyclic Antidepressants and Metabolites in Plasma," 12, 1127 (1999)

"Isocratic Liquid Chromatographic Method for the Determination of Amoxapine and Its Metabolites," 84, 592 (1995)

Journal of Liquid Chromatography

"An HPLC Method for the Determination of Diltiazem and Desacetyldiltiazem in Human Plasma," 21(3), 681–693 (1992)

"An HPLC Method for the Determination of Verapamil and Norverapamil in Human Plasma," 14(9), 1027–1105 (1989)

GEORGE BROWN, Pharm.D.

98 Ben Franklin Drive
Cherry Hill, New Jersey 07896   Email: gbrown@aol.com

Phone: (609) 654-2222
Fax: (609) 654-3333

CLINICAL PHARMACIST

Disease Management Program Development / Drug Information Support / Patient Counseling
Inpatient and Outpatient Dispensing / Exceptional Verbal, Written & Planning Skills / Excellent
Communication & Interpersonal Skills / Patient-Physician Education Materials

LICENSED IN NEW JERSEY AND CALIFORNIA
DOCTOR OF PHARMACY — Rutgers University, 1989
BACHELOR OF SCIENCE, MICROBIOLOGY — Rutgers University, 1985

Highly committed clinical pharmacist with broad experience in managed care / pharmacy benefit management. Strong ability to safely and efficiently dispense drugs. Sound understanding of the principles underlying pharmaceutical care, with an ability to recognize therapeutic incompatibilities. Adept interpersonal and communication skills, with expertise interacting with consumers, medical staff, and administrators. Proactive leadership in the development, implementation, and analysis of disease-management programs.

Career Chronology

Associate Director, Clinical Services — AGI Managed Care, Inc.	1998–2002
Therapeutics & Outcomes Manager — ABC Pharmaceutical Services	1994–1998
Clinical Pharmacy Manager — ABC Pharmaceutical Services	1992–1994
HMO Pharmacy Consultant — New Jersey Pharmacists Association	1990–1992
Hospital Pharmacy Resident — Garden State Community Hospital	1989–1990
Pharmacy Intern — Rutgers University Medical Center	1987–1989

Dispensing Pharmaceutical Experience

NEW JERSEY PHARMACISTS ASSOCIATION (NPA) — Clifton, New Jersey
HMO Pharmacy Consultant
Based on-site at Health Line of New Jersey, a 100,000-member HMO in Flint, NJ. Primary care physicians assumed some financial risk for the amount of money budgeted for health care services per patient enrolled in the health plan.
- Restructured physician prescribing profiles; advised physicians of their outpatient pharmacy costs, recommending alternative efficacious therapies aimed at reducing financial risk.
- Created a survey for data collection to assist improvement of the physician-detailing process.

GARDEN STATE COMMUNITY HOSPITAL — Englewood Cliffs, New Jersey
Hospital Pharmacy Resident
- Promoted a concurrent, hospital-wide reporting program for adverse drug reactions.
- Conducted personal consultations and training on glucometer use to patients with diabetes.
- Provided clinical and distributive services in both the inpatient and outpatient pharmacies.
- Solo pharmacist weekend duty; verified prescriptions and checked medications.

RUTGERS UNIVERSITY MEDICAL CENTER — Bloomfield, New Jersey
Pharmacy Intern
- Performed services related to the preparation and dispensing of drugs and other pharmaceutical supplies in accordance with physician prescriptions.

Strategy: *This resume was designed for a transition back from managed care to practicing pharmacy. Note how the most relevant experience is positioned up front (on page 1) without dates, preceded by a career chronology that clearly spells out details of employment.*

GEORGE BROWN, Pharm.D.

Page 2

Managed Care Experience

AGI MANAGED CARE, INC. — Edison, New Jersey
Large independently managed subsidiary of AGI & Co., Inc. AGI supports clients' outpatient pharmacy coverage via a nationwide network of more than 55,000 retail pharmacies and 13 mail-order pharmacies.

Associate Director, Clinical Services

Based on-site at the Hills Management Program (HMP), AGI's largest client. Provided clinical pharmacy coordination of HMP's mail-order pharmacy benefit.

- Provided clinical pharmacy expertise while accompanying AGI lobbyists to Trenton.
- Ensured timely responses to requests for internal drug information, therapeutic appropriateness, clinical and financial reviews of individual drugs, or current pharmacotherapy for specific diseases.
- Mediated external customer-service follow-ups requiring clinical input; verbal and written to both individual members and program administrators.

ABC PHARMACEUTICAL SERVICES — Bedminster, New Jersey
Formerly a subsidiary of Logan Health Group, now consolidated with Kings Express.

Therapeutics and Outcomes Manager

Spearheaded "BreatheRight," a disease-management program of interventions to promote appropriate, cost-effective therapy and improve outcomes.

- Collaborated with colleagues (clinical, systems, and statisticians) and physicians to develop utilization data "triggers" to identify patients and physicians for inclusion in the BreatheRight program.
- Pioneered the development of patient-education materials and physician correspondence, in collaboration with marketing and legal departments.
- Published joint author of two asthma-management articles, "Evaluating & Identifying the Effects of Asthma," *Annals of Asthma & Immunology*; and "How to Use Claims Databases to Document Cost Centers," *Archives of Asthma Medicine*.
- Planned and coordinated BreatheRight Advisory Panel conference, obtaining endorsement for the program; panel consisted of local and national asthma experts to help in the identification of at–risk asthma patients.

Clinical Pharmacy Manager

- Planned and co-led Pharmacy & Therapeutic Committee meetings, providing accurate, rapid responses to requests for drug information; collaborated in formulary development and evaluated therapeutic benefits and cost-effectiveness of new drugs.
- Assessed data on client HMOs' outpatient prescription drug use during bi-annual on-site visits, presenting recommendations to promote a quality, cost-effective drug-management program to plan administrators.

Publications

Co-authored "Evaluating & Identifying the Effects of Asthma," *Annals of Asthma & Immunology*, 1995
Co-authored "How to Use Claims Databases to Document Cost Centers," *Archives of Asthma Medicine*, 1995

Presentations

ABC's BreatheRight Program: Outcomes Measurement & Tracking, 1996
BreatheRight: The Diversified Process, 1995
Conducted numerous presentations in diverse venues between 1989–1993

REFERENCES AVAILABLE UPON REQUEST

George T. Pollard

8709 Highland Drive
Midland, Michigan 48640

989-555-7666
gtpharm@aol.com

PROFILE

► Accomplished leader with solid track record of retail management and attention to the bottom line.

► Complete understanding of retail pharmacy based on 25+ years of industry experience.

► An experienced supervisor, trainer, team builder, and motivator.

► Earned rapid promotions into positions of increasing scope and responsibility.

► Computer literate.

HIGHLIGHTS OF ACCOMPLISHMENTS

► Successfully turned around poorly performing stores by reducing inventory, increasing gross margins, and building customer base.

► Facilitated opening of two additional units: Designed and developed pharmacy floor plans and traffic flow; ordered initial inventory; hired and trained professional and support staff.

► One of 100 pharmacists from across the state selected to participate on Michigan Pharmacists Association Advisory Board for policy development.

► Developed training guidelines and procedures where none existed.

► Office holder and active member of state-wide professional organization.

SUMMARY OF EXPERIENCE

► Recruited by Pharmacy Department Director to provide operational management of 9-unit retail chain. Maintained responsibility for facilitating and/or monitoring
  - Policy development
  - Recruiting and hiring
  - Scheduling and payroll administration
  - Budget development
  - Purchasing, pricing, and ROI
  - Gross margins
  - P & L
  - Inventory control
  - Third-party audits
  - Goal setting

► Planned and implemented corporate participation in community events such as health fairs and informational presentations. Solicited involvement of appropriate agencies and vendors.

► Recruited and trained staff on computer system, procedures, and policy issues.

► Managed 100+ R.Ph.s and their technicians in 30+ stores located across wide geographic area.

► Contributed to developing incentive program for pharmacists based on sales, inventory levels, payroll guidelines, and other relevant variables.

► Recruited pharmacists from 8 states; developed recruiting materials and attended career fairs.

► Identified methods for increasing and maintaining profit margins; monitored buying patterns.

► Managed all aspects of retail stores, including pharmacies.

Strategy: *This resume was written for a pharmacist who was seeking career advancement in administrative management for a major pharmaceutical chain. The Highlights and Summary sections on page 1 draw attention to relevant qualifications while avoiding repetitive listings of job duties.*

George T. Pollard   989-555-7666

EMPLOYMENT HISTORY

IGA PHARMACY [acquired by Costco in 2000] • Midland, Michigan   1997–Present
Pharmacy Administrator [9 stores]
Pharmacy Manager
Pharmacist

SNYDER DRUG [acquired by Walgreen Pharmacy in 1996] • Mt. Pleasant, Michigan   1982–1997
Pharmacist Recruiter   **Store Manager**
Pharmacy Supervisor [30+ stores/200+ staff]   **Pharmacy Manager**
Super Store Manager [15,000–18,000 sq. ft.]   **Pharmacist**

FAMILY PHARMACY • Auburn, Michigan   1972–1982
Co-Owner/Manager
Pharmacy Manager
Pharmacist

ACADEMIC BACKGROUND & LICENSURE

EASTERN MICHIGAN UNIVERSITY • Ypsilanti, Michigan   STATE OF MICHIGAN
Bachelor of Science — Pharmacy (1972)   **Registered Pharmacist**

AFFILIATIONS

▶ Michigan Pharmacists Association   ▶ Midland County Pharmacists Association
   Lansing, Michigan   Midland, Michigan
   • Executive Board Member (1980–1987)   • President
   • Membership Committee Member
   • Policy Development Member

Excellent professional references available on request

STEVEN A. REYNOLDS

88 Dover Drive
Raleigh, NC 27613

(919) 899-1549
sareynolds@aol.com

CAREER PROFILE

Pharmacy Management Professional with proven ability to impact operations, build revenues/sales, and enhance profitability while enhancing pharmacy service operations.

Strategic planning and operations-management strengths combine with an ability to critically evaluate organizational needs and design effective solutions that achieve performance objectives.

P&L and financial-management expertise includes successes in controlling/reducing cost of goods, increasing operating margins, and reducing accounts receivable.

Instill a customer-driven, total quality management culture through strong leadership, staff development, and empowerment.

Well versed in all reimbursement structures: prospective payment, capitation, risk sharing, per diem, managed care, fee-for-service, federal and state health plans, and third-party plans.

PROFESSIONAL EXPERIENCE

PHARMCARE/SUBSIDIARY OF ADCO CARE
Director of Pharmacy Services – Southeast

Raleigh, NC
1998-present

Senior-level position with strategic, operating, and P&L responsibility for $75 million region with 6 sites, providing long-term-care pharmacy, infusion, home medical equipment, and medical-supply services for 160 nursing centers with 22,000 residents throughout the southeastern U.S. Recruited to turn around failing operation and design strategies to improve the region. Accountable for recruiting, training, development, and management of 300 direct and indirect reports. **Accomplishments:**

- *Merged 4 pharmacies, saving company $1.5 million annually.*
- *Revised pricing structure and reduced cost of goods 25%, saving $50,000 annually.*
- *Improved efficiency through implementation of barcode system, real-time online billing, and new organizational reporting structure.*
- *Led upgrade and consolidation to state-of-the-art computer system at multiple locations for 4 different business lines, reducing costs 15% while increasing efficiency.*
- *Redesigned 2 sites, streamlining workflow and enhancing productivity.*

PHARMCO/SUBSIDIARY OF SOUTHEAST HEALTH
Pharmacy Manager

Raleigh, NC
1995-1998

Recruited to open and direct Pharmco's pharmacy operations in Raleigh, providing pharmaceutical care to residents in long-term-care, sub-acute, and assisted-living facilities. P&L responsibility for entire business, including dispensing pharmacy, consulting pharmacy, quality assurance, IV nursing, billing, medical records, inventory, purchasing, staffing, customer relations, computerized systems, and regulatory compliance. **Accomplishments:**

- *Built profitable operation and grew business 400%, increasing monthly net income from a negative position to a positive 18% by 1998.*
- *Personally generated sales of $5 million and increased prescription volume 93% in 1997.*
- *Created a culture of total quality management through employee empowerment.*
- *Led pharmacy to achieve JCAHO accreditation with commendation in 1997.*
- *Increased inventory turns from 7 to 16 and reduced accounts receivable days from 105 to 40.*
- *Under leadership, pharmacy achieved top ranking in customer satisfaction in 1997-1998.*
- *Won 1998 President's Award out of 25 pharmacists throughout the eastern U.S.*

Strategy: *A chronological format works well for this individual seeking career advancement in pharmacy management. Through formatting enhancements, achievements are clearly distinguished from job activities.*

STEVEN A. REYNOLDS • (919) 899-1549 • Page 2

HOME CARE INFUSION, INC.   Columbus, OH
Home Care Infusion Pharmacist   *1990-1995*

Provided home infusion services for nursing-home residents as member of the healthcare team. Specialized in TPNs, antibiotics, chemotherapy, pain management, and antivirals. Consultant to physicians and nursing staff on home medication therapies. Prepared and documented pharmacy care plans, medications, progress notes, and profiles. Monitored patient outcomes and quality assurance. Managed pharmacy supplies inventory. **Accomplishments:**

- *Selected as one of 2 pharmacists to open company's Columbus pharmacy operations.*
- *Contributed to the successful JCAHO accreditation of the new pharmacy.*
- *Built and maintained excellent relationships with physicians and other healthcare professionals.*
- *Ensured that all pharmacy records met federal and state requirements.*

Prior Experience: Staff Pharmacist, Memorial Hospital, Kettering, OH (1989-1990).

EDUCATIONAL CREDENTIALS

Pharm.D. • 1995
Ohio State University, College of Pharmacy, Columbus, OH

B.S., Pharmacy • 1988
University of North Carolina, Raleigh, NC

PROFESSIONAL LICENSES

North Carolina State Licensed/Registered Pharmacist
Ohio State Licensed/Registered Pharmacist

AFFILIATIONS

American Pharmaceutical Association
North Carolina Pharmaceutical Association

CHAPTER 10

Resumes for Clinical Research Professionals

- Clinical Researcher
- Biotechnology Researcher
- Clinical Research Coordinator
- Public Health Researcher
- Physician Researcher
- Medical Director

Both CV and resume formats are used to present the often complex skills and knowledge of clinical research professionals. In some cases, business results are emphasized; in others, it is the clinical work itself that is the focus.

Simon Carey

2200 E. Twain Street
Tucson, AZ 85716
(520) 555–1212
simoncarey@juno.com

Summary

Biochemistry Research professional with advanced training and professional experience.

- Strong analysis, research, and documentation skills. Experience in laboratory, hospital, and clinical settings ranges from laboratory development and medical research through assisting with surgical procedures.

- Academic studies include biochemistry and medicine of ancient cultures: surgical techniques, herbalism, inorganic pharmaceuticals, and therapeutics.

- Committed to ongoing professional development. Highly motivated, dedicated, and hardworking. Quick to learn new skills and new procedures.

- Widely traveled; accustomed to working with researchers, medical professionals, and patients from many different cultures and backgrounds. Familiar with Spanish, German, and French.

Education

Postgraduate Honours Diploma (equivalent to Master's Degree)
Biochemistry and Ancient Medicine
Mansfield College, Oxford University, Oxford, England (1998)
- Studies included Biochemistry, History of Medicine, Witchcraft and Society in Europe 1450–1700, and Science and Philosophy in Greek and Hellenistic Society.
- Conducted original research and wrote thesis on DNA intercalators—modification of genetic material by carcinogens.
- Intensive study of materials at Oxford's Bodleian Library.
- Active in Oxford Union Debating Society.

Bachelor of Arts with Honors in Chemistry
Duke University, Durham, NC (1990)
- Inducted into Phi Lambda Upsilon Honorary Chemical Society and Phi Eta Sigma Honour Society.
- Won Most Valuable Student Award from Elks National Foundation.
- Won competition for American Heart Association research stipend.

Oxford/Duke Summer Programme
New College, Oxford University, Oxford, England (1993)
- Studied History of Medicine, focusing on late 19th/early 20th Century English medicine.

Salutatorian
Special Projects High School for the Gifted and Talented, Tucson, AZ (1986)

Professional Associations

International Union of Pure and Applied Chemistry
American Chemical Society
Phi Lambda Upsilon Honorary Chemical Society
Duke Alumni Association

Strategy: *The simple yet effective CV format presents a unique clinical, academic, and international background for this individual who is seeking work in the U.S. after several years of work and study abroad.*

Simon Carey

Page 2

(520) 555–1212
simoncarey@juno.com

Professional Experience

Laboratory Development Consultant

International Research Foundation, Nonsuch Hospital, Oxford, England (1998 to 2002)
Calibrated state-of-the-art scientific instruments at craniofacial medicine laboratory. Researched recent developments in craniofacial medicine. Edited teaching materials distributed to students.

Medical Editor

CTC International Research Foundation (1994 to 1995)
Edited teaching materials and orthodontic and craniofacial surgery manuals.

Medical Internships

CTC International Research Foundation (1992)
Assisted with surgical procedures at St. Maurice Hospital and Erasmus Hospital in Brussels, Belgium; University Hospital, Montpellier, France; and Bambino Gesu Hospital (Children's Hospital), Rome. Worked with a wide range of people, from AIDS patients to newborn children.

Therapist

Department of Medicine, University of California at Berkeley (1989)
Provided physical therapy and remedial education for brain-damaged children.

Surgical Volunteer

Duke University Medical Center, Durham, NC (1988 to 1989)
Assisted with surgical procedures and provided post-operative patient care.

Researcher

Research Laboratory, Duke University Medical Center (1987 to 1989)
Researched links between recent blood transfusions and reduced incidence of kidney transplant rejection.

Researcher

University of California at Berkeley (1987)
Participated in American Heart Association–sponsored research concerning physiological effects of drugs on the cardiovascular system.

Volunteer Work

Active in fundraising for Children's House, a Tucson organization serving homeless and abused children. Contributed 2 antique cars to car show—proceeds from ticket sales and concessions supported Children's House.

Traveled to the Dominican Republic to vaccinate children in rural villages against diphtheria, pertussis, tetanus, measles, mumps, rubella, and polio (Sabin). Conducted tuberculosis testing. Reported to UNICEF for aid in proper diet for kwashiorkor victims. Also volunteered at polio hospital.

References Available

SARAH T. MATHEWS, R.N.

2525 Wind Point Place
Cincinnati, OH 45242

Telephone: 513-234-5678
E-mail: smathews@aol.com

BIOTECHNOLOGY RESEARCH

Product Support ◆ Clinical Research ◆ Medical Devices

Dynamic and highly experienced **clinical researcher and registered nurse** with more than ten years of industry experience in drug development. Extensive knowledge of GCPs, FDA regulations, and protocol skills in monitoring diverse drug products. Experience in protocol design, investigator recruitment, and grant negotiations. Highly motivated team player with strong analytical, supervisory, and interpersonal skills. Consistently promoted from Clinical Assistant to Regional Senior Clinical Associate.

PROFESSIONAL EXPERIENCE

The Carone-Tealing Group, Cincinnati, Ohio, 1995–2003
Regional Senior Clinical Research Associate

Created new Midwest office involving the management of Phase III and IV clinical trials of recombinant growth hormone, synthetic growth hormone releasing factor (GRF), and fertility products. Cultivated collaborations with investigators and supported marketing and sales efforts.

- Supervised 10 investigative sites, requiring weekly travel to these sites, major hospitals, and research centers in Midwest. Reported directly to Director of Clinical Trials in R&D, as well as managers of Phase IV studies and corporate staff in Boston.
- Enhanced R&D's efforts and visibility in Midwest with key fertility and growth physicians, accomplished through the development and implementation of Phase IV and post-marketing studies.
- Participated in protocol design and actual conduct of study, assuring compliance with FDA regulations.

Senior Clinical Research Associate

Orchestrated and assisted in the planning of clinical research project, working with leading endocrinologists on recombinant human growth hormone studies for children with secondary growth deficiencies. Supported Phase I, II, and III research activity leading to new-product registration.

- Key player in clinical group that began groundbreaking national multi-center AIDS studies in 1996.
- Identified, interviewed, and recruited investigators; negotiated grants, budgets, and contracts. Surpassed goal, launching sites and securing patients ahead of schedule.
- Assisted in the design and rationale for clinical research protocols and case report forms based on FDA regulations, and monitored progress of study, assuring compliance with protocol.
- Strategized with leading endocrinologists and consulting physicians on new protocol development and redesign, identifying potential on-site problems.
- Supervised and trained study coordinator, CRAs, RNs, and investigators in mandated protocols.
- Collected, analyzed, and interpreted supporting safety and efficacy data in preparation for publication.
- Prepared data summaries and progress reports on all aspects of study projects and presented progress at monthly Carone-Tealing clinical-review meetings.

Strategy: *Because this candidate is seeking a management position, detailed emphasis is placed on her most recent experience, which shows increased responsibility in research. Her early career in hospital nursing is downplayed.*

Sarah T. Mathews, R.N.   page 2   Telephone: 513-234-5678

Clinical Research Assistant

Developed and monitored pivotal studies investigating the safety and efficacy of an immunomodulator in the treatment of AIDS/HIV infections. Coordinated research activities leading to new indications of TP-1.

- Coordinated AIDS multi-center study, having global responsibility for all clinical and administrative aspects of monitoring clinical research and closing out studies.
- Recruited investigators; trained CRAs, study nurse, and pharmaceutical research monitor.
- Instituted major changes in TP-1 drug labeling and packaging system for AIDS and ARC multi-center trials, resulting in a new, cost-effective, and time-efficient procedure.
- Assisted in substantially modifying AIDS data-collection procedures to decrease budgetary costs, maximize efficiency, and obtain concise efficacy data.

Biomedical Research Associates, Boston, MA, 1992–1995
Clinical Research Associate

Represented major pharmaceutical companies to recruit investigators and patients at major hospitals and research institutions to initiate, develop, and monitor protocols for a variety of disease entities. Monitored Phase II and III clinical trials, supervised research associates, and negotiated grants.

- Consistently generated increased revenues by meeting and exceeding territorial goals of initiating, developing, and supervising ongoing clinical studies.
- As top producer, supervised more than 20 different investigative sites, tracking 30 patients per site with six simultaneous protocols representing diverse pharmaceutical companies.
- Improved protocol skills and productivity of CRAs, RNs, investigators, and pharmacists by providing leadership, motivation, and training in FDA regulations and GCPs.
- Interfaced with data management group to perform statistical analysis of data. Oversaw grant payments based on generated data.

Richard Winslow General Hospital, Cranston, MD, 1985–1992
Medical Personnel Associates, Cranston, MD, 1985–1992

As a Registered Nurse, obtained experience in health care at major Maryland teaching hospitals.

EDUCATION

Boston College, Chestnut Hill, MA   Bachelor of Arts in Social Science – 1991
University of Rhode Island, Kingston, RI   Associate of Science in Nursing – 1985

PROFESSIONAL DEVELOPMENT

Adult CPR/AED (Automated External Defibrillation)
Bioethics Seminar, Boston University School of Medicine
Advanced Cardiac Life Support Program, Certified ACLS
"Stem Cell Research and Human Cloning," sponsored by Massachusetts Biomedical Initiative

LICENSE

Massachusetts Registered Nurse, License No. 1658867

LAURA R. MARLIN, R.N.

225 Long Point Drive
Hartsdale, NY 10530

(914) 428-1995
Marlin@healthy.net

CLINICAL RESEARCH COORDINATOR
Attaining Optimal Accuracy, Efficiency, and Productivity

HIGHLY SKILLED HEALTH-CARE PROFESSIONAL with more than 6 years of clinical research experience building productive teams that have set new standards. More than 20 years' practical experience in pioneering health-care programs, services, and technologies. Combined expertise in leading-edge technologies, strategic planning, recruitment, and patient-care management. Combine strong planning, leadership, and consensus-building qualifications with effective writing and presentation skills. Highly articulate, with exceptional communication skills; effective presenter. Consistent contributions in increasing patient census, reducing operating costs, and increasing net revenues in competitive health-care markets. Possess strong clinical and diagnostic expertise.

Expert qualifications in identifying and capturing opportunities to accelerate program expansion, slash costs, increase revenues, and improve profit contributions. Excellent team-building, team-leadership, and interpersonal-relations skills.

Additional expertise includes

- Strategic planning
- Staffing development & training
- Quality & productivity improvement

- Plasmaheresis
- Hemodialysis
- Venipuncture

- Marketing
- Subject recruitment
- Subject compliance & retention

PROFESSIONAL PROFILE	
	- Organized, enthusiastic health-care professional; willing to learn new ideas and go the extra mile to provide quality medical care.
	- Consistent success in surpassing productivity and performance objectives.
	- Demonstrated capability to *resolve problems* swiftly and independently.
	- Possess strong interpersonal skills; able to work effectively with individuals on all levels; effective motivator of self and others.
	- Highly effective in the collection, retention, analysis, reporting, and presentation of data for different aspects of the studies.
	- Demonstrated ability to develop and maintain appropriate therapeutic relationships.
	- Strong problem-resolution skills; able to efficiently and effectively prioritize a broad range of responsibilities to consistently meet deadlines. *"... displays sound judgment in these clinical evaluations." ... "picked up important findings concerning the patient's health and assured timely medical attention."*

SELECTED ACHIEVEMENTS	
	- *Achieved reputation as a resource person, problem solver, troubleshooter, and creative turnaround manager.*
	- *Innovated* setup of blood bank as a clinic stop, thereby enabling revenue to be generated for each patient visit. *"... initiated patient visits to the blood bank as documented outpatient clinic activity; responsible for substantial fiscal benefit."*
	- *Recognized* for *"... surpassing the threshold of enrollment anticipated. On her own initiative, Ms. Marlin has attended weekend health fairs in an attempt to broaden the patient base from which to access candidates."*
	- *Commended* for *"... recognizing opportunities as they occur and taking swift action"... "one of the highest compliance rates among the participating centers."*
	- *Recognized* for ingenious approaches to patient service and problem resolution.
	- *"Consistently exceeds expectations to an exceptional degree."*

Strategy: *An executive CV format was used to project managerial capacity while not overlooking strong clinical qualifications. This job seeker needed to convey her ability to get the job done because she is often competing against individuals with advanced academic degrees.*

Laura R. Marlin, R.N.

**AREAS OF
EXPERTISE**

RESEARCH AND PUBLICATIONS
- Extensive participation in *cutting-edge research.*
- Co-authored three articles for publications that included *Federal Proceedings* and *The Journal of Infectious Diseases.*
- Presented at the American Society of Hematology.

QUALITY IMPROVEMENT
- Set up indicators; monitor all aspects of component therapy.
- Continuously monitor for appropriate blood and component utilization by medical and surgical services.

MEDIA AND REPORTS
- Conceived and developed revolutionary transfusion tag and form to comply with JCAHO, CAP, FDA, and AABB; adopted by other medical facilities.
- Produced highly acclaimed component-therapy slide presentation.
- Designed apheresis worksheet, including standing orders and progress notes.
- Wrote nursing transfusion policy, procedure, and mandatory review.
- Rewrote donor room manual.
- Produce quarterly reports on
  - Appropriateness of Transfusion Therapy (for Transfusion Committee)
  - Monitoring Transfusion Therapy Practices and Procedures (for Transfusion Committee)
  - Monitoring Specific Transfusion Indicators (for Quality Improvement Committee)
  - Nursing-Related Transfusion Issues and Accomplishments (for Nursing Department)

TEACHING / TRAINING / INSERVICE
- Recognized for top-quality presentations *"… contribution to the last Critical Care Nursing Course … required a lot of preparation as evident in the audiovisuals, handouts, and demonstration models."*
- Presented well-received inservice courses on all aspects of Component therapy.

PRECEPTORIAL RESPONSIBILITIES
- Serve as preceptor to Mt. Sinai pathology residents and Lehman nursing students.

BLOOD BANK
- Established donor room as a clinic site, enabling monetary reimbursement for all procedures performed in the donor room.
- Was instrumental in setting up out-patient transfusion program.
- Requested and was granted additional clinical privileges in the areas of
  - phlebotomy—homologous, autologous, and directed donors
  - transfusion therapy
  - therapeutic and donor apheresis

BLOOD DRIVES
- Perform as medical representative on all blood drives with as many as 15 chairs and processing 200 or more donors within 4 hours.

DIALYSIS
- Organized and implemented care plans and machine maintenance regarding all procedures necessary for dialysis. Supervised a 15-bed unit.
- Revamped Peritoneal Dialysis program.
- Wrote the Shiley catheter care procedure for hemodialysis.
- Developed presentations and taught critical-care classes in peritoneal dialysis, care of the patient with renal failure, and AV fistula and AV shunt care.

Laura R. Marlin, R.N.

VASCULAR AND GENERAL SURGERY
- Directed and coordinated three offices.
- Assisted in research surgery with primates.
- Oversaw follow-up and assessment of in-hospital patients.
- Administered patient teaching and discharge planning.
- Performed library research.

COMMITTEES AND CONSULTANCY
- Member of Quality Improvement Committee, 1992-Present
- Member of Transfusion Committee, 1981-Present
- Consultant for Nursing and Medicine
- Liaison between Nursing, Medicine, and Blood Bank

PROFESSIONAL EXPERIENCE

Jun 1994-Present	**RESEARCH NURSE,** Veterans Affairs Medical Center, Bronx, NY
Jun 1993-Jun 1994	**DIALYSIS NURSE,** Veterans Affairs Medical Center, Bronx, NY
Oct 1988-Jun 1993	**TRANSFUSION CLINICIAN,** Veterans Affairs Medical Center, Bronx, NY
Aug 1984-Apr 1988	**STAFF & CHARGE NURSE,** Baumritter Kidney Center, Bronx, NY
Oct 1981-Jul 1984	**TEAM LEADER,** Bronx Hemodialysis Unit, Bronx, NY
Jan 1979-Oct 1981	**STAFF AND CHARGE NURSE, M.S.I.C.U.,** Montifiore Hospital, Bronx, NY

AWARDS

Blood Bank Performance Award 1987
Nursing Performance Award 1987
Special Achievement Awards 1985-1986

RESEARCH & PUBLICATIONS

Jacobson, J.M., Coleman, N., Marlin, L., et al., "HIV Passive Immunotherapy," *Journal of Infectious Disease,* August 1993.

Coleman, N., Marlin, L., et al., "Pharmacokinetics of Serum B12 after Absorption from Nasal Cynanocobalamin Gel in Patients with Gastrointestinal B12 Malabsorption," *Federal Proceedings,* March 1987.

Coleman, N., DeMartino, L., McCleer, E., et al., "Nasal Administration of Cyanocobalamin Gel for Treatment of B12 Deficiency," *Blood,* November 1986. Presented at the American Society for Hematology, December 1986.

EDUCATION

MERCY COLLEGE, Dobbs Ferry, NY	BS Behavioral Sciences, 1985
ST. PETERSBURG JUNIOR COLLEGE, St. Petersburg, FL	AA Nursing, 1979

CONTINUING EDUCATION

Fundamentals of Clinical Research Trials, Association of Clinical Research Professionals—12 CEUs; Nov 1999

AFFILIATION

Member: Association of Clinical Research Professionals

MIR NAHAR, MPH

39 South Potomac Street, Baltimore, MD 21248   (410) 682–1066 — mnahar@aol.com

PROFESSIONAL PROFILE

Dedicated medical professional with a strong commitment to the field of public health research and practice. Results-oriented with a unique combination of clinical, analytical, methodical, and management skills. A demonstrated ability for leadership, rapport, and team building, each impacting on the success of nationally significant health studies. Education, training, and experience in

- design, conduct, and management of epidemiological studies;
- methodology of health services research and evaluation;
- public health policy and management;
- epidemiology of aging, chronic diseases (cardiovascular and cerebrovascular), and mental health;
- use of ultrasonography techniques for cardiovascular research;
- health education and promotion, community building, and public relations.

EDUCATION

MPH (Master of Public Health), **Johns Hopkins University,** Dept. of Epidemiology   1999
MBBS (Doctor of Medicine), **University of Rajasthan,** Sadar Medical College, India   1986

PROFESSIONAL EXPERIENCE

Staff Researcher, *Johns Hopkins University Research Center*, Baltimore, MD   1989–2002

Lead Echosonographer • Director of Recruitment & Retention • Physician's Assistant for the Cardiovascular Health Study (CHS): a landmark epidemiologic study funded by the National Institutes of Health to assess risk factors of cardiovascular and cerebrovascular diseases in an elderly population. Thirteen hundred Baltimore County respondents were recruited for long-term health study and analysis at a community-based clinic.

Selected Achievements

- Conducted and provided leadership to clinical staff in performing various medical procedures, including physicals, BPs, EKGs, Holter monitoring, anthropometry, performance-based measurements, spirometry, audiometry, hematology, and a comprehensive series of medical interviews.
- Dedicated extensive time and energy to maintaining ongoing participation of the study group. Effectively gained the respect and trust of participants. Engaged community leaders, cohort family members, local and national media, and the medical community in promoting participation, acceptance, and long-term success of the study. **Overall result:** +90% retention rate, exceeding previous standards set by any longitudinal medical study.
- Implemented a results-oriented team approach in working with clinic staff; inspired staff to project a warm, friendly, and professional image of CHS to study respondents, ensuring the smooth operation of the center.
- Consistently demonstrated strong problem-solving techniques, interpersonal skills, and ability to work effectively with individuals on all levels. Interfaced with primary care physicians and healthcare institutions to provide them with early notification of alerts and clinically significant findings. **Positive impact:** Coordination of patient care improved; support of CHS was enhanced.

Strategy: *This individual attained a medical degree in India but transitioned to medical research upon immigrating to the U.S. His research project has ended and he's pursuing further work in the public-health arena.*

MIR NAHAR, MPH

(410) 682–1066
PAGE 2

Selected Achievements (continued)

- Performed Echocardiographic and Ultrasonographic screening tests. **Positive outcome:** Research data were analyzed and published by investigators in the *New England Journal of Medicine,* suggesting the clinical relevance of ultrasonographic screening as a predictor of subsequent strokes. Represented CHS in national media coverage of this finding.

- Instrumental in the support of CHS sister-studies (Women's Health and Aging and Artherosclerosis Risk in Communities); the development and support of CHS ancillary studies (MRI, Sleep Apnea, Caregivers) through recruitment of participants; development and implementation of questionnaires; quality control supervision; preliminary EKG interpretation; staff training staff; and exit interviews.

- Conducted ongoing evaluation of adherence to and compliance with CHS protocol through supervision of test procedures, staff training, quality-control measures, daily maintenance of participant data files, and case management. Facilitated the design and drafting of a baseline procedural manual for conducting home visits.

- Successfully led and directed an initiative to re-recruit the entire cohort during the final year of operation of the community clinic, to ensure long-term follow-up through access to medical records.

Junior Resident, *G.B. Pant Hospital, New Delhi*   1987–1988
Department of Cardiothoracic and Vascular Surgery

- Provided PreOp and PostOp assessment and management of cardiac patients in an ICU setting.

- Assisted with cardiothoracic and vascular surgical procedures.

- Participated in the implementation of departmental research studies.

PROFESSIONAL AFFILIATIONS

American Public Health Association
Metropolitan Washington Public Health Association
Mental Health Association of Maryland
American Heart Association Council on Epidemiology & Prevention

COMPUTER PROFICIENCY

MS Office • WordPerfect • Graphics • Stata • EpiInfo 6

Yuen Shun-Yi, MD/Ph.D.

Department of Pathology and Immunology
The University of Chicago
5841 S. Maryland, Room P212, MC4092
Chicago, IL 60637

773-702-1031
shun-yi@midway.uchicago.edu

MEDICAL RESEARCH PHYSICIAN/LECTURER
Award-winning, Widely Published Cancer Researcher
Postdoctoral Experience at MD Anderson Cancer Center, Nation's Top Cancer Hospital

Discovered New Human Gene Family Involved in Skin Differentiation
Developed and Patented Novel Technology to Detect Global Gene Expression
Currently Engaged in Ongoing Laboratory Projects in Carcinogenesis and Cancer Research

EDUCATION

MD/Ph.D., *Pathology,* Gifu University School of Medicine, Japan—1996

Master of Medicine, *Pathology,* Zhejiang University School of Medicine, China—1987

Bachelor of Medicine, *Pathology,* Zhejiang University School of Medicine, China—1982

SELECTED ACCOMPLISHMENTS & RESEARCH

❏ Developed original technology, dubbed Rapid Analysis of Gene Expression, to investigate global gene expression pattern.

❏ Cloned three mouse genes (whole length cDNA) using RACE, and gene promoters using genome walking technology.

❏ Studied human colon cancers, applying molecular tools (SSCP for point mutation detection, direct DNA sequencing, Southern blot, and Western blot).

❏ Used molecular tools to set up cell lines expressing p450 isoenzyme for mutagenesis study (RT-PCR, cDNA cloning, and Northern blot).

❏ Screened down targets of ATF3 and E2A in mRNA level with mouse microarray, and in protein level with protenomics tool.

❏ 30 publications from 1988 to present, covering broad range of subjects in cancer research in such journals as *Genomics, Journal of Biological Chemistry,* and *J. Cancer Research & Clinical Oncology,* among others.

❏ **CLONED GENES AND EST**
  - E2F1-inducible gene 2 GenBank Number AF176514 (EST)
  - E2F1-inducible gene 3 GenBank Number AF176515 (EST)
  - E2F1-inducible gene 4 GenBank Number AF176516 (EST)
  - Mouse E2F1-inducible gene 5 promoter GenBank Number AY007216
  - Mouse EIG3 genomic DNA sequence including promoter GenBank Number AF303430
  - Whole Mouse EIG3 cDNA sequence GenBank Number AF303034
  - Whole Mouse EIG5 gene cDNA sequence
  - Mus musculus E2F1-inducible (Eig4) mRNA, complete sequence GenBank AF176516
  - Human SPRL genes (EST) GenBank Numbers BI670513-BI670520

Continued

Strategy: *A functional-chronological hybrid format was chosen for this individual, whose previous document was a lengthy, traditional CV. Impressive career achievements are spotlighted in the introduction.*

RESUME 72, CONTINUED

Yuen Shun-Yi, MD/Ph.D.

PAGE TWO

CAREER CHRONOLOGY

THE UNIVERSITY OF CHICAGO   2002–Present
Dept. of Pathology and Immunology, Chicago, IL
Assistant Professor

MD ANDERSON CANCER CENTER   2001–2002
Dept. of Carcinogenesis, Houston, TX
Research Associate

MD ANDERSON CANCER CENTER   1998–2001
Dept. of Carcinogenesis, Houston, TX
Postdoctoral Research Fellow

ZHEJIANG UNIVERSITY SCHOOL OF MEDICINE   1996–1998
Dept. of Medical Molecular Biology/Dept. of Pathophysiology, China
Associate Professor

ZHEJIANG UNIVERSITY SCHOOL OF MEDICINE   1987–1991
Dept. of Pathology, China
Lecturer

ZHEJIANG UNIVERSITY SCHOOL OF MEDICINE   1983–1984
Dept. of Pathology, China
Teaching Assistant

AWARDS & GRANTS

Functional Genomics Study on k5-ATF3 Transgenic Mice, NIESH ES07784, USA—2001–2003
Young Investigator Award, 90th AACR Annual Meeting, Philadelphia—1999
Outstanding Young Researcher in Medical Science, Zhejiang Province, China—1997
Establishment and Application of Cell Lines Expressing p450 Isoenzymes,
Cash Grant ($40,000), National Science Foundation of China—1997

PROFESSIONAL AFFILIATIONS

American Association for Cancer Research, 1999–Present
American Association for the Advancement of Science, 1995–Present
International Association of Pathophysiology, 1996–2000
Chinese Association of Pathophysiology, 1996–1998
Japanese Association for Cancer Research, 1991–1996
Chinese Association of Pathology, 1983–1991

CHARLOTTE HASSON, M.D.

714-822-3540
drhasson@email.com
56 Ocean Drive, Placentia, CA 92870

MEDICAL PROFESSIONAL
Drug Development ... Medical Affairs ... Clinical Research

Well-respected and knowledgeable medical doctor with an extensive research background in radiation oncology, conformal radiation, and intensity modulation. Fluent in English and French. Career highlights include ...

Leadership ... Led the 4-year national irradiation oncology project. Partnered with contractors, architects, and the Tunisia Ministry of Health to build the facility and hired and trained technicians, nurses, and residents, establishing the country's first total-body irradiation facility for bone-marrow transplant patients.

Initiative ... Established Tunisia's first and only retinoblastoma facility, eliminating the need for children to travel to Paris or Geneva for treatment.

Noted Researcher and Author ... Selected as a key member of the South African team to conduct the hematology research and write that chapter for *Hodgkin's Disease in Africa* published in 1999 by Lippincott Williams & Wilkins.

Cross-functional Teams ... Collaborated with multidisciplinary committees and established therapeutic strategies for patients with breast, lung, and oral-cavity cancers.

Organizational, Project Management, and Relationship Competencies ... Partnered with the Tunisian Cancer Society to teach doctors and nurses how to screen for breast and cervical cancers and initiated anti-smoking techniques for children. Pioneered fund-raising lectures and seminars to teach patients how to deal with cancer.

PROFESSIONAL EXPERIENCE

MEDICAL ACTION COMMUNICATIONS, Placentia, California
Associate Medical Director — since 2002
Hired to manage medical and scientific communications for oncology projects and serve as the liaison for sponsor representatives, opinion leaders, and intradepartmental representatives. Developed the program and scientific content for a major international symposium. Organized advisory boards, including setting the agenda, selecting appropriate opinion leaders, preparing background scientific and slide material, overseeing slide review session, and producing the advisory board executive report. Developed and maintained a product reference database.

DEPARTMENT OF RADIOTHERAPY, CURIE INSTITUTE, Paris, France
Clinical Instructor of Oncology Radiotherapy — 1998–2000
Participated in clinical research work on breast, ENT, and lung cancers. Consulted and diagnosed cancer patients, and liaised with multidisciplinary committees on treatment and follow-up.

Strategy: *This resume was intended to help this very accomplished foreign doctor get her foot in the door with an American company with a future goal of moving into R&D. The traditional CV format is preceded by a striking introduction.*

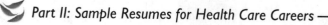

CHARLOTTE HASSON, M.D.   Page 2   714-822-3540

DEPARTMENT OF RADIOTHERAPY, INSTITUT SALAH AZAIZ, Tunis, Tunisia
Assistant Professor in Oncology — 1995–1998
Assistant Attending Physician — 1994
  Promoted within one year to assist the professor in directing a clinic seeing 10,000 patients yearly. Supervised a 30-person cross-functional team of nurses and technicians. Selected to serve a 6-month term as temporary department head with full accountability for the budget and management of six doctors and two residents. Taught oncology to medical students and radiology personnel; conducted clinical research on breast, hemato-oncology, ENT, and uterine cancers.

DEPARTMENT OF RADIOTHERAPY, CURIE INSTITUTE, Paris, France
Clinical Fellow in Radiotherapy — 1991–1993

DEPARTMENT OF ONCOLOGY, Hôpital Henri Mondor, Créteil, France
DEPARTMENT OF RADIOTHERAPY, Institut Salah Azaiz, Tunis, Tunisia
Resident in Oncology Radiotherapy — 1987–1991

EDUCATION & TRAINING

Clinical Trials for Anti-Cancer Drugs — 2002
Institute for International Research, San Francisco, California

Drug Development for Pharmaceutical Physicians and Scientists — 2001
Pharmaceuticals Education & Research Institute (PERI), Washington, D.C.

Diploma of Advanced Study of Oncology — 1999
Paris Sud Medical School, University of Paris XI, France

Board Certification in Oncology-Radiotherapy — 1992
University René Descartes Paris V, France

Doctor in Medicine, graduated *magna cum laude* — 1987
Tunis Medical School, University of Tunis II, Tunisia

Medical School — 1987
Tunis Medical School, University of Tunis II, Tunis, Tunisia

TEACHING & MENTORING

Faculty of Medicine, Tunis, Tunisia
Ecole Supérieure des Sciences et Techniques de la Santé de Tunis, Tunis, Tunisia
Department of Radiotherapy, Institut Salah Azaiz, Tunis, Tunisia

LECTURER HIGHLIGHTS

- Environmental Exposure and Carcinogenesis
- Treatment of Gynecologic Tumors

CHARLOTTE HASSON, M.D.   Page 3   714-822-3540

- The Role of Nursing Staff Before and After Gynecological Curietherapy
- Diagnosis Methods and Classification of Uterine and Cervical Cancers
- Radiotherapy: Its Indication and Use in Treating Hodgkin's Disease
- Total Body Radiation (TBR): Principles, Protocol, and Side Effects
- Use of Radiotherapy in Treating Aggressive Lymphomas
- Use of Radiotherapy in Treating Giant Cell Tumors
- The Quadratic Linear Model: Its Principles and Uses in Radiotherapy
- Predictive Value of Potential Doubling Time in Radiotherapy
- Indications and Uses of Radiotherapy in Treating Hodgkin's Disease
- Chondrosarcoma
- Radiotherapy and the Treatment of Hodgkin's Disease
- Non-Hodgkin's Bone Lymphomas

SELECTED PUBLICATIONS

Hodgkin's Disease in Africa. PETER JACOBS, WERNER BEZWODA, GEOFFREY FALKSON, AND CHARLOTTE HASSON, in *Hodgkin's Disease,* PETER M. MAUCH, JAMES O. ARMITAGE, VOLKER DIEHL, RICHARD T. HOPPE, LAWRENCE M. WEISS. Lippincott Williams & Wilkins, 1999.

Emergency Planning in Cancerology. CHARLOTTE HASSON, HAMOUDA BOUSSEN, in *Cancérologie Pratique,* MONGI MAALEJ. Centre de Publication Universitaire, 1999.

Ductal Carcinoma *In Situ*: Conservative Treatment or Mastectomy?. C. HASSON, F. FEUILHADE, in *Breast Cancer: Prognostic Factors and Therapeutic Strategy,* F. FEUILHADE, E. CALITCHI, J.P. LEBOURGEOIS. Sauramps Medical, 1993.

CONGRESSES

ASCO Annual Meetings
French Society of Oncology Radiotherapy (SFRO) Annual Meetings
2nd Journées Scientifiques, Centre Henri Becquerel — Institut Salah Azaiz

PROFESSIONAL MEMBERSHIPS

American Society of Clinical Oncology
French Society of Radiation Oncology
European Society of Radiation Oncology

CHAPTER 11

Resumes for Health Care Administrators, Managers, Administrative Support Staff, and Consultants

- Medical Transcriptionist
- Medical Translator
- Medical Records Manager
- Medical Auditor/Case Manager
- Health Information Manager
- Volunteer Services Coordinator
- Practice Administrator
- Director of Practice Management
- Hospital Chaplain
- Health and Science Media Consultant
- Health Care Management Consultant
- Health Policy Executive
- Home-Care Executive
- Director of Emergency Services
- Director of Food and Nutritional Services
- Hospital Services Administrator
- Veterinary Hospital Manager
- Health Care Management Executive

Because the focus of these professionals is the business side of health care, a business-oriented, accomplishment-rich resume is the best choice.

CLARA BRIGHTMAN

12332 Valleyheart Avenue
Sherman Oaks, CA 91423

(818) 555-1111
cbright@email.com

MEDICAL/PATHOLOGY TRANSCRIPTIONIST

In-depth Knowledge of Medical Terminology and Laboratory Procedures
Combined with Strong Secretarial and Transcription Skills.

- 14 years' medical-related background, including 5 years of transcription experience.

- Consistently meet deadlines in a high-pressure environment, with attention to detail and accuracy.

- Well organized; able to handle a variety of responsibilities simultaneously.

- Strong computer skills, including Microsoft Word and Excel, and WordPerfect.

- Experienced in all general office equipment and procedures. Possess excellent telephone and customer-service skills.

PROFESSIONAL EXPERIENCE

WESTSIDE MEDICAL CENTER, Beverly Hills, CA • 1998 to Present
Pathology Secretary/Transcriptionist
- Transcribe high volume of pathology, EEG/EMG reports.
- Type laboratory procedures; log and monitor all pathology and cytology records.
- Handle clinical laboratory correspondence.

SANTA MONICA COMMUNITY HOSPITAL, Santa Monica, CA • 1995 to 1997
Pathology Assistant
- Maintained histological and cytological stains; prepared cytology specimens; filed pathology and cytology slides.
- Prepared daily pathology and cytology charges for data processing and billing.

ALLSTATE THERAPEUTIC CORPORATION, Los Angeles, CA • 1989 to 1995
Pharmaceutical company, manufacturers of biological products from human plasma
Senior Lab Technician—Quality Control Sterility Lab (1994–1995)
Lab Technician—Quality Control Microbiological Monitoring Lab (1989–1994)

EDUCATION

CALIFORNIA STATE UNIVERSITY, Los Angeles • 1989
B.S. Degree in Medical Technology

Strategy: *The introduction to this resume presents a strong case for this medical transcriptionist with five years of professional experience in her field. Note how earlier clinical background is downplayed.*

Beverly Garris, LVN

423 Isla Vista   Home: 949/381-1127
Huntington Beach, CA 92605   bgarris@aol.com   Cell: 949/758-2532

MEDICAL TRANSLATION SERVICES

A compassionate individual with 25 years of nursing experience and a high level of integrity who possesses skills necessary to provide quality translation services and confidentiality to Spanish-speaking patients in all types of medical facility settings, including inpatient and outpatient care.

AREAS OF EXPERTISE

- Excellent communication skills and bilingual abilities: English/Spanish.
- Substantial experience with patients on a one-on-one basis.
- Assisted patients and families to minimize their stress levels.
- Related doctors' instructions to patients as a telephone advice nurse.
- Translated for patients at their bedsides in hospitals and medical clinics.
- Assisted patients with their DME needs and/or continuing medical services.
- Administered care and assisted Spanish-speaking patients in home settings.
- Helped patients with consent forms and to understand necessary medical care.
- Coordinated with agencies and companies to provide health services and durable medical equipment to patients.
- Gathered information, conducted medical history intakes, and related after-care instructions to patients and family members.

EDUCATION

- Continuing-education courses at local hospitals and colleges:
  — Seminars include Medical/Legal Issues and Patient Communications.
  — 30+ hours every two years.

- Vocational Nursing (1976–1978)
  — Citrus College, Azusa, CA

LICENSES

- Currently enrolled in Medical Interpreter Certification Program, 2004
  — Southern California School of Interpretation, Santa Fe Springs, CA
- Current California LVN License VN30527
- Intravenous Therapy & Blood Withdrawal Certificate
- Current CPR

Strategy: *This resume was written to support a career transition from nursing to medical translation services. The extensive nursing background is relegated to page 2 so that it does not distract the reader from the current career emphasis.*

Beverly Garris, LVN

Resume — Page 2

PROFESSIONAL EXPERIENCE

Medpartners, Temecula, CA
Nurse, 3/97–1/98
General back-office nursing duties in a family/pediatric practice.
- Assisted physician in all aspects of patient care.
- Educated patients and their families in care procedures in English and Spanish.
- Administered injections, medications, and lab draws; carried out doctors' orders.
- Interfaced with other departments, retrieved data, fielded phone calls, and ordered supplies.

David Rayne, M.D., Upland, CA
Nurse, 9/95–3/97
Back-office and light front-office procedures; marketing and customer relations.
- Set up and coordinated community health fairs.
- Assisted physician in all aspects of patient care.
- Prepared patients for examinations; obtained medical history and vital signs.
- Scheduled patients for further procedures as needed.
- Checked charts for accuracy regarding ICD-9 and CPT coding.

Yorba Park Medical Group, Orange, CA
Nurse (Temporary), 3/95–9/95
Team leader in an urgent-care setting during evening and weekend shifts.
- Assisted physicians in all aspects of patient care and triage protocol.
- Interfaced with families, physicians, pharmacies, laboratories, and referrals.
- Assisted Spanish-speaking patients to complete paperwork for Worker's Comp-related injuries.

Elder Care Services, Orange County, CA
Self-Employed Nurse, 12/82–1/95
- Evaluated and assessed patients' physical, cognitive, social, and emotional functional levels and impairments.
- Identified patients' needs, interests, problems, current capacity, and support needs.
- Interfaced with family members and the healthcare team to determine the best recovery program for each patient.

Temporary Staffing Services, Orange County, CA
Self-Employed Nurse, 12/82–8/95
Staff relief in the private practices of
— Stan Landers, M.D. — Family Practice
— Michael Josephs, M.D. — Family Practice
— Ann Bennett, M.D. — Gynecology
— Newport Walk-In Clinic

Anaheim Hills Medical Group, Anaheim Hills, CA
Nurse, 1/80–12/82
General office nurse in the private practices of Phillip Charles, M.D.; William Landers, M.D.; and the industrial medical clinic.
- Interfaced with insurance companies and employers.

RUBY F. HALLIDAY, A.R.T.

347 Cotter Avenue, San Mateo, California ~ 94040   [650] 594-2214

MEDICAL RECORDS MANAGER

Proven combination of management and organizational abilities in Health Information Services. Strong problem-solving, communication, analytical, negotiation, and development skills. Computer literate: Excel, Word, WordPerfect, Windows 95; Internet proficient.

◆ Energetic   ◆ Enthusiastic   ◆ Dependable   ◆ Optimistic   ◆ Dedicated   ◆ Conscientious

QUALIFICATIONS SUMMARY

Management/Supervision

- Successfully managed technical and clerical operations at two hospitals and maintained primary work load.
- Assisted in planning staff reduction without reduction in service or patient care.
- Addressed problems quickly; followed through until issues were resolved.
- Demonstrated exemplary interviewing techniques; excelled at evaluating prospective employees.
- Maintained excellent rapport with staff, co-workers, patients, and physicians.
- Assisted in budget planning and kept supplies well within budget.

Training/Development

- Assisted in revising employee tasks prior to layoff and trained staff in new functions.
- Collaborated with I.S. analyst to prepare chart-tracking training and implementation.
- Planned, implemented, and trained staff on new Phamis chart tracking system.

Organization/Planning

- Initiated and managed implementation of standardized medical records procedures resulting in multiple system-wide benefits, including
  - ◆ increased productivity and quality, especially in records transfer and billing
  - ◆ smoother work flow, less time to prepare
  - ◆ consistency and uniformity of process
- Successfully revised clerical-related patient care process. Widely accepted by patients and implemented system-wide.
- Participated in smooth transition to "in-house" outpatient coding.
- Facilitated effective transition of birth certificate function to Perinatal Department.

PROFESSIONAL EXPERIENCE

HILLVIEW SONOMA HEALTH SYSTEM, Burlingame, CA   1990–Present
Assistant Director, Medical Records (1996–Present)
Manage technical and clerical operations of Medical Records Department for both Hillview and Sonoma Hospitals.
- Prioritize, schedule, and assign workload.
- Liaison between Medical Records Department and Information Systems.
- Develop departmental policies and procedures, revising and updating as needed.
- Assist in budget preparations.

Strategy: *Using a combination format, this resume clearly highlights relevant areas of expertise in an expanded Qualifications Summary and then details experience in a chronological work history.*

RUBY F. HALLIDAY, A.R.T.   Page Two

Medical Record Specialist (1990–1996)
Provided supervision to the Medical Records Department; liaison with Business Services.
- Ensured accurate submission of all medical data necessary to properly bill patient accounts.
- Performed technical backup to department positions; managed work flow.
- Monitored systems to ensure accuracy and adequacy of department functions.
- Trained, supervised, and developed staff.

CODING UNLIMITED, Palm Springs, CA   1986–1990
Consultant
Participated in specialized health information projects throughout the Bay Area, including:

Interim Manager (1988–1990)
Stanford Health Services, Palo Alto, CA
Managed successful implementation of Clinical Data Abstraction Program.
- Hired and trained staff, coordinated activities, and formulated procedures. Liaison with software provider and Santa Clara County Office of Vital Records.
- Reviewed and made recommendations for improvement of Health Information Management Services process, including chart completion, physician suspension, and customer service.
- Provided comparative analysis of data associated with medical transcription (i.e., turnaround time and employee productivity).

Medical Records Analyst (1986–1988)
Sequoia Hospital, Redwood City, CA
Analyzed medical records for quality of content. Maintained daily hospital inpatient census. Interfaced with physicians and other departments.

RECOVERY INN OF LOS GATOS, Los Gatos, CA   1985
RECOVERY INN OF MENLO PARK, Menlo Park, CA
Consultant
Established policies and procedures for two new outpatient surgical facilities, following Title 22 requirements and JCAHO guidelines. Assisted with selection of filing and record-management systems.

PROFESSIONAL AFFILIATIONS
California Health Information Association
- Delegate, Annual Meeting, 1996, 1999   President, Local Chapter, 1994–1995
- Annual Symposium Committee, 1992   Education Chairman, 1991–1992

EDUCATION
Zenger-Miller Frontline Leadership; 1998
A.S., Accredited Record Technician, Chabot College, Hayward, CA; 1989
Medical Record Technology courses, Bellevue Area College, Bellevue, WA; 1988
Business Administration courses, University of Puget Sound, Tacoma, WA; 1986–1988

Mary Kelner, RN
113 Normal Avenue, Passaic, NJ 07055
(201) 757-5555 Home ▪ mjkelner@optonline.com

PROFILE

Medical Auditor ▪ **Case Manager** ▪ **Registered Nurse** with clinical/auditing experience that includes medical treatment documentation reviews, DRGs, CPT coding, and ICD-9-CM coding. Knowledgeable of the disease process, findings, course of treatment, quality assurance, and risk management. Demonstrated track record in

✓ Medical Records Auditing ✓ Practice Compliance Auditing ✓ Medical Bill Auditing
✓ Practice Site Reviews ✓ Managed Care Case Management ✓ HEDIS Assessment
✓ Medicaid Auditing ✓ Field Utilization Review ✓ Electronic Chart Review

Background in insurance company–based managed-care protocol and case management for catastrophic trauma, soft-tissue damage, and complicated orthopedic injuries. Skilled in M&R guidelines, Interqual criteria, and new-hire orientations. Proven ability to interact effectively with healthcare and office staff professionals.

PROFESSIONAL EXPERIENCE

QUALCARE, INC. (healthcare accreditation firm), Bloomfield, NJ   1998–present
Nurse Reviewer
Field position with multiple long- and short-term assignments. Audited, examined, and verified medical records, and monitored practice sites to ensure documentation accuracy and compliance with standard medical practices and criteria. Conducted 15–18 on-site appointments weekly at medical clinics, hospitals, health plans, and physicians' offices. Reviewed 40–70 charts daily. Completed 3–4 practice site reviews daily.

▪ **BlueKey Health Plan.** Performed HEDIS effectiveness-of-care audits, Medicaid audits, and Healthy Start Initiative and follow-up visit tracking. Practice compliance audits involved medical record reviews for specific disease conditions and/or routine care, including diabetes foot, eye, and blood work status; asthma management; immunizations; and OB-GYN well visits and OB care.

▪ **Americaid.** Conducted medical record documentation reviews and practice site reviews for medical standards and credentialing purposes.

▪ **American Medical Accreditation Program (AMAP)** — Iowa foundation for medical care information system. Performed environment-of-care data collection for the New Jersey Medical Society. Conducted medical record review and site assessment to determine clinical performance, based on set standards and criteria.

SENTINEL INSURANCE COMPANY, Nutley, NJ   1987–1998
Out-of-Network Utilization Review Specialist — Sentinel Healthcare, Cedar Grove, NJ (1997–1998)
▪ Identified and implemented appropriate level of care, based on health insurance policy provisions and medical need. Scope of authority included pre-authorization, review, and discharge planning.

▪ Monitored for quality of care based on ethical and medical standards and criteria, as well as timeliness and cost-effectiveness. Ensured compliance to federal, state, and industry medical management regulations. Utilized computer-based records-management procedures for documenting and retrieving clinical data.

Page 1 of 2

Strategy: *This resume was written to help a Utilization Review Specialist transition to a full-time Medical Auditing position. Highlighted keywords are most appropriate to the new field, while extensive RN experience is also included as a strong qualifier.*

201

Mary Kelner, RN

(201) 757-5555 Home ▪ mjkelner@optonline.com   Page 2

PROFESSIONAL EXPERIENCE

Field Concurrent Review Nurse — Sentinel Healthcare, Newark, NJ (1993–1997)

▪ Performed on-site concurrent chart review for in-patient populations at area teaching medical centers, investigating medical status, appropriateness of stay, and quality of care.

▪ Monitored clinical outcomes and consulted with network physicians and medical director for case-management review, ensuring timely delivery of optimum-level patient care.

▪ Proactively addressed network gaps by researching and recruiting specialty physicians and facilities to provide continuum of care within the network.

▪ Effectively balanced patients' medical needs with health plan benefits to appropriately implement discharge planning to home or alternate-level setting.

Rehabilitation Coordinator — Property & Casualty Insurance Division, Nutley, NJ (1987–1993)

▪ Designed and delivered field case management within the Personal Injury Protection (PIP) unit. Caseload consistently averaged 40–55 catastrophic and/or traumatic personal injury cases. Coordinated client benefits between Sentinel and the State of New Jersey.

▪ Audited medical bills and hospital charts, evaluating coding and reviewing all related medical treatment documentation. Negotiated and resolved discrepancies.

▪ Monitored cases from initial medical assessment through ultimate disposition, coordinating healthcare at all levels in compliance with the New Jersey No-Fault statute.

▪ Received Sentinel's **Quarterly Quality Service Leadership Award** in 1991.

REHABILITATION PARTNERS, INC., Newark, NJ   1983–1987
Insurance Rehabilitation Specialist. Consultant for NJ-based insurance companies. Managed traumatic injury cases from initial assessment through resolution, addressing all medical, legal, and financial issues.

CEDAR GROVE HOSPITAL, Cedar Grove, NJ   1981–1983
Staff Nurse — Medical / Surgical and Orthopedic Units.

EDUCATION

Diploma — Nursing, Montclair State College, Upper Montclair, NJ
Seton Hall University — College of Nursing, Continuing Education Certificates:
The Nurse as Case Manager (43 contact hours), 2001; RN Re-Entry into Practice (140 contact hours), 1998;
Professional development (clinical experience and seminars) in healthcare delivery practices.

CERTIFICATIONS

Registered Nurse — New Jersey (License # 55555)
Certified Case Manager — 1993 (Certification # 55555)

Melanie Kaiser, RHIA

1872 Royal Forest Drive
Memphis, TN 38120

(901) 689-0443 Home
MKaiserRHIA@msn.com

HEALTH INFORMATION MANAGER

HIGHLIGHTS OF QUALIFICATIONS

- Energetic, enthusiastic, and articulate business professional with a B.S. in Health Information Management and 12+ years of experience, including Organizational & Process Improvement; Cost Reduction & Budget Management; Quality Assurance/JCAHO Standards Compliance; and Staff Recruiting, Training, & Development.
- Resourceful problem solver with a talent for identifying needs and presenting effective solutions.
- Decisive manager with a unique blend of business and healthcare experience.
- Entrepreneurial spirit with a proven record of successfully promoting the rapid and profitable growth of a startup company marketing physicians' records services. Ambitious, adventurous, and goal-oriented.
- Ability to convey a warm yet professional image and easily establish a rapport with people from multicultural backgrounds.

PROFESSIONAL EXPERIENCE & ACCOMPLISHMENTS

STATIONED OVERSEAS   October 1994 to December 2002

- Recently returned to the USA after living overseas with my family in Lagos, Nigeria, and Brunei Darussalam. Active in several volunteer organizations and held the office of Secretary for the American Women's Club in Nigeria, while also home-schooling my two children for two of these years.

ST. LUKE'S CHILDREN'S HOSPITAL—Houston, TX   February 1993 to September 1994

Director, Health Information Management Department

- Staffed and managed the organizational and administrative operations of the HIM Department.
- Oversaw coding and record completion of all inpatient, emergency, and outpatient records, ensuring compliance with all regulatory agencies. Established policies and procedures and quality-assurance initiatives.
- Planned and organized monthly medical record committee meetings for physicians and hospital staff.
- Recognized for improvement of department operations. Reduced bill-hold status (for Medicare unbilled accounts) by approximately 75%. Reduced physician-incomplete chart count by approximately 65% to bring HIM Department and hospital into compliance with JCAHO standards. Reduced full-time employee count and department overhead by reviewing and negotiating contracts with outside vendors. Simultaneously improved turnaround time on transcribed reports and release of medical information.

ALPHA MICROGRAPHICS—Houston, TX   June 1991 to February 1993

Health Information Management Consultant/Sales

- Responsible for forming and maintaining business relationships with HIM staff at hospitals and clinics in the Houston metropolitan area. Assessed and recommended record storage solutions—microfilm, digital/optical imaging, or off-site storage.

Strategy: *To avoid raising red flags because of a long period of unemployment, this job seeker includes a brief explanation of the eight-year period when she was out of the country.*

Melanie Kaiser, RHIA   Page 2

HRS (Health Records Services)—New Orleans, LA   January 1989 to May 1991

Owner

- Strategic planning for new business startup. Development and implementation of marketing plan. Wrote proposal letters, followed up to set appointments, and gave presentations to physicians and office managers regarding services offered. Directed company-wide operations (budgeting; AR/AP; recruiting, hiring, and training staff; QA; and customer service).

- Dictated discharge summaries on hospital inpatient medical records on an ongoing basis. Reports were formatted to meet JCAHO standards, Medicare, and Peer Review Organization (PRO) guidelines. No clinical judgments or assumptions were made in reporting, only a summary of the patients' actual hospital course as clearly documented in the medical records.

- Business grew exponentially to serve 15 physicians and employ a staff of 8 records specialists, including RHIAs, RNs, and medical residents.

ALLIED HEALTHCARE CORPORATION   June 1986 to January 1989

Director, Health Information Management Department/ Quality Assurance Coordinator, Overland Park Hospital (Covington, LA)

Director, Health Information Management Department and Interim Director, Admitting Department, St. Francis Medical Center (Kenner, LA)

- Initiated and directed the conversion from manual tracking of incomplete patient records to an automated tracking system.

- Appointed interim director of the Patient Admitting Department in the absence of a director due to layoffs.

- Prepared the Health Information Management Department for successful JCAHO survey, resulting in HIM department and hospital commendations.

- Contributing member of numerous multidisciplinary hospital committees (Quality Assurance, Utilization Review, and Medical Records).

MELTZER FOUNDATION HOSPITAL—New Orleans, LA   March 1983 to May 1985

Tumor Registrar for the Cancer Institute

- Abstracted relevant statistical information from oncology patient records into a computerized database.

- Assisted the hospital pathologist in planning and presenting oncology cases at monthly tumor board conferences.

EAST JEFFERSON GENERAL HOSPITAL—New Orleans, LA   January 1982 to March 1983

Hospital-wide Quality Assurance Coordinator/ICD-9-cm Coder

EDUCATION/SPECIALIZED TRAINING

UNIVERSITY OF TENNESSEE CENTER FOR HEALTH SCIENCES—Memphis, TN
Graduated Cum Laude with B.S. in Health Information Management
Passed National Registration Exam for certification as RHIA
Competent computer user familiar with MS Windows, Word, and Excel

PROFESSIONAL AFFILIATIONS

American Health Information Management Association

DELORES A. STOCKDALE

4245 Jessica Drive • Meriden, Kansas 66512
H: 785-246-3346 • deecares@hotmail.com

OVERVIEW

Cross-culturally sensitive **VOLUNTEER SERVICES COORDINATOR** experienced in recruiting, screening, placing, and retaining volunteer candidates in positions to support or care for the needs of patients with terminal illnesses and their families. Outstanding ability to work with community and professional groups. Develop excellent rapport with individuals of all socio-economic levels. Loyal, honest, and dedicated professional possessing an exemplary reputation for providing quality volunteers to assist patients/families in experiencing life to the fullest and facing death in comfort and dignity. Promote the program creed to all volunteers:

Holds the dignity of the patient sacred

Offers hope and affirms life

Surrounds the patient with a familiar environment

Participates with the family in providing care

Initiates and maintains pain and system control

Cares for the emotional needs of the family unit

Extends bereavement care for a year after death

Recognized as a resource and problem solver. Genuine concern and sensitivity for others. Extraordinary communication and listening skills.

PROFESSIONAL EXPERIENCE

Community Care Hospice, Topeka, KS   May 1999 to present

VOLUNTEER COORDINATOR (August 2000 to present)
HOME HEALTH AIDE (May 1999 to August 2000)

Instrumental in the conception, development, and implementation of the Volunteer Program for Community Care Hospice. Oversee all aspects of recruitment, placement, orientation, training, coordination, and administration of 75–100 hospice volunteers serving a client population of 95 within ten counties in the Topeka area. Recipient of Community Care Hospice Award for 2001.

Program Management: Increased volunteers from initial 3 to over 100 in the past 24 months.
- Manage volunteer program administration and development in all service areas, including but not limited to general office work, public relations, committee work, planning/coordinating special functions, special projects, volunteer training, motivational meetings, and bereavement support.
- Screen volunteer applications and reference letters, matching volunteers' interest and skills with program needs to ensure that patient/family needs are met appropriately.
- Conduct pre-training, training, and post-training workshops, providing in-depth knowledge and skill base needed to service patient needs.
- Plan and conduct volunteer support meeting once a month.
- Provide motivational support to volunteers by sending words of encouragement and appreciation notes; recognize volunteers annually at Volunteer Appreciation Banquet.
- Maintain effective working relationships between Topeka's and Perry's personnel/volunteers.

Let us outdo each other in being helpful and kind to each other and in doing good. Hebrews 10:24

Strategy: *This resume clearly shows both tangible and intangible qualifications for the desired role as a hospice volunteer coordinator. In the Professional Experience section, subheadings call attention to key skills and experience.*

DELORES A. STOCKDALE   Page 2

Program Design: Researched, designed, and implemented volunteer training and orientation program.
- Wrote and revamped program policies, procedures, and guidelines.
- Selected, adapted, and applied a combination of instructional methods and techniques.
- Lead and supervise volunteer orientations/training seminars held four to five times a year.
- Participate in orientation program for new hospice staff personnel.

Public Relations: Boosted visibility and established volunteer programs for community groups.
- Work in collaboration with Topeka Girl Scouts Troop 303 to provide motivational visits to individuals in assisted living centers and area nursing homes.
- Assist Hospice educator with community awareness program by speaking at senior centers.
- Serve as a liaison between volunteers and staff.
- Participate in professional and community health and welfare activities.

Administration
- Prepare and administer a $15,000 annual operating budget for the volunteer program.
- Compile statistical data for cost saving and service reports as required weekly by the Administrator.
- Evaluate performance of program assistant and volunteers.
- Maintain compliance with Kansas State regulation 420-5-17.10 for volunteer services and ensure volunteers comply with agency policies and procedures.
- Schedule required testing to include TB test or chest X ray and Hepatitis B vaccinations.
- Assess and monitor a record-keeping system.
- Handle highly confidential patient and volunteer records.

WORK HISTORY

HOME HEALTH AIDE, Shawnee County Health Department, Topeka, KS, 1994 to 1998
MANAGER, Blends and Trends, Topeka, KS, 1976 to 1988

PROFESSIONAL DEVELOPMENT & TRAINING

Completed, Basic Life Support for Healthcare Provider Program, expires 02/2005
Completed, Model Curriculum Course of Training for Home Health Aides, 1999

Completed the following Community Care Hospice Development Programs:
    Use of Opiates in Pain Management, 2002
    Nursing Assessment and OSHA Update, 2002
    Blood Borne Pathogen Training, 2002
    Treatment and Care of the Patient with Endstage Colon Cancer, 2002
    Sign, Symptoms, and Care of the Patient with Endstage COPD, 2001
    Sign, Symptoms, and Treatment of Patients with Alzheimer's Disease, 2001
    Volunteer Training Seminar, 2001
    Managing Oxygen in the Home Environment, 2001
    Personal Care Skills, 1999
    Confidentiality: Is It Still Around?, 1999
    Volunteer Training Program, 1998
Attended National Hospice Conference, 2001 and 2002
Attended Alabama Hospice Conference, Birmingham, AL, 2000
Group Member, National Hospice Organization
Member, National Council of Hospice and Palliative Professionals

Let us outdo each other in being helpful and kind to each other and in doing good. Hebrews 10:24

LEDA WEITLAND

631 Randall Drive • Brentwood, NY 11717 • (631) 777-6004 • ledaweitland@health.com

Healthcare Management

Highly capable healthcare professional offering five years of multiple-practice management experience, clinical proficiencies, and a Bachelor's degree in Health Science with a concentration in Healthcare Management.

Business Unit Management…Continuous Quality Improvement…Patient Care & Relations…
HR/Staff Training & Supervision…Data and Records Management…Budget Control…Cost Analysis…
Billing…Accounts Payable/Receivable…Payroll…Purchasing…Inventory Control…Sales…Marketing

Windows XP; Microsoft Word, Excel, PowerPoint; QuickBooks; Data Management Systems

Professional Experience

Dr. William R. Berger & Associates, Brentwood Station, New York   2/98–present
Long Island's leading experts in Laser Vision Correction for nearsightedness, farsightedness, and astigmatism.

Practice Administrator   2/00–present
Supervisor Technician   8/98–2/00
Technician   2/98–8/98

- Fully direct the management of three high-volume optometric practices, promoting superior vision care for 150–200 weekly adult/pediatric patients through supervision of 35–40 administrative and technical staff.
- Coordinate multiple office functions that focus on computerized scheduling, electronic billing, reimbursements, collections, accounts payable/receivable, patient records, data management, and payment plans. Demonstrated knowledge of insurance carriers, medical terminology, and CPT/ICD-9 codes.
- As Human Resources Administrator, oversee staff recruitment, training, supervision, and appraisals; develop job descriptions; advertise open position announcements; and address employee issues with confidentiality.
- Serve as primary point of contact with and liaison between patients, administrative staffs, physicians, therapists, and technicians to facilitate proper lines of communication and expedite problem resolution.
- Implement Continuous Quality Improvement (CQI) guidelines to measure the performance of business operations; prepare monthly financial reports; and manage internal credentialing verification procedures.
- Educate patients, providing explanations of test results and therapeutic treatment plans; participate in weekly meetings to evaluate patient cases and determine the need for referrals.
- Clinically assist during eye-health examinations and treatments, expertly operating (and training technicians on) an HRT Laser Scanner, Canon Digital Retinal Camera, and Visual Field Frequency Doubler.
- Collaborate with Social Services and charitable organizations to provide free eye-care examinations.

Office Support Associate, e-Wireless, Brentwood, New York   9/97–11/99
- Provided diversified office support in areas of accounts receivable, inventory control, and marketing for this authorized dealer/wholesale distributor of Motorola, Nokia, and Diva wireless products.

Special Events Coordinator, Fundraisers of America, The Islips, New York   6/94–11/97
- Coordinated on-site special events in the areas of customer needs assessment, event planning, inventory control, vendor relations, purchasing, accounts payable, and weekly payroll for 10–15 employees.

Education

Bachelor of Science degree in Health Science, *Concentration in Healthcare Management,* **2002**
State University *of* New York *at* Farmingdale, Farmingdale, New York

Strategy: With strong medical office management experience and a recent degree in health care management, this candidate is ready to advance her career to the next management level.

Curriculum Vitæ

Janet Grady, RN, MSN

1215 Norwood Lane   ✦   Montgomery, Alabama 36100   ✦   [334] 555-5555

VALUE TO GLIDE MEMORIAL: As your **Director of Practice Management,** direct nursing care that gives peace of mind to patients, families, and your board of directors.

CAPABILITIES YOU CAN USE AT ONCE:

✦ **Vision** to see how people can focus themselves toward excellence.

✦ **Leadership** to build, guide, and maintain very high quality nursing services.

✦ **Energy** to overcome challenges quickly and correctly.

✦ **Poise** in helping everyone—from senior decision makers to nurses' aides—achieve goals they are proud of.

WORK HISTORY WITH EXAMPLES OF SUCCESS:

More than 20 years of increasing responsibility with the Department of Veterans' Affairs, including these most recent assignments:

✦ *Promoted to* Chief, Nursing Service, VA Medical Center, Norman, Oklahoma, 99–Present

  ✦ Led sluggish medical center to its **highest accreditation score ever.**
  ✦ **Cut critical shortage of 52 RNs** to 15 in two years.
  ✦ **Arranged $100,000 in** VA-sponsored **tuition reimbursement awards** for students seeking nursing degrees. Recruited 72 students. During the first year, 12 LPNs completed an accredited RN program.

✦ Associate Chief, Nursing Service, VA Medical Center, Groton, Connecticut, 98–99

  ✦ Guided groups to **solve problems in every area.** Sample: Cut admission time in half.
  ✦ **Increased patient satisfaction** in psychiatry wards from 55% to 98%.
  ✦ Placed ward secretaries on each nursing team. **Saved cost of 6 positions.** Order-entry **error rate dropped from 31% to 8%.**

✦ Assistant Chief, Nursing Service, VA Administration Central Office, Austin, Texas, 98

  ✦ Produced first major study of patient falls in VA medical centers during this preceptorship. **My recommendations and findings adopted for further study at all 172 centers.**

At the VA Medical Center, Logansport, Ohio:

✦ *Promoted to* Associate Chief for Clinical Practice, Surgery Ambulatory Care, and Patient Attendant Service, 95–98

  ✦ Built system to get patients to the right appointment on time: **nearly doubled rate at which patients could be seen.**
  ✦ Introduced nurse practitioners to **free physicians for other tasks** and allow patients to be seen by same caregiver consistently.

✦ *Promoted to* Acting Assistant Chief, Nursing Service, 92–95

Strategy: *The strategy for this resume was to overcome the VA hospital stereotype perceived by some private-sector health care professionals. An additional challenge was to make long service time attractive while avoiding potential age discrimination.*

| Janet Grady, RN, MSN | **Director of Practice Management** | [334] 555-5555 |

EDUCATION:

- M.S.N., Carlisle College of Nursing, Carlisle, Pennsylvania, 88
- B.S.N., Michaels College of Nursing at Central University, Laneton, Vermont, 84

ADJUNCT FACULTY APPOINTMENTS:

- School of Nursing, Central State University, Central, Alabama
- Selton University School of Nursing and Allied Health, Selton, Alabama

PUBLICATIONS IN THE FIELD OF NURSING:

- "An Educational Partnership/Tuition Reimbursement Project," Journal of Nursing Education, October 99
- "Patient Fall Prevention Study at One VA Medical Center," VA Preceptorship Training Archives, November 97
- With Camilla Bowles, "The COPD Patient's General Knowledge of His Health Problems and His Re-admission to a Pulmonary Disease Service," Unpublished thesis, 88

COMPUTER LITERACY: Fully proficient in proprietary scheduling, budgeting, resource control, and education software.

AWARDS AND HONORS:

- Leadership VA: One of 30 selected from 5,000 eligibles to attend four workshops on national-level issues, 01
- Director's Commendation: The highest award the VA gives, 00
- Distinguished Black Woman in Health Care, Marlin State University School of Social Work, Marlin, Louisiana, 99
- Nurse of the Year: Chosen by 150 colleagues, Marlin Chapter, National Black Nurses' Association, 92
- "Who's Who in America," 90–91
- Achievement Award, Chamber of Commerce, Marlin, Louisiana, 91

MEMBERSHIPS:

- First President and co-founder of The Association of Chiefs of Nursing Services, an organization consisting of all 172 chief nurses from VA medical centers nationwide.
- Chair, Professional Organization for Health Care Issues, Shelton County Women's Commission, 99–02.
- President, Marlin Chapter of the National Black Nurses Association, 95–99.
- Life member, American Lung Association.
- Member, Sigma Theta Tau nursing society. Increased membership from 75 to 300 in one year.

SERVICE TO MY COMMUNITY:

- Created community-based hypertension screening for 200–275 elderly citizens.
- Organized two annual on-the-spot screenings for breast cancer, AIDS, and blood pressure. Screened 5,000 women the first year; nearly 10,000 the second year.

Rev. Benjamin Dupree

5402 Kings Highway
Jackson, MS 39213
(601) 555-1212

SUMMARY

Hospital Chaplain with extensive professional experience, training, and community involvement.

- Highly trained in clinical pastoral education and counseling; experienced at helping people in crisis situations. Offer pastoral care to patients who are expiring and assist family members throughout the bereavement process.

- Maintain sound judgment and presence of mind in highly stressful, often traumatic conditions. Perceptive and insightful; an attentive listener.

- Experience facilitating workshops and discussions concerning grief, near-death experience, spirituality, and other issues.

Ready to apply acquired ministry skills as a chaplain in a multi-service healthcare system.

CLINICAL TRAINING

Clinical Member · Association for Clinical Pastoral Education (2000 to Present)

Clinical Pastoral Education · University Medical Center, Jackson, MS (2000 to 2001, 4 units)
- Trained in Emergency Department of Level One trauma center.
- Specialty area: Pediatrics and General Surgery.
- Advanced Status training includes Ministry Formation, Crisis Management, Crisis Counseling/Intervention, and Pastoral Care in a Hospital Setting.

Clinical Pastoral Education · Baptist Medical Center, New Orleans, LA
- Advanced Unit (Summer 1995) and 2 Basic Units (1999 and Spring 2000).
- Pastoral Care unit assignments included Adult Intensive Care, Oncology, Surgery, Pediatrics, Pediatric Intensive Care, Neonatal Intensive Care, Coronary Care, Emergency Room, Restorative Care, and Orthopedic Surgery.
- Advanced Specialty Area: HIV ministry. Counseled and visited HIV patients. Participated in a weekly HIV support group. Attended rounds and conferred with healthcare team.

EDUCATION

Master of Divinity, Biblical Studies · New Orleans Baptist Theological Seminary, LA (1988)
Bachelor of Arts, Biblical Studies · Copiah College, Clinton, MS (1985)
Associate of Science · Lincoln Community College, Clinton, MS (1984)
Licensed and Ordained · First Baptist Church, Copiah, MS (1983)

CLINICAL EXPERIENCE

Chaplain Resident · University Medical Center, Jackson, MS (2000 to Present)
Provide on-call, hospital-wide coverage. Serve as pastor for patients, their families, and staff. Consult with doctors, nurses, and other medical professionals as part of the healthcare team. Compile verbatim records of counseling sessions; meet with other chaplain residents and supervisor to evaluate and share insights. Coordinate ministry needs with other chaplains, social workers, and ministers in the community.

Strategy: *The first page of this resume highlights relevant health care–related pastoral information, while additional details of a lengthy ministerial career appear on page 2.*

Rev. Benjamin Dupree   Page 2

Family Counselor-in-Training · Baptist Chemical Dependency Center, Jackson, MS (1998 to 1999)
Provided support to chemically dependent patients and their families. Conducted intake interviews and psychosocial assessments of patients. Co-facilitated support groups for family members of patients.

ADDITIONAL PASTORAL EXPERIENCE

Interim Pastor · Third Baptist Church, Jackson, MS (1999 to 2000)
Preached and led worship services for the congregation. Provided pastoral leadership and guidance in administration of the church. Made pastoral visits to sick and inactive members.

· Initiated Sunday night worship service/Bible study and Wednesday night prayer meeting services. Increased congregational attendance and awareness of ministry needs in the community.

Teacher · Forrester Christian School, Jackson, MS (1992 to 1993; 1997 to 1999)
Taught courses in the Life of Christ and Physical Science. Created an interactive, participatory atmosphere in classes. Organized and conducted chapel services and other school functions. Assistant Coach of football team.

· Arranged and facilitated an international dialogue focused on religion in Great Britain between students from England and Forrester Christian School.

Program Director · Boys & Girls Clubs, Flagstaff, AZ (1996 to 1998)
Directed week-long camp programs for 90 children, ages 6 to 12. Led morning devotionals for entire camp. Recruited and trained 20 college students to serve as Camp Counselors, emphasizing children's safety. Planned a wide range of activities, including riflery, swimming, canoeing, crafts, and other sports. Promoted Boys & Girls Clubs at United Way functions. Member, Arizona Camping Association.

· Successfully organized programs for 900 children during the summer.

Interim Pastor · Pine Baptist Church, Jackson, MS (1993)

Interim Pastor · Morton Baptist Church, Jackson, MS (1991 to 1992)
Preached in Sunday services. Made pastoral visits. Employed by the Mississippi Baptist Convention and led summer youth workshops on drug-abuse prevention and church-music study for groups of 100 children at Baptist Assembly, Jackson, MS.

Group Director · Camp Black Rock, Old Mountain, NC (Summer 1991)
Implemented camp programs for 90 children, ages 6 to 8. Directed staff of 8 college-age counselors. Led interdenominational ministry services.

Pastor · Second Baptist Church, Jackson, MS (1989 to 1990)

Pastor · First Baptist Church, Jackson, MS (1979 to 1982)
Preached and led Sunday services. Provided pastoral care to members of the community. Developed active youth ministry and achieved 30% growth in Sunday-school attendance.

Associate Pastor/Youth · First Baptist Church, Tallahassee, FL (1978 to 1979)
Directed college and career ministry. Organized and directed youth ministry. Co-directed Vacation Bible School. Recruited and trained 30 youth workers. Preached in youth-led worship services monthly.

· Served as summer Camp Director for 100 young people. Grew youth ministry from 2 departments to 4. Increased Sunday school attendance by 50%.

REFERENCES AVAILABLE

RESUME 83: TEENA ROSE, CPRW, CEIP, CCM; HUBER HEIGHTS, OH

Rianne Rivera, MS, RD

2575 Kings Highway, Loveland, OH 45140
Phone: (513) 245-0921 Cell: (513) 404-7310

HEALTH AND SCIENCE MEDIA CONSULTANT and CORPORATE SPOKESPERSON
Corporate Communications / Media Outlets / Public Relations / Communications Strategies

Media specialist serving as a spokesperson, columnist, author, and communications expert regarding science and medical issues. Key media involvement, including the *Washington Post*, the *Journal of the American Dietetic Association*, CNBC, NPR, *Larry King Live*, the *Cincinnati Enquirer*, and *Hardball with Chris Matthews*. Author of topical articles and panelist for Q&A sessions regarding health and medical topics: gather facts, develop research statistics, and create customer-ready content for company newsletters. Devise and implement programs to educate the public on health concerns.

Education & Certifications

Master of Arts Degree, Science and Environmental Reporting Program, 2001
The Ohio State University, Graduate School of Journalism, Columbus, OH
Associate Producer Internship: NPR, summer 2001

Bachelor of Arts Degree, Nutrition, 1987
University of Cincinnati, Cincinnati, OH
President, Phi Upsilon Omicron Honor Society, 1986–87
Minor: Communications, graduated with honors

Registered Dietitian, American Dietetic Association, 1991

Professional Experience

MEDIA CONSULTANT / COLUMNIST / WRITER, 1992–present
Rivera Health Communications, Loveland, OH
Contribute articles to key health forums, with a history of participating in the American Dietetic Association as an expert panelist and serving as an interviewee to many area and national newspapers and television stations. Currently authoring a book, titled "Beauty from the Inside Out," expected to be completed in the winter of 2004.

SPOKESPERSON, 1992–1994
Ohio State Dietetic Association, Columbus, OH
Prepared and submitted press kits, press releases, and pitch letters for the media. Interviews: The *Washington Post, Columbus Dispatch, Cincinnati Enquirer, Cleveland Plain Dealer*, and *Akron Beacon Journal* newspapers, NPR and numerous Ohio radio stations, and the PBS television network.

PUBLIC RELATIONS / HEALTH COMMUNICATIONS AGENT, 1990–1992
Ohio University, Athens, OH
Advisory member to the update of Ohio University's manual, "Control Your Weight—Control Your Life." Developed and implemented biannual blood-pressure screening in cooperation with the American Heart Association, and headed two-hour "Eating Out Sensibly" tours (highlighted in national newspapers). Instructed 10-hour healthy eating classes, and spoke to corporations on health and medical-related topics. Created, wrote, and edited the "Take It Off" newsletter.

Media Involvement / Freelance Writing

Detailed portfolio is enclosed, featuring sample writings and project documentation.

- Contributed articles to key online health icons: WebMD.com, Dietetics.com, and CookingLightMagazine.com.

Strategy: *This resume was written for a registered dietitian who has transitioned to a career as a public-relations and media consultant. The summary is peppered with notable TV, radio, and print references.*

Rianne Rivera, MS, RD

(Media Involvement / Freelance Writing, cont'd)

- Nutrition Counselor and Corporate Wellness Speaker, 1992–present
- Editor / Researcher, "Smart Foods," Tufts University Medical Press, 1996
- Diet Consultant, *Larry King Live*, 1995
- Recipe Analyst, "Lighten Up," the food section of the *Columbus Dispatch*, 1995
- Guest Expert, CNBC live broadcast, "Taking It Off," 1994
- Health columnist, *Cincinnati Enquirer*, 1993–1994
- Guest Speaker (weekly), WVXU radio station, 1992–1994

Business Affiliations & Awards

Member, American Association for the Advancement of Science
Member, National Association of Science Writers
Member, American Dietetic Association
Member, Ohio State Dietetic Association
Dietitian of the Year, American Dietetic Association, 1998

Program Implementation

Created and coordinated program that raised more than $50,000 worth of food products for the hungry. Earned coverage in local and national media; expanded program statewide in second year. Recruited and supervised more than 200 volunteers.

Other Experience

Corporate Communications Associate, 2002–present
Queen City Associates, Cincinnati, OH
Write press releases, prepare press kits, arrange interviews, and conduct other media-related activities—researching stories, verifying statistics, and creating clip books for high-end presentations.

Software & Industry Specifics

MS Office, Lexis/Nexis, Adobe Acrobat (PDF), Lotus Notes

Well-versed on American Medical Association (AMA), the *New York Times* and Associated Press style guidelines, and Food and Drug Administration regulations.

Willing to Travel

Florence Knight

4 Red Cross Avenue
Greenwich, CT 06830

(203) 861-1111

knight@earthlink.net

Health-Care Consultant: Clever, results-driven strategist who uses resource optimization, cost control, and quality management techniques in health-care operations problem-solving, policy development, market planning, and program design.

Experience

Health-Care Management Consultant, 1993 to Present

Planned and implemented new functions reflecting the contemporary resource-conscious, highly competitive environment.

- Served as transitional operations director at an entrepreneurial, privately held, $2M consulting practice. Responsible for professional and support staff; recruiting functions; liaison with legal, benefits, and accounting advisors; systems protocols; client product quality assurance; and daily management of headquarters office. Established marketing campaign and collaterals. Emphasis on physician practice management, strategy and business development, and financial outsourcing services.

- Re-engineered a well-respected but financially unstable rehabilitation center to provide a surplus of income over expenses by refocusing services, drastically reducing overhead expenses, dramatically increasing service volume, and securing successful networking relationships.

- Conducted a detailed operations review at a specialty hospital, netting significant payroll savings by eliminating mandatory overtime assignments while simultaneously increasing staffing coverage within the existing budget; also forecasted major A/R-related expense reductions and revenue enhancements through conversion to a POS cashier function instead of routine patient invoicing.

- Created professional seminar curricula and conference presentations on managed-care issues that included organizing physician networks, successful financial management under capitation, and new approaches to quality assurance/outcome measurement studies.

- Completed a comprehensive business plan for a profit-making nurses' registry and nursing private practice, including financial feasibility, market opportunities, operations requirements, and staffing needs.

- Assumed financial management of medical college division, realizing almost $1M (about 40%) in additional revenues within first year through improved third-party reimbursement, innovative billing, and revised payment policies; also introduced budgeting and inventory control methods.

- Directed the design, development, implementation, conversion, and user training of a custom payroll/personnel/budgeting system that monitors expenses against income and service effort at a large hospital chain.

- Developed and implemented complete practice policies and procedures to create a new department at an urban teaching hospital; standards encompassed routine office systems, banking, legal and accounting requirements, specifications for patient billing, evaluation of proposed managed-care affiliations, and review of outside billing vendor's performance.

Strategy: *This resume highlights the many projects and assignments completed by a health care management consultant. Measurable results make a good case for her ability to get results for her clients.*

Florence Knight

- Staffed Board of Directors, Trustees, and other executive-level committees at an inner-city medical complex and was principal contact with community interests and regulatory groups.

- Prepared numerous Certificate of Need applications for both hospital-based and independent organizations; developed narrative portion, staffing, program, facility, and financial sections.

- Designed an interactive, transaction-oriented database to capture consumer encounters for front-end billing and research queries.

- Prepared an extensive annotated bibliography summarizing over 200 articles and citations on health-care quality assurance design, implementation, and utilization methods.

Senior Associate, American Practice Management; New York, NY, 1990–1993

Assigned to the financial and ambulatory care practice groups whose clients included private practitioners, institutional providers, and hospital suppliers.

- Increased service volume and revenues for outpatient treatment areas by restructuring appointment calendars, revising staffing schedules, reallocating room assignments, and changing patient and information flow patterns.

- Identified target markets and performed financial feasibility studies.

Utilization Review Director and Operations Analyst, Columbia-Presbyterian Medical Center; New York, NY, 1987–1990

- Instituted first utilization review/quality assurance department and ensured continuity through ongoing internal audits.

- Created an automated length-of-stay database profiling practitioners by diagnostic, procedural, and demographic variables.

Regional Administrator, Department of Health, State of New York; New York, NY, 1983–1987

- Reviewed written documentation submitted by Medicaid and Medicare providers for adherence to care standards.

- Reported on site visits, itemizing cost components that subsequently evolved into the DRG concept.

Education

Columbia University Graduate School of Business Administration, 1983–1985
Columbia University School of Public Health, M.P.H., 1983, NIMH Fellow
Columbia University, B.S., R.N., 1980, Sigma Theta Tau Honor Society

Research Assistant, Columbia University Center for Community Health Systems, 1983

- Contributor to a project that evaluated the scope of health services available to an inner-city population and specified requirements for a pilot Health Maintenance Organization.

RESUME 85: CORY EDWARDS, CRW, CECC, CCMC, MBTI; STERLING, VA

BARBARA A. DENTONE

10 Jones Street, Suite 123, Cambridge MA 02142
Phone: 617-494-1996 • Cell phone: 617-718-1765

PROFESSIONAL PROFILE

Senior health policy executive with extensive experience in coalition building, policy development, strategic planning, program implementation and evaluation, and clinical practice in public, private, and not-for-profit sectors and at international, federal, state, and local levels. Directed successful international relief and refugee operation, saving thousands of lives.

CAREER HIGHLIGHTS

➢ Directed international relief operation team in West Africa during time of famine and extreme malnutrition. Provided diagnostic services in clinics, represented team, and negotiated contracts at all levels of civilian and military government.

➢ Extensive knowledge of healthcare. Earned doctorate in health and social welfare for studies assessing cost factors in managed-care environments.

➢ Led policy team at National Institute of Alcohol Abuse and Alcoholism, selected for detail to Congress. Implemented very successful, historic food-safety hearings and influenced development of legislation.

PROFESSIONAL EXPERIENCE

Consultant, Cambridge, MA   1997–Present

Director of Public Policy, National Programs, and Public Relations for international organization dedicated to education, research, and advocacy of the prudent use of antibiotics. Collaborate with government organizations, legislative and regulatory branches. Promote and present education for health professionals. Exhibit at trade shows. Serve as the organization's point person on bioterrorism. Provide consulting services to strengthen business performance and adapt business procedures to comply with state and federal regulations.

➢ Collaborate in strategic planning for organization.

➢ Direct international surveillance study, The Global Advisory on Antibiotic Resistance Data, in cooperation with major pharmaceutical companies and CDC and WHO as advisors.

➢ Detect resistant pathogens and antibiotics and compare across companies.

➢ Spearhead profitable fundraising and development activities.

➢ Assist clients in establishing electronic businesses in diverse fields, often allied to healthcare services.

➢ Consulted with information technology firm to target healthcare, insurance, and state legislatures to implement workflow applications and e-commerce across business enterprises.

WORKGROUP FOR ELECTRONIC DATA INTERCHANGE (WEDI)

Executive Director, Boston, MA   1995–1996

Directed establishment and operations of non-profit association to conduct research and public education regarding key provisions of the Health Insurance Portability and Accountability Act (HIPAA). Developed strategic and operating plans, including long- and short-term goals, membership criteria, budget planning and execution, recruitment, and development of human and information resources to support intensive operation. Managed 4 technical advisory groups, comprising approximately 100 individuals representing different participants in healthcare.

➢ Developed 25-member board of directors broadly reflecting divergent concerns about electronic standards and privacy provisions governing transmission of financial data in healthcare. Conducted effective liaison with House and Senate Committees, providing frequent technical briefings on issues and ensuring presentation of coalition witnesses at key hearings and meetings.

➢ Sustained coalition through enactment of law, successfully doubling membership during leadership.

Strategy: Notable career achievements—some from many years ago—are highlighted on page 1 so they are not overlooked. This detailed three-page resume is appropriate for a senior health care policy executive with diverse global experience.

BARBARA A. DENTONE

THE TRAVELERS INSURANCE COMPANY

Division Vice President and Counsel to the President, Hartford, CT   1992–1995

Served as Travelers' key strategist on administrative simplification and formulation and execution of Workgroup for Electronic Data Interchange (WEDI) mission, and on public policy affecting healthcare information technology and healthcare reform for the five largest insurers. Proposed and drafted legislation at federal and state levels to maintain private-sector flexibility and role.

➤ Developed and published coalition blueprint for reform in healthcare information exchanges.

➤ Successfully presented completed concept report to the Secretary of Health and Human Services within six months of project kickoff.

➤ Developed and published 400-page report to the Secretary of Health and Human Services providing foundation for policies governing electronic exchange of information in healthcare. Incorporated effective privacy protections while facilitating effective implementation of emerging technologies.

➤ Effective coalition leadership recognized as influential in transforming complex national healthcare initiative into practical incremental reform strategy.

Director of Health Issues, CORPORATE COMMUNICATIONS, Hartford, CT   1989–1992

Supervised development of healthcare policy studies to assess complex range of community, state, and national legislative and regulatory provisions affecting the company and the health-insurance industry. Worked closely and collaboratively with other members of the Health Insurance Association of America (HIAA) on managed care policies and information technology at the state and federal levels.

➤ Trained staff of 11 government affairs specialists in health issues. Increased ability of staff to negotiate and secure legislation more favorable to private-sector interests.

➤ Testified as expert witness in major state legislative hearings, successfully limiting state activities to facilitate future development of national standards for information exchange and privacy protection.

➤ Led study by Hartford's Chamber of Commerce assessing the impact of building a high-technology children's hospital in Hartford. Redirected resources to programs that successfully reduced high infant-mortality rates.

NATIONAL INSTITUTE ON ALCOHOL ABUSE AND ALCOHOLISM

Deputy Director, OFFICE OF POLICY ANALYSIS, Rockville, MD   1983–1989

Assisted management and coordinated legislative activities of the Institute. Analyzed and interpreted the implications of alcoholism and alcohol abuse–related legislation, regulations, and related policy proposals. Collaborated with the Director and key Institute staff in planning and coordinating legislative programs.

➤ Reviewed draft legislation, regulations, and program decisions of other agencies that affected the Institute's programs and mission.

➤ Provided advice on legislative and policy changes to state and local officials, agency heads, and officers of professional organizations and advocacy groups.

Legislative Analyst, Rockville, MD   1978–1983

Analyzed legislation and regulations affecting Institute interests and programs. Collaborated in planning and coordinating Institute's legislative programs, drafted legislative proposals, and coordinated development of testimony and briefing materials for Congressional hearings. Developed testimony and briefed Institute's Director for all Institute's reauthorization hearings and alcohol warning labels hearings. Developed plans for implementation of statutes authorizing Institute programs. Coordinated development of program regulations.

➤ Persuaded Institute's congressional authorizing committee to repeal provisions having unintended consequences and enact other initiatives within the Department's plan.

BARBARA A. DENTONE

CHURCH WORLD SERVICE, CHRISTIAN COUNCIL OF NIGERIA
INTERNATIONAL COMMITTEE OF THE RED CROSS (Geneva, Switzerland)   1968–1971
International Relief Team Director, Nigeria, West Africa

Directed team responsible for the medical and feeding needs of the population in capital city, Enugu, and a five-mile radius. After war, relocated team to rehabilitate another devastated city, Onitsha, and the surrounding county, of which only 1/4 was accessible by land. Populations totaled approximately 500,000. Analyzed needs (in a war zone and without guidance), developed a plan—including surveying needs, allocating scarce resources, and hiring and managing over 200 African medical aides and relief workers— and administered payroll. Treated the sick and malnourished. Managed a weekly mass-feeding program of 75 tons per week. Established a pharmacy and ordered supplies. Wrote reports for country and international organizations. Represented in-country organization, Christian Council of Nigeria, at governmental and ICCR meetings. Along with other NGOs, rehabilitated a major TB hospital nearby.

- Managed six U.S. team members; found and modified housing in war-devastated area. Employed several hundred Africans. Sensitive to local politics, frequently working and negotiating through church leaders and local chiefs.

- After the war, developed plan to rehabilitate the country. Focus shifted to decisions around which pre-war health facilities should be rebuilt, what new ones needed to be built, and which ones should be repaired. Supervised staff of health centers, dispensaries, and maternities. Opened and managed TB units, maternities, and geriatric wards.

EDUCATION

Ph.D.   ***Brandeis University,*** Waltham, MA   *Health and Social Welfare*   1989
         Florence Heller Graduate School for Advanced Studies in Social Welfare

         Pew Scholar: ***Doctoral Dissertation:*** "Characteristics of Case Management Contributing to Savings in High-Cost Illnesses."

M.P.H.   ***Johns Hopkins University***   *Public Health Planning and Administration*   1973
         School of Hygiene and Public Health, Baltimore, MD

AWARDS AND RECOGNITION

➤ ***Who's Who Worldwide Registry of Global Business Leaders,*** 1993/94
➤ Elected to ***New York State Committee on Healthcare Data Automation*** and ***Florida Governor's Advisory Committee on Data***
➤ Outstanding Contribution Bonuses—The Travelers Companies
➤ Pew Scholarship, ***Brandeis University,*** 1985–1989
➤ Alcohol, Drug Abuse, and Mental Health Administrator's ***Meritorious Achievement Award,*** 1985
➤ Outstanding Performance Awards, ***National Institute on Alcohol Abuse and Alcoholism*** (Five consecutive years)
➤ Quality Increase Awards, ***National Institute on Alcohol Abuse and Alcoholism***
➤ ***Health Resources Administration*** Cash Award
➤ ***Outstanding Young Woman of the Year in America,*** 1971

RESUME 86: DEBI BOGARD, CCMC; SAN DIEGO, CA

NICKOLE SCHLOTMAN

113 N.E. 21st Street Portland, Oregon 97201	nickole@yahoo.com	Home (503) 894-2646 Cell (503) 226-7315

HOME-CARE EXECUTIVE

● Prominent home-care leader, driving advancement of personal-care industry through federal, state, and local legislative activities ● Top-flight administrator dedicated to promoting impeccable standards of care within the industry ● Recognized speaker at workshops throughout the United States ● Business owner in home-care industry
● Published author, teacher, trainer

PROFESSIONAL ACHIEVEMENTS

Founder / Vice President   **1999–2003**
Homecare Incorporated   Portland, Oregon

Co-founded company to provide quality home-care services for elderly and disabled. Grew from start-up to $45 million in three years by launching key initiatives: set industry standard for quality, training, innovation, and professionalism; streamlined and standardized operating processes and procedures to improve quality and consistency and overall patient care; integrated new acquisitions into company; incorporated back-office functions into centralized delivery systems; developed team of patient-focused management and staff.

- Managed annual budget of $2,250,000.
- Supervised department of 18 with 9 direct reports.
- Designed and successfully implemented company-wide, standardized policies, procedures, and processes.
- Successfully completed software conversion of 18 locations in 6 months, with support staff of 6, achieving company's strategic goal of centralizing back-office functions.
- Managed HR, Operations, and Systems Departments for 5 newly acquired companies.
- Restructured Risk Management Department, reducing Workers' Comp Experience Modification Rating from 123 to 55 in two and one-half years, with a projected savings of $950,000 annually.
- Spearheaded change in background-check vendor, increasing efficiency and reducing cost by $83,560 annually.

Owner / Executive Director   1992–2002
Health Care for the Handicapped   Seattle, Washington

Grew, from start-up, successful business providing in-home personal-care services to elderly and disabled. Directed all aspects of business start-up and growth, including operations, strategic planning, business development, budgeting, hiring, and training. Established and implemented quality standards specific to home-care organizations.

- Tripled growth in one and one-half years and grew from start-up to $6 million in six years.
- Campaigned for home-care legislative concerns, lobbying local, state, and federal legislators.
- Credited with being Washington's first health-care company to implement industry-specific scheduling, billing, and payroll software.
- Pioneered IVR technology (Interactive Voice Response) in home-care industry.

Strategy: *Solid achievements are the focus of this executive's resume. The bulleted lists are packed with numbers and results.*

NICKOLE SCHLOTMAN, PAGE 2

Special-Needs Teacher   1988–1999
Seattle Union School District   Seattle, Washington

- Engaged in eight district-wide committees for development of programs, processes, and curriculum for special-needs children, ages three to five.
- Played significant role in grant-writing projects resulting in $3 million for Special Education programs.

Special-Needs Teacher   1981–1988
Northwest Washington Board of Cooperative Educational Services   Seattle, Washington

- Coordinated speech and language services for nine rural districts.
- Served as member of nine-district team selected to write and implement $90,000 grant proposal to develop innovative programs for special-needs students.
- Provided speech and language services to six school districts, preschool through 12th grade, integrating speech and language services into the classroom.

EDUCATION

M.A. Speech Pathology   **1984**
Arizona State University; Flagstaff, Arizona

B.S. Speech Pathology / Audiology   **1975**
Oklahoma State University; Stillwater, Oklahoma

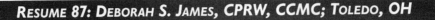
RESUME 87: DEBORAH S. JAMES, CPRW, CCMC; TOLEDO, OH

CLAIRE LYNNE LINCOLN

1414 Oakmont Street • Columbus, OH 43235
Mobile: (419) 666-4518 • Email: clincoln@yahoo.com

DIRECTOR EMERGENCY / TRAUMA SERVICES

Healthcare executive with more than 15 years' experience serving in leadership capacities and nursing positions in a technologically advanced and competitive medical environment. Comprehensive experience in Level I Trauma environment, planning, organizing, coordinating, directing, and evaluating programs. Excellent communication, leadership, and motivational skills to effectively interact with staff, clients, and executive management team. Proven track record building a team-spirited atmosphere based on open communication and mutual respect. Strong background in interdisciplinary project management, re-engineering, management, facilitation/presentation, operational systems, and staff development programs. Willing to relocate.

EDUCATION

Master of Healthcare Administration, University of Michigan, Ann Arbor, MI • 1996

Bachelor of Science in Nursing • The Ohio State University, Columbus, OH • 1990

LICENSURES / CERTIFICATIONS

State of Ohio Nursing Administration Certification • Ohio & Michigan Board of Nursing Licensure
PALS • ACLS • CPR • BTLS

CAREER PROFILE

UNIVERSITY HOSPITAL, Columbus, OH • 1999–Present
Director of Emergency Services / Administrative Director of Trauma Program

Recruited to provide leadership and professional guidance for this Level I Trauma Center with pediatric commitment and affiliation with a critical-care transport network and Air Ambulance Service. Departments include an Emergency Department that records more than 105,000 visits per year, a Pediatric Emergency Center, Observation Unit, and Express Care service. Oversee 20 direct reports, 215 full-time staff members, and 95+ part-time employees. Provide oversight for a $9.5M operating budget and annual revenue of $54M.

- **Guided $80M emergency pavilion project—completed on time and under budget; facility opened to the public in June 2001.**
- **Survived reorganization of ER physicians on three separate occasions without major incidents.**
- **Slashed employee turnover from more than 22% in 1998 to less than 3% in 2002.**
- **Implemented a computerized patient-tracking system (IBEX) in the new ER facility.**
- **Played an instrumental role in planning for Trauma Survey—June 1999.**
- **Received Level I Trauma Designation with Pediatric Commitment in June 1999 and passed re-verification as an Adult and Pediatric Trauma Level I in June 2002.**

Strategy: *This resume highlights the candidate's ability to steer capital-improvement projects, achieve and maintain accreditation, and maintain outstanding employee relations during turbulent times.*

RESUME 87, CONTINUED

CLAIRE LYNNE LINCOLN
(419) 666-4518 • Email: clincoln@yahoo.com

ST. ANN'S MEDICAL CENTER, Ann Arbor, MI • 1987–1999

Director of Emergency Services, Level I Trauma w/Pediatric Commitment (1995–1999)

Directed department recording more than 70,000 visits per year, with life-flight affiliation and mobile intensive-care transport services. Emergency Department housed a Fast-Track Program, four-bed observation unit, and Chest Pain Emergency Center. St. Ann's Medical Center consists of three hospitals with more than 30 ambulatory care units.

- **Maintained 24-hour management services. Designed working budgets; hired, supervised, and counseled staff; and managed a variety of projects and capital improvements.**
- **Consistently received successful JCHAO, AOA, and Trauma reviews.**
- **Design team leader for 38,000-square-foot ER Department construction project.**
- **Slashed cost-per-visit over 3-year period by 13.5% despite increases in employee wages and supplies; cut staff turnover from 35% to 8% per year.**
- **Appointed Team Leader for Emergency Department Reengineering Project (1997–1998).**

Nurse Manager—Sylvan Outpatient Surgery Center (1992–1995)
Hospital-affiliated freestanding outpatient surgery center housing four operating rooms, treatment room, and 24-hour recovery center. OSC handled mix of ophthalmology, plastic surgery, EENT, orthopedic, general surgery, and GYN-surgeries. Center records approximately 5,000 cases per year.

Managed opening for this freestanding 24-hour overnight recovery center. Supervised daily operations; hired and supervised personnel; prepared and planned budget; and implemented new programs.

- **Increased caseload from 3,000 per year in 1992 to more than 5,000 in 1995.**
- **Instituted staff cross-training program for all functions in all areas of the Surgery Center.**

Interim Assistant Vice President, Medical-Surgical Division (1987–1992)

Assumed administrative and leadership responsibilities for Medical Surgical nursing units that included Medical Intensive Care, Neuro ICU, Arthritis Treatment Center, and Nursing Resource/Education Center.

- **Successfully completed accreditation process for the JCHAO.**
- **Provided budget guidelines for 1990 Med-Surg Division, winning the unanimous approval and support of the Board of Directors.**

AFFILIATIONS

American Nursing Association (ANA)
Emergency Nursing Association (ENA)
Operation Smile (Ann Arbor, Michigan Chapter) — Medical Review Board, 1994–2002

TONI M. DEMARCO

452 Burns Court • Port Washington, New York 11554 • (516) 535-6221
tmdemarco@optonline.net

HEALTHCARE / NUTRITIONAL SERVICES MANAGER

Proactive MBA Management professional with expertise in process and performance improvement, administration, human resources, training and development, and creative business channeling. Excellent team-building and interpersonal relations skills. Ability to provide a team-oriented management style focused on motivation and success. Precise, resourceful problem-solver. Effective leader and mentor.

PROFESSIONAL EXPERIENCE

SLOAN KETTERING HOSPITAL • New York, NY   **1978 to Present**
Assistant Director / Food Nutritional Services • 2000 to Present
Production Manager • 1994 to 2000
   Co-direct, coordinate, and supervise the general production of the Food & Nutritional Services Department. Service approximately 1,200 to 1,600 meals per day for patients, staff, employees, and off-site meal service hospitalization program. Provide sit-down service for up to 100 people daily. Train, schedule, mentor, and supervise staff of 30–32 per shift, including cooks, cooks' helpers, nutritional service aides, and cafeteria staff. Recruit, train, and schedule new employees.

- Provide catering for in-service medical programs, partial-hospitalization meal programs, snack programs, fund-raising events, and community affairs.
- Organize projects and service with all departments.
- Participate in $3,000,000 capital budget and special functions planning.
- Purchase food/supplies/equipment and maintain inventory control; review cost-control records.
- Create and implement departmental job descriptions, evaluation forms, and competency testing. Formulate safety program and departmental recording procedures.
- Oversee safety and sanitation procedures; enforce New York State Department of Health and JCAHO mandates, and interpret guidelines for staff.
- Continually develop new menu selections; research recipes, survey patients for input, and coordinate menu planning.
- Facilitate "Meals-On-Wheels" service as part of community outreach, continuum-of-care program sponsored by hospital. Plan menus and supervise staff production.
- Conduct weekly patient rounds.
- Confer with Infection Control Director for patient-related safe food handling protocol.
- Serve on Environment of Care Committee, Wellness Committee, and Performance Improvement Committee.

   ~ *Played key role in Performance Improvement Program for Food & Nutritional Services Department.*
   ~ *Pioneered and streamlined Dysphasia Food Program with Clinical Nutrition Manager and Speech Pathologist.*
   ~ *Spearheaded Mentor Program for administrative rotation of Suffolk County Community College Diet Technician Program and New York Tech's Dietetic Master's Program.*
   ~ *Developed Emergency Preparation Plan for Food & Nutritional Services Department.*
   ~ *Developed Heart Healthy Menu Program for employee dining.*
   ~ *Developed and executed 15 standardized forms to maintain HACCP compliance.*
   ~ *Participated in capital campaign for the ambulatory surgical pavilion as team captain, committee member for hospital fund-raising event, and family-walk committee team captain.*

Strategy: *Experience, achievements, and advanced business education are all emphasized in this resume for a seasoned management professional.*

RESUME 88, CONTINUED

TONI M. DEMARCO
- Page Two -

Diet Technician • 1989 to 1994
Supervisor • 1981 to 1989
Nutrition Service Aide • 1978 to 1981

RESIDENTIAL CARE FACILITY • Bay Shore, NY   **11/97 to 1/02**
Consultant Nutritionist
    Consulted in preparation of meal service to clients in residential treatment center. Coordinated nutritional care of residents.

- Formulated menu and production sheets for School Lunch Program and residential living for residents, mindful of cultural diversity and age-specific population.
- Performed nutritional screening and recorded nutritional care intervention in medical records.
- Maintained list of residents with special nutritional needs.
- Visited with clients to obtain food preferences and tolerances.
- Provided nutritional counseling for staff, clients, and family.
- Planned in advance for both general and therapeutic diets.
- With nursing staff, coordinated the nutritional care and recording of information related to nutritional needs.
- Posted current menus in food preparation area for staff review and information.

EDUCATION

Dowling College, Oakdale, NY
Master of Business Administration, 1999
Bachelor of Business Administration, 1996

Suffolk County Community College, Riverhead, NY
Associate of Applied Science, 1980

CERTIFICATIONS

New York State Certified Dietitian Nutritionist, 1996

MEMBERSHIPS / ASSOCIATIONS

American Dietetic Association
Long Island Dietetic Association, Registered Dietetic Technician
Hospital Federal Credit Union, Board Member

COMPUTER SKILLS

MS Word/Excel/PowerPoint • TimeCare for Windows • WordPerfect • Internet

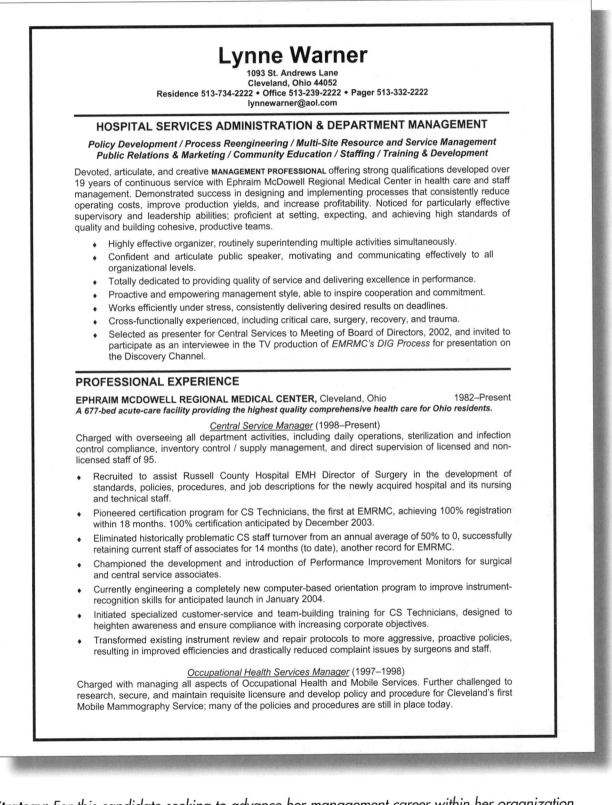

Lynne Warner

1093 St. Andrews Lane
Cleveland, Ohio 44052
Residence 513-734-2222 ♦ Office 513-239-2222 ♦ Pager 513-332-2222
lynnewarner@aol.com

HOSPITAL SERVICES ADMINISTRATION & DEPARTMENT MANAGEMENT

Policy Development / Process Reengineering / Multi-Site Resource and Service Management
Public Relations & Marketing / Community Education / Staffing / Training & Development

Devoted, articulate, and creative **MANAGEMENT PROFESSIONAL** offering strong qualifications developed over 19 years of continuous service with Ephraim McDowell Regional Medical Center in health care and staff management. Demonstrated success in designing and implementing processes that consistently reduce operating costs, improve production yields, and increase profitability. Noticed for particularly effective supervisory and leadership abilities; proficient at setting, expecting, and achieving high standards of quality and building cohesive, productive teams.

- Highly effective organizer, routinely superintending multiple activities simultaneously.
- Confident and articulate public speaker, motivating and communicating effectively to all organizational levels.
- Totally dedicated to providing quality of service and delivering excellence in performance.
- Proactive and empowering management style, able to inspire cooperation and commitment.
- Works efficiently under stress, consistently delivering desired results on deadlines.
- Cross-functionally experienced, including critical care, surgery, recovery, and trauma.
- Selected as presenter for Central Services to Meeting of Board of Directors, 2002, and invited to participate as an interviewee in the TV production of *EMRMC's DIG Process* for presentation on the Discovery Channel.

PROFESSIONAL EXPERIENCE

EPHRAIM MCDOWELL REGIONAL MEDICAL CENTER, Cleveland, Ohio   1982–Present
A 677-bed acute-care facility providing the highest quality comprehensive health care for Ohio residents.

<u>*Central Service Manager*</u> (1998–Present)
Charged with overseeing all department activities, including daily operations, sterilization and infection control compliance, inventory control / supply management, and direct supervision of licensed and non-licensed staff of 95.

- Recruited to assist Russell County Hospital EMH Director of Surgery in the development of standards, policies, procedures, and job descriptions for the newly acquired hospital and its nursing and technical staff.
- Pioneered certification program for CS Technicians, the first at EMRMC, achieving 100% registration within 18 months. 100% certification anticipated by December 2003.
- Eliminated historically problematic CS staff turnover from an annual average of 50% to 0, successfully retaining current staff of associates for 14 months (to date), another record for EMRMC.
- Championed the development and introduction of Performance Improvement Monitors for surgical and central service associates.
- Currently engineering a completely new computer-based orientation program to improve instrument-recognition skills for anticipated launch in January 2004.
- Initiated specialized customer-service and team-building training for CS Technicians, designed to heighten awareness and ensure compliance with increasing corporate objectives.
- Transformed existing instrument review and repair protocols to more aggressive, proactive policies, resulting in improved efficiencies and drastically reduced complaint issues by surgeons and staff.

<u>*Occupational Health Services Manager*</u> (1997–1998)
Charged with managing all aspects of Occupational Health and Mobile Services. Further challenged to research, secure, and maintain requisite licensure and develop policy and procedure for Cleveland's first Mobile Mammography Service; many of the policies and procedures are still in place today.

Strategy: *For this candidate seeking to advance her management career within her organization, clinical-care experience is downplayed while administrative activities and accomplishments are emphasized.*

RESUME 89, CONTINUED

Confidential Résumé of Lynne Warner   **Page 2**

Ephriam McDowell Regional Medical Center, Continued ...

Unit Facilitator Recovery Services (1992–1997)
Reporting to the Director of Surgery, entrusted with 24-hour responsibility and accountability for providing leadership and supervision of EMRMC's Recovery Services, including nursing staff of 12.

◆ Established ACLS and PALS certification requirements for all staff.

◆ Served as Chair for Pain Management DIG. Formulated new policy and initiated pain-management focus groups, recognized for our utilization of pain scale in post-surgical patients.

◆ Introduced EMRMC's first observation unit, "Recovery 3," providing extended-stay capabilities for surgical and medical patients.

◆ Assisted in the organization of the first ACLS classes, serving as an instructor since 1987.

◆ Assisted also in coordinating the first ACLS Instructor Training Course at EMRMC.

Hospital Supervisor 1990–Present
University of Kentucky, Staff Nurse, Outpatient Surgery 1990–1993 (Flex Position)
Critical Care Nursing Agency 1989–1995 (Flex Position)
Staff Nurse, Surgical Services 1989–1992
CCU Staff / Shift Charge Nurse 1982–1989

EDUCATION AND SPECIAL TRAINING

Case Western Reserve University — Cleveland, Ohio
Accepted to Master of Nursing (MSN) Program, to commence in August 2003

University of Kentucky — Lexington, Kentucky
Bachelor of Science, Nursing — 1989

Centre College — Danville, Kentucky
Bachelor of Science, Biology — 1987

Lexington Community College — Lexington, Kentucky
Nursing Associate's Degree — 1982

Creating the New American Hospital, Clayton Sherman
Raising Standards in American Healthcare, Clayton Sherman
Project Management Training, Fred Pryor Seminars
Seven Habits of Highly Effective People, Stephen R. Covey
Frontline Leadership, EMRMC
How to Be an Effective Manager, EMRMC

LICENSURE AND CERTIFICATIONS

Registered Nurse, State of Ohio — Current Status — License #1048534
Central Service Technology Certification (IAHCSMM)
Certified Legal Nurse Consultant
ACLS and PALS Certifications

PROFESSIONAL AFFILIATIONS AND COMMUNITY ACTIVITIES

Member, Business and Professional Women — Cleveland Chapter
Member, Ohio Nurses Association (ONA)
Member, Association of Operating Room Nurses (AORN)
Member, Association of Occupational Health Professionals (AOHP)
Recorder, Value Analysis Committee, EMRMC
Instructor, Member, and Fundraiser, American Heart and Lung Associations

Daniel Harrington

45 Hancock Street • Needham, MA 02494 • (781) 555-4321 • dharrington@verizon.net

Veterinary Hospital Management

SUMMARY

Five years' experience in veterinary medicine and veterinary hospital management, including both start-up and long-term operating facilities. Proven ability to meet financial objectives and to establish procedures that ensure smooth operations. Background includes veterinary technician studies, animal research, and animal management in zoo and research facilities. Key accomplishments include

- Increased business through targeted and creative marketing programs.
- Developed inventory-control system that tracked and maintained required levels of supplies.
- Established and implemented quality assurance procedures.
- Managed and trained professional and support staff to meet top standards of care.

RELATED EXPERIENCE

PETCARE CORPORATION, Allston, MA   2001–2003
Manager

- Key member of acquisitions team that introduced PetCare policies and procedures to 4 acquired hospitals and one start-up facility, achieving cooperation and compliance with new corporate concept.
- Managed day-to-day financial operations—including accounts receivable, approval of invoices and bills, and inventory control—for facilities that averaged up to $600,000 annual income.
- Ensured that expenditures and costs met predetermined financial guidelines.
- Managed 1–2 doctors and 10–12 support staff per facility, including hiring and firing responsibility, scheduling, and training all levels of staff in new management and operating systems.
- Oversaw construction of new facility, monitoring multiple contractors and coordinating activities toward scheduled start date.
- Assisted in developing corporate policies and procedures.
- Created marketing program that increased business 15%.

WELLESLEY ANIMAL HOSPITAL, Wellesley, MA   1997–2001
Manager/Senior Veterinary Technician

- Oversaw $60,000 in inventory; developed inventory-control system that ensured adequate levels of supplies.
- Scheduled and trained new staff.
- Developed procedures for emergency, after-hours staff to ensure accurate transmission of information concerning ongoing cases and smooth transition of care.
- Introduced a referral-reward program that generated a 7% increase in new business.
- Administered medications and X rays; assisted during surgical procedures; monitored ICU patients; set up daily schedule; maintained all equipment and utilities; performed dentistry.
- Performed veterinary nursing duties; greeted patients and set them up in examination rooms; assisted doctors in examinations and treatment rooms.

Strategy: *A chronological format emphasizes managerial experience related to career target, while earlier direct-care experience appears on page 2.*

Daniel Harrington – (781) 555-4321   **Page 2**

TUFTS UNIVERSITY MEDICAL CENTER,
LABORATORY ANIMAL SCIENCE CENTER, Medfield, MA   1995–1997
Lab Animal Technician
- Performed general husbandry duties of primate colony, including feeding and cleaning and maintaining cages and equipment.
- Conducted field research in Thailand, studying population densities and behavior patterns of tiger populations.
- Developed and implemented enrichment activities.

MIDDLESEX COUNTY ANIMAL HOSPITAL, Newton, MA   1993–1995
Veterinary Technician
- Assisted doctors with examinations and medical treatments and procedures.

STONE ZOO, Stoneham, MA   1990–2000
Educator–Animal Keeper (volunteer staff)
- Provided a variety of animal care services, including husbandry and medical care, behavioral modification, and static colony and breeding colony management with special emphasis on non-human primates.
- Instructed zoo visitors and patrons on a variety of zoo topics, such as animal histories, research activities, and breeding practices.

BENSON'S WILD ANIMAL FARM, Hudson, NH   1982–1985
Animal Keeper (volunteer staff)

EDUCATION
  Certification: Veterinary Technician I, Animal Behavioral Science, Middlesex Community College, Bedford, MA
  Other Certifications: Animal CPR, Dentistry, Anesthesia
  Ongoing continuing-education seminars on veterinary technician topics

AFFILIATIONS
  Member: American Association of Zoo Keepers, Stone Zoo Task Force, Franklin Park Zoo Advisory Committee

MILITARY
  E5 — U.S. Marine Corps   1986–1988

Keith F. Hammoth

5751 S. Holt Road
Indianapolis, Indiana 46241

317-375-9219
kfhammoth@aol.com

Healthcare Senior Management / Financial Operations / Executive Administration

Professional career reflects more than 20 years of management, administration, operations, marketing, public relations, research, and strategic planning in the highly competitive and diligently regulated industries of medical practice management and healthcare services.

Leadership has been utilized in finance, negotiations, regulatory compliance, construction, policy, and zoning issues for regional medical networks. Administrative management ranged from a 6-state multi-specialty group with 80 physicians providing services in 12 operating centers to an internationally renowned Retina Institute with 6 satellite facilities. Fiscal responsibilities extended to all operational, marketing, and personnel functions, with budgets in excess of $100M and revenue growth ranging from 25%–72%.

Credentials

Awarded a **Master of Arts** degree in Business Administration from Christian Brothers University. Graduate studies are supported by a **Bachelor of Arts** in Human Relations from the University of Kansas. Have enhanced academic and professional credentials with additional practical training in marketing, demographic research, organizational design, medical regulatory supervision, information management, technology strategies, and public/corporate relations.

Selected Accomplishments

- Designed organizational structure and business plan to merge 3 physicians into a single practice; 8-month project resulted in a 3-year revenue increase from $5.5M to $10M.

- Developed organizational restructuring plan for national specialty group, turned a near-bankrupt corporation profitable, overhauled all expense categories, reduced costs 20%, and increased revenues 25%.

- Completed regulatory compliance to achieve new licensure for regional hospital with limited growth capacity and restricted certification. Acquired largest expansion approval in Tennessee state history.

- Implemented technology overhaul for entire medical practice group. Selected products and vendors; completed installation, testing, and training within 5 months of project launch. Increased operational efficiency and enhanced the access to necessary shared information by all parties.

- Turned struggling hospital with poor physician satisfaction scores into a multi-service care provider, increased occupancy from 55% to 75%, and increased operating revenues 20% in the first 12 months.

- Established centralized billing systems and protocol design for 12 diagnostic-services joint ventures.

- Spearheaded all organizational plans for the merger of 18 medical practices into one corporation with 92 staff.

Strategy: *A combined functional/chronological style permits placement of strongest achievements on page 1 while providing a full explanation of career history.*

Keith F. Hammoth   Page 2

Detailed Career History

Executive Director   1999–2002
Chicago Vision, Inc.   Chicago, Illinois
- Researched physician needs, revised organizational structure, and negotiated 3 parties into 1.
- Drafted 29 sets of legal documents over a 7-month period to complete reorganization.
- Took financial initiatives to increase annual revenues from $5.5M to $10.8M over 36 months.
- Modified all forms and medical documentation, following an unsatisfactory audit; established new procedures and training for personnel; brought organization to 98% compliance in 6 months.

Regional Administrator   1997–1999
Prime Health   Wilmington, North Carolina
- Held operational supervision for 13 physician practices and 3 ASC units in 6 states.
- Coordinated and managed a $100M budget with 25% growth year over year.
- Served as the point of contact for patient/practice surveys and due diligence for practice mergers.
- Performed cost/budget analysis and determined that three practice groups were operating at costs of 80%—75%—65% against a national average of 53%; brought all centers to 55% operating cost in 90 days.
- Developed a 4-day training seminar for practice administrators that increased efficiency, enhanced consistency between practice locations, and increased the ownership of corporate goals and objectives.
- Identified 2 key competing practice groups and developed merger plan that created 1 major service provider with 70% of regional market share.
- Designed personnel, operational, and performance descriptions for 14 administrators, 3 surgery-center directors, and 300 support staff, including but not limited to nurses, technicians, and clerks.

Executive Director   1990–1997
Tennessee Vision Institute   Memphis, Tennessee
- Conducted internal financial audit and determined 35% of charges were missed. Revised forms and procedures to capture charges, and increase collections and revenues.
- Designed preferred-provider referral partnership with key optometrists within a 200-mile radius to increase referral business by 35%, including patients from 35 states and 20 countries.

Partner   1986–1990
Medical Management Associates   Nashville, Tennessee
- Established start-up company to provide diagnostic imaging and healthcare consulting.
- Coordinated 12 joint ventures for diagnostic ultrasound services with a centralized billing service.
- Upon discovery of increased competition, led 15 providers to develop a plan that interfaced their practices, hospital contracts, and diagnostic and treatment centers to growth stage of 25 physicians.

Executive Director   1982–1986
Nashville Physicians Group   Nashville, Tennessee
- Functioned as organizational coordinator for 85 physicians with corresponding documentation to merge services, procedures, and treatment under one structural system.
- Established work-flow efficiency and space-utilization plans that increased usability of existing space and provided framework for 40% additional growth.

Vice President/Director of Medical Services & Cardiopulmonary Research   1974–1982
Baptist Memorial Healthcare   Memphis, Tennessee
- Identified growth restrictions of a regional hospital running 98% occupancy, with minimal regulatory credentials and a 40-bed emergency room holding area; acquired largest expansion approval in Tennessee state history and expanded services from 5 to 7 days per week.

Edith P. Weed, MBA, MPA

68 Charlie Drive
East Hanover, New Jersey 07936

Residence: 973–666–5551 • *E-mail: WeedEP@yahoo.com* • *Cellular: 973–555–5552*

HEALTHCARE INDUSTRY EXECUTIVE

Managed Care / Contract Service Organizations / Hospital Organization / Government Entities
Healthcare Systems Design & Administration / Logistics Management / Materials Management

Senior Director with expertise in the strategic planning, development, and leadership of innovative healthcare networks. Integrated and standardized systems to enhance total quality of care while maximizing human and financial resources. Strong business and financial management expertise; able to achieve objectives without compromising healthcare quality through effective utilization of managed-care concepts, contract services, and delivery systems.

PROFESSIONAL EXPERIENCE

VETERANS ADMINISTRATION, SENIOR EXECUTIVE SERVICE, East Hanover, New Jersey

Network Director   1996 to Present

Recruited to lead the revitalization and growth of Veterans healthcare service options by integrating eight autonomous facilities into a vast network that now includes 8 hospitals, 30+ community clinics, and 7 medical-school affiliations in six states. Challenged to reduce service/ equipment/commodities costs, enhance productivity, and improve service availability utilizing existing staff and facilities.

Scope of responsibility includes budget management, delivery-systems development and implementation, emergency medical preparedness, and vendor/contractor relations. Work in cooperation with hospital administrators, financial executives, government agencies, veterans service organizations, legislators, and policymakers to propel innovative managed-care programs that serve nearly one million veterans annually. Accountable to the National Administrator of Health. Directly accountable for a staff of 15 and indirectly responsible for more than 7,000 corporate, medical, and support staff throughout the system.

Achievements:

❖ Integrated all database systems and standardized procedures/processes throughout the network in several service areas. Reaped multiple benefits, including:

  ✓ **Reduced annual laboratory costs $15 million by establishing centralized lab.**

  ✓ **Identified and eliminated nearly 4,500 instances of multiple facility use and prescription redundancies.**

  ✓ **Cut resource costs by converting to a paperless system.**

❖ Saved more than $6 million annually by cutting contracting staff, standardizing commodities, and facilitating group equipment purchases. Cut administrative overhead nearly 13% in three years, enabling a redirection of more than $65 million to patient care.

❖ Championed the development of the most sophisticated telemedicine system in the country and opened 25 community-based clinics throughout network area. Generated nearly $40 million in revenues, exceeding targets 25% despite double-digit increases in medical care costs and minimal budget increases.

❖ Restructured operations at several facilities to meet demands for outpatient, short-term, and long-term care. Transformed marginal hospital into a high-quality outpatient clinic by integrating two facilities to form one healthcare system, reducing redundancies and overhead costs.

❖ Achieved national distinction among 22 Veterans Administration networks by being the first of only two networks to attain NCQA accreditation.

Strategy: *A bold-looking presentation that highlights executive management skills, this resume was written for a health care executive seeking a position with the federal government. Early career experience is tightly condensed.*

EDITH P. WEED, MBA, MPA
— *continued* —

VOLUNTARY HOSPITALS ASSOCIATION, East Hanover, New Jersey

Vice President, Managed Care and Business Development   1990 to 1996

Senior Executive with full responsibility for business development and procurement of contract services for a member network of 40+ hospitals in a tri–state area. Orchestrated the successful integration of delivery systems between member systems and hospitals. Directed revenue maximization and generation efforts.

Achievements:

❖ Credited with facilitating more than $5 million in cost savings annually for four consecutive years by centralizing service contracting system within Business Office.

❖ Dramatically improved and standardized customer services by establishing a uniform customer-satisfaction survey that offered comparable data throughout member network. Encouraged member–to–member collaboration to enhance quality and uniformity in customer service. Scores improved year–over–year for five consecutive years.

❖ Negotiated shrewd product contracts by utilizing previous industry relationships, knowledge, and experience within the managed-care system.

PREVIOUS EMPLOYMENT includes 12 years' experience within the Healthcare/Health Insurance industry during the development years of managed-care systems.

PROFESSIONAL/CIVIC ACTIVITIES

Affiliations:
Member, American Association of Health Plans
Member, American Legion

Community:
Volunteer, East Hanover Red Cross
Volunteer, Golden Age Games
Volunteer, Wheelchair Olympics

EDUCATION & PROFESSIONAL DEVELOPMENT

MBA–Finance, SMITH COLLEGE, 1997
GPA 4.0

MPA–Healthcare Management, UNIVERSITY OF SOUTHERN CALIFORNIA, 1994
GPA 3.8

BA–Liberal Arts, SMITH COLLEGE, 1986
GPA: 4.0

Additional training/coursework includes
❖ **Executive MBA**
❖ **Mediation Training**
❖ **Terrorist Response Training**

TERRENCE WONSEN, M.D., M.B.A., F.A.C.O.E.M.

1057 Forest Park Boulevard
St. Louis, MO 63104

E-mail: wonsenMD@earthlink.net

(314) 699-9287 (home)
(314) 424-3127 (pager/cell phone)

CAREER PROFILE

SENIOR EXECUTIVE — OCCUPATIONAL AND ENVIRONMENTAL MEDICINE

Corporate Medical Director / Corporate Health Services Director / Vice President of Medical Affairs

Distinguished 22-year career as manager and practicing physician in corporate and hospital settings. Combine business acumen with medical/clinical expertise. Excel at aligning medical goals with business objectives. Record of implementing cost-effective programs and processes that improve employee health and safety, reduce expenses from absenteeism, and cut healthcare costs. Strong operational, project management, team-building, and leadership skills. Experienced in managing international, multi-site, employee-health delivery systems. Skills and areas of expertise include:

- Policy & program development
- Strategic planning
- Project management
- Process improvement
- Workers' compensation
- Disability management
- Health & disability benefits

- Medical surveillance testing
- Wellness & health promotion
- Travel medicine
- Immunization programs
- Ergonomic issues
- HMO, indemnity & commercial insurance

- Bioterrorism readiness
- Regulations — OSHA, EPA
- Industrial hygiene & safety
- Toxicology
- Sick building syndrome
- FAA & FHWA drug/alcohol testing programs

PROFESSIONAL CREDENTIALS

Education
M.B.A. School of Business Administration, Washington University, St. Louis, MO 1989
M.D. School of Medicine, Washington University, St. Louis, MO 1985
B.A. Yale University, New Haven, CT 1978

Medical Licensure MO, IL, FL

Certifications
American Board of Preventive Medicine/Occupational Health 1999
American Board of Emergency Medicine 1996
American Board of Medical Management 1992
Fellow, American College of Occupational and Environmental Medicine 2002

Affiliations
President, Midwest College of Occupational and Environmental Medicine 1998–Present
Fellow, American College of Occupational and Environmental Medicine
Member, American College of Physician Executives

PROFESSIONAL EXPERIENCE

CONSOLIDATED INDUSTRIES, INC., St. Louis, MO   1997–Present
Multibillion-dollar global engineering and construction company.

Medical Director — Midwest Region (seven sites, 15 staff)

Manage occupational and environmental medicine (OEM) operations and drive strategic initiatives at multiple sites in the U.S. and internationally. As lead physician, supervise and mentor healthcare professionals. Treat patients. Serve as an expert clinical resource for multi-site health-services personnel and as internal consultant on high-level corporate projects. Oversee health and safety issues related to overseas travel. Provide consulting services to the Environmental Health and Safety Department on environmental health issues and to the corporate legal department on ADA, FMLA, workplace violence, and environmental-exposure litigation. Member of the Medical Standards Committee.

Strategy: The challenge with this resume was to position Dr. Wonsen as possessing all the competencies needed to make a step up from regional medical director to a corporate-level director position.

TERRENCE WONSEN, M.D., M.B.A., F.A.C.O.E.M.   PAGE 2

PROFESSIONAL EXPERIENCE (CONTINUED)

Selected Achievements — Consolidated Industries, Inc.

Strategic Planning and Internal Consulting
- Identified the strategic OEM requirements of a complex global organization. Defined short- and long-term organizational and business goals.
- Reviewed and updated corporate medical policies and procedures. Ensured OSHA compliance.
- Collaborated with environmental health and safety executives to establish criteria for medical surveillance.
- Provided expertise on the potential impact of bioterrorism. Contributed to development of a corporate response.
- Key player in developing and piloting a corporate wellness program.

Program Reengineering and Process Redesign
- Reengineered clinic operations — identified and captured opportunities for efficiency and quality improvements.
- Created a high degree of uniformity throughout the 26-clinic program, reducing risk of error, improving quality of patient care, and decreasing costs of medical-director-level oversight.
- Achieved impressively high "retention of care" metrics. Enabled the manufacturing-facility clinic with the heaviest caseload to handle 95% of injuries onsite in 2002 (industry standard for excellence is considered to be 80%+). Result: reduced absenteeism and slashed costs previously incurred by relying on offsite treatment.
- Redesigned staffing model. Instituted nurse-based patient-care guidelines with oversight by a consulting physician. Defined and developed a position for a disability nurse case manager.

Program Initiatives
- Created a detailed disability training manual. Standardized processes and procedures for performing disability evaluations and handling insurance issues. Trained physicians. Results: streamlined operations, returned employees to work earlier, and increased number of modified-duty solutions.
- Rolled out the AED (automatic external defibrillator) Program in the Midwest in 2001.
- Collaborated on a corporate-wide, 26-site initiative to vaccinate employees against influenza. Achieved an aggressive 30% target for employee participation, significantly exceeding corporate benchmarks.
- Developed an overseas assignment and travel immunization program. Served as physician-consultant to troubleshoot and solve expatriate medical emergencies and problems.
- Launched company's first integrated disability program. Results: saved on direct costs of disability and medical payments by enabling employees to return to work with modified duties; saved on indirect costs related to lost productivity, replacement hiring, and overtime; and reduced costs of Workers' Compensation payments.

ILLINOIS GENERAL MEDICAL CENTER, Chicago, IL   1994–1997
Associate Medical Director for the Corporate Health Program

Accountable for both management and clinical roles. Developed policies and procedures, visited client company sites, conducted evaluations, and treated patients. Worked closely with the PT and OT teams to coordinate efforts.

- Increased the number of workers who returned to full- or modified-work duties.
- Decreased the number of days workers missed work due to disability.
- Achieved high levels of customer satisfaction.
- Made key contributions to growing the client base and increasing program revenues.

ST. JOSEPH HOSPITAL, Chicago, IL   1989–1994
Chairman, Department of Emergency Medicine
Director, Occupational Health Program

- Conceived, developed, and implemented the hospital's first occupational health program.

CHICAGO GENERAL HOSPITAL, Chicago, IL   1985–1989
Director, Emergency Department

- Reengineered the E.D. delivery system. Results: increased patient volume and revenues by 15%, raised customer satisfaction levels, enhanced the E.D.'s reputation, and improved Quality Control.

HARVARD MEDICAL SCHOOL, BETH ISRAEL HOSPITAL, Boston, MA   1983–1985
Intern and Resident in Surgery

DR. ERIC J. LEVY

3925 Seminole Drive
Canfield, Ohio 44406

docericlevy@ms.com

Home: (330) 702-6636
Office: (330) 799-9090

SENIOR-LEVEL HEALTHCARE EXECUTIVE
Chief Executive Officer...Chief Operating Officer...Consultant

Proven leader in recognition and implementation of current and future healthcare industry trends ...
Accomplished "outside-the-box" thinker with more than two decades of progressively responsible and diversified administrative and clinical experience directing medical facilities. Diverse background in financial management, strategic market penetration, technology procurement, and staff development. Extensive negotiating skills with insurance and government healthcare contracts to optimize reimbursement status. Broad experience directly interfacing with high-level physician specialists, boards of directors, and executive leadership. Highly skilled in evaluating and implementing mergers and acquisitions focused on regional expansion.

AREAS OF EXPERTISE

- ✓ **Strategic Planning & Analysis**
- ✓ **Cost-Benefit Analysis**
- ✓ **Project Management**
- ✓ **Medicare Guidelines**
- ✓ **Contract Negotiations**
- ✓ **Operations Management**

- ✓ **Financial Funding Strategies**
- ✓ **Financial Budgets/Forecasting**
- ✓ **Resident Staffing/Training**
- ✓ **Community/Media Relations**
- ✓ **Presentations & Public Speaking**
- ✓ **Integrated Healthcare Delivery**

CAREER PROGRESSION

RIVERKNOLL HEALTH, Mahoning County – Trumbull County – Columbiana County, Ohio
Combined resources of area hospitals, medical centers, ambulatory campuses, home-care agencies, and other clinical services with approximately 5,000 employees and nearly 30 locations. Riverknoll Health is the third-largest integrated healthcare delivery system in northeast Ohio.

Division Chief of Podiatry (1999 – Present)
Tasked to engineer strategic visions for podiatric department including budget forecasting, community program development, media outreach, and services and technology procurement. Act as mediator between physicians and hospital administration addressing issues related to pay-scale increases, tenure retention, and various related issues. Participate as member of several steering committees, directing long-term plans focusing on utilization of future needs and services and preparation of cost/benefit analysis of multiple facilities, including a hospital concentrating on heart development/ailments and orthopedic ambulatory surgery center.

Founding Residency Director of Podiatric Medicine and Surgery (1995 – 1999)
Amidst turbulent and volatile market conditions, realized potential for new-graduate medical education division. Successfully presented concept to CEO and Department of Surgery Chairman, resulting in "go-ahead" from executive staff. On first attempt favorably spearheaded appropriate tasks (providing HFCA guidelines and petitioning the Council of Graduate Medical Education) to receive required credentials. Secured **$1.3 million** annual funding for resident salaries and education expenses for 12 residents.

- ✓ **Accountable for hospital- and clinic-related curriculum design, assignments to instructing physicians, and staff evaluations.** Oversaw and steered resident publications, weekly journal clubs, and staff development meetings. Ultimately responsible for graduate residents' performance focused on patient care.

- ✓ Promoted community-relations campaigns by providing residents and founding director as judges in city science fairs and assisting in "help-hotlines" for healthcare organization outreach programs. **Recognized as "Outstanding Program Director" by Department of Surgery and Institution Chairman.**

Strategy: *This resume presents dual expertise in management and clinical areas as both a nurse and a doctor, with the goal of giving this job seeker a competitive advantage over more experienced administrators who lack deep clinical background.*

DR. ERIC J. LEVY   Page 2 of 2

EPSTEIN HEALTHCARE RESERVE SYSTEM, JEWISH HOSPITAL – Youngstown, Ohio
Combined 300+ bed campus of inpatient and outpatient care serving acute, chronic, and rehabilitative services. Provider of multiple medical and surgical clinics focusing on society's less fortunate. Education programs include dental, podiatry, family practice, pediatrics, internal medicine, and general surgery with more than 120 residents.

Podiatric Clinic Director (1987 – 2000)
Served as podiatry department chief responsible for daily operations, compliance with budget parameters, strategic marketing and planning, patient and staff education, technology purchases, contract negotiations, and staffing and development of 12 residents. Managed seven associates—including nursing, billing, and ancillary personnel—while overseeing patient caseload of 30–40 per day. Positioned as Medicare Peer Review Physician to interpret and uphold Medicare guidelines. Actively participated in all aspects of Porter model, including analyzing, buying, selling, and substituting in clinic implementation and management. Executed multiple presentations to vascular symposiums.

✓ **Clearly visible leading community support promotions and fund-raising campaigns while simultaneously participating in telethons and public-service television to raise public awareness and acquire donations and grants to meet $200,000 annual operating budget.**

✓ **Published in the *American Podiatric Medical Association Journal* with surgical case presentations.**

CONSULTING PROJECTS

BENJAMIN PHARMACEUTICALS
Hillsborough, New Jersey
Managing Project Consultant (October 2000 – Present)
Appointed to identify international pharmaceutical companies attempting to penetrate markets within the United States. Evaluate and research existing product lines and create marketing strategies to capture a desired market share. Steer through federal approval process to ensure fast results.

✓ **Led major push to assist Canadian pharmaceutical firms to fill supply void created by high-priced medicines. Push was successful in increasing stock availability to target population through reduced rates, as well as creating a viable position for incoming firms.**

MASSACHUSETTS MEDICAL, INC.
Somerset, New Jersey
Managing Project Consultant (September 2000 – Present)
Positioned to define and evaluate goals relative to corporate visions. Scrutinize feasible research data to verify goals and develop alternative scenarios related to vision.

✓ **Most recently supported efforts to identify pertinent data utilized in offering platform of safer tobacco by creating and offering products with fewer carcinogens. Efforts proved positive and led to 15% sales growth through aggressive marketing.**

EDUCATION

Seton Hall University—South Orange, New Jersey
Master of Healthcare Administration

Ohio College of Podiatric Medicine—Cleveland, Ohio
Doctorate of Podiatric Medicine
Winner of Baird-Johnson Award

Kent State University—Warren, Ohio
Bachelor of Science, Biology

Youngstown State University—Youngstown, Ohio
Associate Degree in Applied Science—Nursing

Chapter 12

Resumes for Health Care Educators

- Diabetic Instructor/Educator
- Neonatal Nurse Educator
- Instrument Educator/Consultant
- ATOD Educator/Counselor
- Health Trainer/Success Coach

Although they do not provide direct care, health care educators use their expertise to broaden the knowledge of other health care professionals and the general public. Subject-matter expertise and communication and presentation skills are always important to highlight in these resumes.

Emilie Nicholds

111 Shawns Avenue • Orlando, Florida 34109 • nic31@aol.com • (941) 593-2222

Diabetic Instructor / Educator

Highly self-motivated professional with demonstrated health experience coupled with the confidence and perseverance to exceed in all endeavors. Ten years of industry background providing education / understanding of related pharmaceuticals / equipment.

➢ Expert knowledge in field of diabetes with comprehensive experience teaching self-management skills and presenting innovations through seminars / lectures.

➢ Outstanding organizational and time-management abilities utilized to quickly resolve problems for optimum improvement and patient service.

➢ Exceptional presentation, negotiation, and interpersonal skills; quick to develop positive rapport with healthcare / business professionals within any healthcare environment.

➢ Proven track record of consistently achieving goals, operating easily and effectively with minimum supervision and maximum responsibility.

Education

Master of Science, 2001—Health Education / Gerontology
Florida Gulf Coast University, Fort Myers, Florida

Bachelor of Science, 1990—Major: Medical Dietetics
Queens University, Kingston, Ontario

Certified Diabetes Educator—2000
American Association of Diabetes Educators

PROFESSIONAL EXPERIENCE

ORLANDO COMMUNITY HOSPITAL, Orlando, Florida   1999–Present
Diabetes Educator

Responsible for providing education within the field of diabetes, one-on-one to clients within outpatient clinic, to community at large through lectures / seminars, and to professionals within the hospital. Increased patient satisfaction with implementation of check-in and follow-up procedures.

♦ Instrumental in increasing referral numbers to diabetes program through the launch of an innovative marketing plan.

♦ As industry expert, utilized extensive knowledge to ensure dissemination of up-to-date information to clients and professionals.

♦ Streamlined administrative tasks for efficiency; organized educational materials.

♦ Increased department productivity and revenues by implementing group counseling sessions and limiting individual counseling.

♦ Coordinated ADA-accredited diabetes program, evaluated success of program, and presented results to advisory board.

Strategy: *This resume portrays nearly ten years of experience as a diabetic instructor. Note that the achievement statements focus on results.*

Emilie Nicholds

COMMUNITY HOME SERVICE, Orlando, Florida   1996–1999

Dietician / Diabetes Educator

Provided diabetes education to homebound patients, ensuring their education on the various nutritional / diet concerns and products available, as well as performing screening on criteria for agency.

♦ Developed professional in-service, facilitating spread of knowledge within the agency.

SELF-EMPLOYED, Orlando, Florida   1994–1996

Consulting Dietician / Diabetes Educator

(Private practice with various clients, including Ace Care Home Healthcare, Collins Home Healthcare, Queens Retirement Communities, and Heritage Home Health) Established a successful entrepreneurial practice specializing in outpatient diet and diabetes education. Developed continuing-education series for staff and external healthcare professionals.

♦ Forged alliances with physicians and other health organizations, building a solid referral base.

♦ Presented statistical analysis to stakeholders, maintaining quality assurance.

KINGSTON GENERAL HOSPITAL, Kingston, Ontario   1990–1994

Clinical Manager (1991–1994)
Clinical Dietician (1990–1991)

Quickly promoted through increasingly responsible positions leading up to management of clinical nutrition department. Ensured the complete delivery of staff and patient in-service and community education including promotion at health fairs. Developed and implemented computerized screening protocols.

Professional Associations

American Association of Diabetes Educators, 1996–Present
American Diabetes Association, 2000–Present
Canadian Diabetes Association, 2001–Present

References

References are available and will be furnished upon request.

JANICE KRAMER, RN

2615 SW Juniper Street
Seattle, WA 98503
(206) 527-1453 Home
jkramer@yahoo.com

Neonatal Nurse Educator

SUMMARY OF QUALIFICATIONS

Energetic nursing professional with 8+ years as an RN with clinical expertise in neonatal nursing, 4+ years as an adult education instructor. Act as change agent to improve health and well being of infants by developing innovative courses and teaching baby care to new parents. M.S. in nursing; licensed Registered Nurse. Proven communication skills, working easily with doctors, nurses, patients, and families. Strong PC skills. Enthusiastic, positive, hardworking.

AREAS OF EXPERTISE

- Critically ill newborns
- Premature infants
- Low-birth-weight infants
- Life-threatening complications
- Congenital malformations

- Parent education
- Adult learning theory
- Dynamic teaching strategies
- Curriculum development
- Active learning methods

EDUCATION/LICENSURE

Master of Science in Nursing, University of Washington, Seattle, WA, 1997

Bachelor of Science in Nursing, Yakima College, Yakima, WA, 1994
Graduated Cum Laude

Registered Nurse, licensed in Washington

PROFESSIONAL TEACHING EXPERIENCE

NORTH SEATTLE COMMUNITY COLLEGE, Seattle, WA   1998–Present
Community Education Instructor

Design, develop, and deliver courses in prenatal/postnatal care, pregnancy preparation, and Lamaze techniques.

PROFESSIONAL NURSING EXPERIENCE

UNIVERSITY HOSPITAL, Seattle, WA   1995–Present
Registered Nurse

Care for critically ill infants in intensive-care unit, coordinating with staff, infection control, and quality control. Mentor staff and act as role model in care provision. Keep abreast of new trends in the field of neonatal care. Foster effective interpersonal relationships among patients, families, and other health team members. Act as education resource to all members of the neonatal intensive-care team.

YAKIMA VALLEY MEMORIAL HOSPITAL, Yakima, WA   1994–1995
Registered Nurse

Cared for neonatal intensive-care-unit patients.

PROFESSIONAL AFFILIATIONS/COMPUTER SKILLS

American Nurses Association/National Association of Neonatal Nurses/Lamaze International

Strong PC skills, including MS Windows, MS Word, Internet, and e-mail

Strategy: *Seeking a transition from nurse to nurse educator, this job seeker highlighted her extensive expertise in neonatal nursing. Her teaching experience is a plus that gets prominent placement.*

CAPLA JOY

23365 Stiles Place
Santa Clarita, CA 91387

661-777-5320
e-mail: joyc@sr.sticare.com

INSTRUMENT EDUCATOR / CONSULTANT

Dynamic, self-directed, goal-oriented, hands-on professional with a varied background in leading-edge technologies, clinical research, laboratory, and nursing. Committed to pioneering research and product development.

Excellent problem-solving skills and a strong orientation in customer service/satisfaction. Demonstrated planning, organizational, oral and written communication, and interpersonal skills. Professional and articulate; able to interact with physicians, nurses, and clients at all levels. Conscientious application of policies and procedures; detail-oriented individual with demonstrated success in managing diverse priorities. Work well with a team, yet decisive and self-starting in implementation.

LICENSURE

Registered Nurse, California License 510628
BLS and ACLS Certified

SUMMARY OF QUALIFICATIONS

Well-qualified and technically proficient Research Scientist with nursing experience and strong academic qualifications. Expertise in lab and field research, enzyme assay, data collection/analysis, and projects. Substantial experience in sophisticated research techniques and technologies.

Clinical Laboratory Skills
Extensive hands-on skills with a variety of equipment acquired as **Licensed Vocational** and **Registered Nurse,** as well as **Veterinary Assistant.**

▪ Cell Biology	▪ Autoclave Instruments	▪ Spectrophotometer
▪ Microbiology	▪ Aseptic and Sterile Techniques	▪ Microscopic Analysis
▪ Anatomy / Physiology	▪ Process X Rays	▪ Biochemistry
▪ Mixing Solutions	▪ Staining Techniques	▪ Incubators
▪ Table Top Centrifuge	▪ Genetics	▪ Pipetting

Computer Technology
Windows 2000, Microsoft Office 2000, database applications, and Internet research.

EDUCATION

Bachelor of Science, Biology; Minor: Chemistry; Cum Laude
University of Southern Montana, Bozeman, MT

Experimented with basic and advanced life forms. Worked in cooperation with a multidisciplinary scientific and research team

Associate of Science, Mathematics
Associate of Arts, Nursing (Licensed Vocational Nurse and Registered Nurse)
College of the Canyons, Santa Clarita, CA

Currently taking an Operating Room course at College of the Canyons, Santa Clarita, CA

Strategy: *A functional format on page 1 allows qualifications to be combined into one strong section. Details of employment history are spelled out on page 2.*

CAPLA JOY Page 2

PROFESSIONAL EXPERIENCE

On-Call Representative / Instrument Educator 2001–Present
Trellis • Redlands, CA
    Instruct hospital staffs in the use of **Alaris** infusion pumps, **Lifescan** blood glucose monitors, and **BD** IV therapy products.

Registered Nurse 2000–2002
Valley Presbyterian Hospital • Van Nuys, CA
    Administered patient care and ensured that proper policies and procedures were applied.

Lab Technician 2000
Santa Clarita Community College • Santa Clarita, CA
    Set up and tore down molecular cellular laboratories. Maintained MSDS files, prepared microbiology media, inventoried new chemical and lab supplies. Handled all greenhouse duties.

Instructor 2000
Chino Career College • Chino, CA (concurrently)
    Covered all medical assisting requirements; venipuncture; injection techniques; ECG; laboratory procedures, including use of laboratory equipment; and pharmacology. Prepared and delivered all lecture and lab instruction. Counseled students.

Veterinary Assistant 1996–1998
Bozeman Veterinary Hospital • Bozeman, MT
    Assisted with surgeries, X rays, and animal treatments; set up rooms, prepped animals, and cleansed teeth and wounds. Restrained, bathed, fed, and exercised animals. Injected animals with vaccinations and medications, including subcutaneous hydration. Worked on projects to determine whether there was increased risk in combining vaccines with surgical procedures in cats and dogs.

Registered Nurse / Full Time in Postpartum/Nursery Unit
IP RN / Intensive Internship Program in Maternal/Child Unit 1995
Holy Cross Medical Center • Mission Hills, CA

- Instructed patients on signs and symptoms of premature labor, labor process, Cesarean post-op, postpartum care, and breastfeeding. Diabetic teaching regarding insulin, diet, and exercise.
- Provided nursing care to patients with acute toxemia, hypertension, and insulin-dependent diabetes.
- Performed well-baby examinations and assisted neonatal nurses with procedures on high-risk infants.

Licensed Vocational Nurse / Women's Nursery Unit 1993–1995
St. Joseph's Hospital • Burbank, CA
Telma Sanchez, M.D., OB-GYN • Burbank, CA

- PRCU and rotations to MSU, DOU, and TCU.

Veterinary Assistant Prior to 1993
Mid Valley Veterinary Assistant, Van Nuys, CA

PAMELA M. FREED
ATOD Educator / Counselor

1234 First Street, N.E.
Washington, DC 20006

Home: (202) 709-0157
Work: (703) 716-0077

OBJECTIVE
*Educating and counseling underserved or special populations
on substance-abuse, perinatal, and occupational concerns.*

CERTIFICATIONS
Certified Prevention Specialist (1995)
Certified Intervention Specialist (1992)
CSAC (Certified Substance Abuse Counselor) (1990)
Certified Relapse Prevention Specialist (1988)

EDUCATION
M.A., Psychological Services (1996) — Virginia Tech University (Falls Church, VA)
Substance Abuse (30 hours) (1988–1990) — Virginia Tech University (Falls Church, VA)
Bachelor of Arts Degree, Speech (1986) — University of North Texas (Denton, TX)

PROFESSIONAL SUMMARY
Top-notch ATOD Educator and Counselor with 25 years of experience in the field of mental health, substance-abuse, and crisis management.

Broad range of critical skills earned working with a variety of special populations, including perinatal (women and children), dually diagnosed, and physically disabled substance abusers; HIV-positive clients; and workers in crises. Experience includes

- **Thirteen** years providing clinical assessments, crisis management, and emergency assistance to substance abusers, including self-referrals and referrals by employers.
- **Ten** years educating families and businesses on substance-abuse signs and symptoms and facilitating crisis interventions at home and at work.
- **Seven** years counseling health professionals (e.g., hospital and clinical staffs, doctors, health departments, and social workers) on issues facing chronic substance abusers.
- **Five** years running clinical relapse and prevention groups for substance-abusing women and children, and helping clients identify and plan to prevent relapse triggers.
- **Three** years developing and running clinical programs on relapse and prevention for HIV-positive clients and the dually diagnosed (e.g., mental health and substance-abuse issues).
- **Developing** vocational rehabilitation programs and helping workers with job transitions (e.g., testing, searching, placement strategies) and workforce re-entry after interventions.

CURRENT ASSIGNMENT

Fairfax Hospital, CATS Treatment Program
Substance Abuse Prevention Specialist (1995 to Present). Manage a caseload of 100 substance abusers—from intake to discharge, and individual to group counseling. Emphasize women-specific addiction issues, recovery planning, and independent-living skills.
- Trained and supervised health professionals, local health groups, and women's programs on perinatal addiction.
- Selected as program developer and consultant for the State Task Force on Perinatal Addiction.
- Acted as the CATS liaison to local Head Start Programs, Health Departments, and HIV Clinics regarding substance-abuse issues.
- Helped plan and execute the annual Substance Abuse Awareness Week event.

Strategy: *Because credentials are important in the field of substance-abuse treatment, this resume emphasizes certifications, education, and direct experience with special populations up front.*

PAMELA M. FREED   Page Two

PRIOR PROFESSIONAL EXPERIENCE

ATOD Volunteer (1992 to 1995)
- Conducted 30+ voluntary training classes on a variety of ATOD topics, including the family and substance abuse, enabling and co-dependency, substance abuse and women, recovery and relapse, relapse prevention, perinatal addiction, violence and addiction, intervention, and the overall addiction process.
- Provided ATOD training for various state and government institutions, including the Center for Substance Abuse Training; the Alcohol and Drug Services Forum; the Virginia Council of Social Workers; the Metropolitan Council of Governments; the Defense Nuclear Agency; the Governor's Task Force on Perinatal Addiction; and the Departments of Housing, Transitional Housing, Human Development, Employment and Training, Mental Health, and Mental Retardation.
- Trained community businesses on EAP and ATOD issues, as well as HR requirements under substance-related programs.
- Trained several private organizations on ATOD topics. Clients included the Virginia Employment Commission, George Washington University, and local United Way–affiliated businesses.
- Counseled patients in treatment at Northern Virginia Counseling Group on relapse and prevention strategies.
- Assisted the United Way Advisory Council with allocation of funds for ATOD issues.
- Developed programs and curriculum for use by ATOD professionals on seven topics:
  - Overview of Substance Abuse
  - Women's Issues in Substance Abuse
  - Family Issues Relating to ATOD
  - The Intervention Process
  - Relapse Prevention (for special audiences)
  - Violence and Substance Abuse
  - The Workplace and Substance Abuse (currently under development)

Virginia Mental Health Association
  Director, Work Adjustment Training Program (1990 to 1992). Assisted a caseload of 50 substance abusers re-entering the workforce.
- Facilitated the workforce re-entry process for substance abusers—from start to finish.
- Conducted job training and facilitated job search and start-up for clients.

  Association Director (1988 to 1990). Hired as Assistant Director and promoted to Executive Director in one year. Responsible for day-to-day running of the organization.
- Assisted dually diagnosed clients with various mental-health/substance-abuse challenges.
- Ensured that the association adhered to state and federal regulations and mandates regarding training and program development.

State Department of Vocational Rehabilitation (Virginia)
  Vocational Counselor (1986 to 1988). Managed a caseload of 60 substance abusers.
- Conducted intakes and assessments, and referred clients for basic services (e.g., medical, social, and housing). Also verified abstinence by monitoring urine screens.
- Conducted vocational testing, developed vocational plans, and assisted clients with job search and placement. Also provided post-placement follow-up and assistance for clients.

S. K. TRAN

2307 King
Alexandria, VA 22314

E-mail: sktran2003@aol.com

Home: (703) 709-0157
Mobile: (703) 719-5115

SENIOR PROFILE	

HEALTH TRAINER/PROGRAM DEVELOPER • SUCCESS COACH
Goal: To deliver and/or develop training in communication, conflict resolution, and stress management.

- **Certified success coach and health trainer** of 20 years. Deliver custom or pre-packaged training to public/private businesses to help meet employee health challenges. Effectively train diverse audiences on health topics, facilitate practical goal-setting and solutions, and address both mental and physical limitations and challenges.
- **Training specialties** include communication, one-on-one and group problem-solving, goal setting and achievement, conflict resolution, life skills and coaching, psychological and physical ergonomics and stress management, and occupational therapy.
- **Teaching style** integrates auditory, visual, and tactile learning with holistic, mind-body-spirit connection.
- **Creative program developer** with a passion for out-of-the-box thinking and motivation through personal empowerment. Blend health and metaphysical therapies with coaching and training. Skillfully coach toward acceptance of meaningful choice and change. Come with enthusiasm, energy, and intuition—no batteries required.

AREAS OF EXPERTISE

- Diverse Group Training
- Corporate Training
- Training Program Development
- Individual Training & Coaching
- Goal-Setting & Achievement
- Occupational Therapy

- Ergonomics & Stress Management
- Team & Interpersonal Communication
- Conflict Resolutions
- Mind-Body-Spirit Connection
- Influencing for Choice & Change
- Motivation & Empowerment

EXPERIENCE

HEALTH TRAINING—Alexandria, VA
Private provider of coaching, training, and training development for individuals/businesses.
Trainer and Success Coach, 1997 to Present
Launched business in 1997 to deliver health coaching and training to individuals and businesses. In 1998 expanded business to include business training, success coaching, and personal effectiveness and empowerment.

- **Developed workshops on communication, stress management, self-empowerment, and spirituality** and trained the general public, for Arlington County Wellness Program.
- **Using pre-packaged training, trained admin team of 25 on burnout prevention** and time/stress management, for Arlington County Parks and Recreation. Included learning styles, supervisory feedback styles, motivating, and exploring motivation with personnel.
- **Trained staff on stress management/self-empowerment,** for Fairfax County personnel. Developed training and delivered ongoing workshops and training for 5 years.
- **Taught team communication for 8 managers/social workers** dealing with mental health, ECHO (Every Citizen Has Opportunities), and disadvantaged clients—for private training contractor Clarity. Developed and delivered the training, including training on dealing with supervisors. Led to improved teamwork and increased clarity for trainees.
- **Successfully coached 25 individuals to career or personal goals.** Involved clarification of goals, goal setting and achievement, support, and practical problem-solving for issues such as career change, single parenting, and work/life balance.

OCCUPATIONAL CONSULTING—Alexandria, VA
Contract provider of in-home occupational therapy training and treatment services.
Occupational Therapist/OT Consultant, 1997 to 2000
Provided occupational therapy and training for various medical contractors, businesses, and individuals, while building HEALTH TRAINING business.

Strategy: *The profile emphasizes this individual's unique blend of health training, training-program development, and personal success coaching. The rest of the resume shows how she gained this breadth of experience.*

S. K. TRAN

Résumé—Page Two

EXPERIENCE	OCCUPATIONAL CONSULTING (continued)

- **Assessed medical/dental office for body mechanics and ergonomic improvements,** and conducted workshops on ergonomics, stress management, and work/life balance, for Dental Assistants Association and Diabetic Centers of America.
- **Developed individualized ergonomic program to lower psychological/physical stress** for workers at Big Six accounting/brokerage firms. Led to group training at both companies.
- **Performed productivity analysis/ergo redesign for physically challenged worker,** and motivational assessment/ergonomic redesign for government worker with back surgery.
- **Standardized and delivered training/rehabilitation to 25 patients** recovering from immune-systems cancer, neurological, or orthopaedic disorders, and **provided in-home training/rehab for 10+ patients/week** with cardio, diabetic, and spinal conditions, for contractors I-Care and Mobile Therapies. Encompassed eldercare, body movement, EC/WS, equipment usage, and dealing with physical disadvantages.

FAIRFAX HOSPITAL—Fairfax, VA (www.inova.org/ifh)
Provider of state-of-the-art medical care to Fairfax County residents.

Occupational Therapist (OT), Rehabilitation Department, 1989 to 1996

Delivered patient care, rehab quality assurance, adherence to quality-care regulations, and internal/external lectures on ergonomics, spine/hand injuries, and trauma.

- **Trained and rehabilitated 20 patients/week** with cardiopulmonary, diabetic, and spinal conditions or injuries. Included patient evaluations and training on ergonomics, body movement, elder care, stress management, and mind-body somatics.
- **Assisted task force to establish hospital's pain-management/charting protocol.**
- **Established ergonomics/stress-management training program for HR and Rehab staff.** Also trained rehab patients on ergonomics and proper body movement for spine, hand, and upper-extremity trauma.
- **Earned merit salary increase that was three times the norm,** for developing spinal education program that increased revenue and funded additional OT staff.
- **Reputation among peers as pace setter, QC provider, and OT trainer/expert.**

INOVA ALEXANDRIA HOSPITAL—Alexandria, VA (www.inova.org/iah)
Provider of medical care for Alexandria residents, with 365 trained staff and state-of-the-art technologies.

Director, Occupational Therapy (OT) Department, 1980 to 1989

- **Developed/delivered hospital-wide training on body movement, ergonomics, and quality care.** Training included doctors, nurses, OTs, interns, and HR.
- **Planned departmental programs in cardiopulmonary care and psychological rehab.**
- **Oversaw team of 6 OTs with caseload of 50 neuro/ortho/cardio patients.**

EDUCATION/ AFFILIATIONS	**Certified Success Coach,** 1998—SUCCESS DYNAMICS NETWORK—MD

Certified Success Coach, 1998—SUCCESS DYNAMICS NETWORK—MD
Minister of Metaphysics, 1997—COLLEGE OF METAPHYSICAL STUDIES—VA
B.S., Occupational Therapy, 1980—UNIVERSITY OF UTAH, COLLEGE OF HEALTH
Computer Skills: MS Word, e-mail, Internet browsing, and Windows 98/2000

Member, American Occupational Therapy Association, 1980 to Present
Member, Success Dynamics Network, 1998 to Present

Contact Data—E-mail: sktran2003@aol.com • Home: (703) 709-0157 • Mobile: (703) 719-5115

APPENDIX

Internet Career Resources

With the emergence of the Internet has come a huge collection of job search resources. Here are some of our favorites.

Job Search Sites

You'll find thousands and thousands of current professional employment opportunities on these sites.

HEALTH CARE/MEDICAL/PHARMACEUTICAL CAREERS

For additional information on specific-health related occupations, contact

American Medical Association
Health Professions Career and Education Directory
515 N. State St., Chicago, IL 60610
www.ama-assn.org/ama/pub/category/2322.html

For information on health care scholarship opportunities, contact the U.S. Department of Health and Human Services at (301) 443-4776. Be sure to ask about both the National Health Services Corps and the Undergraduate Education of Professional Nurses Grant Program.

Absolutely Health Care	www.healthjobsUSA.com
Academic Physician & Scientist	www.acphysci.com
All Nurses	www.allnurses.com
American Medical Association (JAMA)	www.ama-assn.org/ cgi-bin/webad
Aureus Medical	www.aureusmed.com
CareerBuilder Health Jobs	www.healthopps.com
CompHealth	www.comphealth.com

Cross Country TravCorps	www.crosscountrytravcorps.com
Employ MED	www.employmed.com
GreatNurse	www.greatnurse.com
Great Valley Publishing	www.gvpub.com
Healthcare Consultants (pharmacy staffing)	www.pharmacy-staffing.com
HealthCare Hub	www.healthcarehub.com
Health Care Job Store	www.healthcarejobstore.com
Health Care Jobs Online	www.hcjobsonline.com
Health Care Recruitment Online	www.healthcareers-online.com
HealthECareers	www.healthecareers.com
HealthJobSite.com	www.healthjobsite.com
Health Leaders	www.HealthLeaders.com
Health Network USA	www.hnusa.com
HireHealth	www.hirehealth.com
Hospital Jobs OnLine	www.hospitaljobsonline.com/jobsearch.aspx
HospitalLink	www.hospitallink.com
Hot Nurse Jobs	www.hotnursejobs.com
J. Allen & Associates (physician jobs)	www.NHRphysician.com
Legal Nurse.com (National Certification for Legal Nurse Consultants)	www.legalnurse.com
LocumTenens.com (physician jobs)	www.locumtenens.com
MedCAREERS	www.medcareers.com
MedHunters.com	www.medhunters.com
Medical-AdMart	www.medical-admart.com
MedicalJobSpot	www.medicaljobspot.com
MedJump	www.medjump.com
Medzilla	www.medzilla.com
Monster Health Care	www.monsterhealthcare.com
NP Jobs (jobs for Nurse Practitioners)	www.npjobs.com
Nurse Recruiter.com	www.nurse-recruiter.com

NurseVillage.com	www.nursevillage.com
Nursing Spectrum	www.nursingspectrum.com
PeerCentral	www.peercentral.com
Pharmaceutical Company Database	www.coreynahman.com/ pharmaceutical_company_database.html
Physicians Employment	www.physemp.com
PhysicianWork	www.physicianwork.com
PracticeChoice	www.practicechoice.com
RehabJobsOnline	www.rehabjobs.com
rnjobs.com	www.rnjobs.com
RTjobs.com	www.rtjobs.com
Rx Career Center	www.rxcareercenter.com

GENERAL SITES FOR ALL CAREERS

6FigureJobs	www.6figurejobs.com
All Star Jobs	www.allstarjobs.com
America's CareerInfoNet	www.acinet.org/acinet
America's Job Bank	www.ajb.dni.us
BestJobsUSA	www.bestjobsusa.com/index-jsk-ns.asp
BlackWorld Careers	www.blackworld.com/careers.htm
Canada WorkInfo Net	www.workinfonet.ca
CareerBuilder	www.careerbuilder.com
Career.com	www.career.com
CareerExchange.com	www.careerexchange.com
Career Exposure	www.careerexposure.com
Careermag.com	www.careermag.com
CareerShop	www.careershop.com
CareerSite.com	www.careersite.com
Contract Employment Weekly	www.ceweekly.com
Digital City (jobs by location)	home.digitalcity.com
EmploymentGuide.com	www.employmentguide.com
Excite	http://careers.excite.com
FlipDog	www.flipdog.com
Futurestep	www.futurestep.com

GETAJOB!   www.getajob.com

Help Wanted   www.helpwanted.com

HotJobs.com   www.hotjobs.com

It's Your Job Now   www.ItsYourJobNow.com

JobBankUSA   www.jobbankusa.com

JobHuntersBible.com   www.jobhuntersbible.com

Job-Hunt.org   www.job-hunt.org

JOBNET.com   www.jobnet.com/philly

JobWeb   www.jobweb.com

Kiwi Careers (New Zealand)   www.careers.co.nz

LatPro   www.latpro.com

Monster.com   www.monster.com

NationJob Network   www.nationjob.com

NCOA MaturityWorks   www.maturityworks.org

Net Temps   www.net-temps.com

Online-Jobs.Com   www.online-jobs.com

The Riley Guide   www.rileyguide.com

Saludos Hispanos   www.saludos.com

SIRC Internet Resume Center   www.inpursuit.com/sirc

TrueCareers   www.truecareers.com

Wages.com   www.wages.com.au

WorkTree   www.worktree.com

ENTRY-LEVEL CAREERS

CampusCareerCenter.com   www.campuscareercenter.com

College Grad Job Hunter   www.collegegrad.com

College Job Board   www.collegejobboard.com

MonsterTRAK   www.jobtrak.com

GOVERNMENT AND MILITARY CAREERS

Federal Jobs Net   www.federaljobs.net

FedWorld   www.fedworld.gov

FRS Federal Jobs Central   www.fedjobs.com

GetaGovJob.com   www.getagovjob.com

GovExec.com   www.govexec.com

HRS Federal Job Search	www.hrsjobs.com
Military Career Guide Online	www.militarycareers.com
PLANETGOV	www.planetgov.com
USAJOBS (United States Office of Personnel Management)	www.usajobs.opm.gov

Company Information

Outstanding resources for researching specific companies.

555-1212.com	www.555-1212.com
Brint.com	www.brint.com
EDGAR Online	www.edgar-online.com
Experience	www.experiencenetwork.com
Fortune Magazine	www.fortune.com
Hoover's Business Profiles	www.hoovers.com
infoUSA (small business information)	www.infousa.com
Intellifact.com	www.igiweb.com/intellifact/
OneSource CorpTech	www.corptech.com
SuperPages.com	www.bigbook.com
U.S. Chamber of Commerce	www.uschamber.com/
Vault Company Research	www.vault.com/companies/ searchcompanies.jsp
Wetfeet.com Company Research	www.wetfeet.com/asp/ companyresource_home.asp

Dictionaries and Glossaries

Outstanding information on key words and acronyms.

Acronym Finder	www.acronymfinder.com
AltaVista's Babelfish Foreign-Language Translation Service	http://babelfish.altavista.com/
CIGNA Glossary of Health Terms	www.cigna.com/consumer/ education/glossary/
ComputerUser High-Tech Dictionary	www.computeruser.com/resources/ dictionary/dictionary.html

Dave's Truly Canadian Dictionary of Canadian Spelling	www.luther.ca/~dave7cnv/cdnspelling/ cdnspelling.html
Department of Defense Glossary of Healthcare Terminology	www.tricare.osd.mil/imtr/gloss3.html
Dictionary of Investment Terms	www.county.com.au/web/webdict.nsf/ pages/index?open
Duhaime's Legal Dictionary	www.duhaime.org
eHealthCoach Glossary	www.ehealthcoach.com/Glossary_ healthcare.asp
High-Tech Dictionary Chat Symbols	www.computeruser.com/resources/ dictionary/chat.html
InvestorWords.com	www.investorwords.com
Law.com Legal Industry Glossary	www.law.com
Legal Dictionary	www.nolo.com/lawcenter/ dictionary/wordindex.cfm
Medical Lexicon	www.pharma-lexicon.com/
Merriam-Webster Collegiate Dictionary & Thesaurus	www.m-w.com/home.htm
Refdesk	www.refdesk.com
Technology Terms Dictionary	www.computeruser.com/
TechWeb TechEncyclopedia	www.techweb.com/encyclopedia/
Verizon Glossary of Telecom Terms	www22.verizon.com/wholesale/glossary/ 0,2624,0_9,00.html
The Virtual Reference Desk-Dictionaries	http://thorplus.lib.purdue.edu/ rguides/guides.html
Washington Post Business Glossary	www.washingtonpost.com/ wp-srv/business/longterm/ glossary/index.htm
Webopedia: Online Dictionary for Computer and Internet Terms	www.webopedia.com
Whatis?com Technology Terms	whatis.techtarget.com
Wordsmyth: The Educational Dictionary/Thesaurus	www.wordsmyth.net

Interviewing Tips and Techniques

Expert guidance to sharpen and strengthen your interviewing skills.

About.com Interviewing	www.jobsearch.about.com/business/jobsearch/msubinterv.htm
Bradley CVs Introduction to Job Interviews	www.bradleycvs.demon.co.uk/interview/index.htm
Dress for Success	www.dressforsuccess.org
Job-Interview.net	www.job-interview.net
Northeastern University Career Services	www.dac.neu.edu/coop.careerservices/interview.html

Salary and Compensation Information

Learn from the experts to strengthen your negotiating skills and increase your salary.

Abbott, Langer & Associates	www.abbott-langer.com
America's Career InfoNet	www.acinet.org/acinet/select_occupation.asp?stfips=&next=occ_rep
Bureau of Labor Statistics	www.bls.gov/bls/wages.htm
Clayton Wallis Co.	www.claytonwallis.com
Consultant Salaries	www.cob.ohio-state.edu/~fin/jobs/mco/salary.htm
Economic Research Institute	www.erieri.com
Health Care Salary Surveys	www.pohly.com/salary.shtml
Janco Associates MIS Salary Survey	www.psrinc.com/salary.htm
JobStar	www.jobstar.org/tools/salary/index.htm
Monster.com Salary Info	salary.monster.com/
Salary and Crime Calculator	www.homefair.com/homefair/cmr/salcalc.html
Wageweb	www.wageweb.com
WorldatWork (The Professional Association for Compensation, Benefits, and Total Rewards)	www.worldatwork.org

INDEX OF CONTRIBUTORS

The sample resumes in chapters 4 through 12 were written by professional resume and cover letter writers. If you need help with your resume and job search correspondence, you can use the following list to locate a career professional. Many, if not all, of these resume professionals work with clients long-distance as well as in their local areas.

A note about credentials: Nearly all of the contributing writers have earned one or more professional credentials. These credentials are highly regarded in the careers and employment industry and are indicative of the writer's expertise and commitment to professional development. Here is an explication of each of these credentials:

Credential	Awarded by	Recognizes
CAC: Certified Accredited Consultant	California Staffing Professionals	Certification to work as a recruiter in California
CBC: Certified Behavioral Consultant	The Institute for Motivational Living and Target Training International	
CCM: Credentialed Career Master	Career Masters Institute	Specific professional expertise, knowledge of current career trends, commitment to continuing education, and dedication through *pro bono* work
CCMC: Certified Career Management Coach	Career Coach University	Training and expertise in career coaching
CCRP: Certified Career Research Professional	Professional Resume Writing and Research Association	Expertise in helping job seekers develop and execute a career research plan

(continues)

Credential	Awarded by	Recognizes
CECC: Certified Electronic Career Coach	Professional Resume Writing and Research Association	Expertise in job-search-related Internet technology and electronic communications
CEIP: Certified Employment Interview Professional	Professional Association of Resume Writers and Career Coaches	Expertise in interview preparation strategy
CERW: Certified Expert Resume Writer	Professional Resume Writing & Research Association	Advanced expertise in resume writing
CFCM: Certified Federal Contracts Manager	National Contract Management Association	Knowledge in all facets of federal contracts
CFRWC: Certified Federal Resume Writer and Coach	The Resume Place	Expertise in the intricacies of federal government resume writing
CIPC: Certified International Personnel Consultant	National Association of Personnel Services	Expertise in staffing and placement
CJST: Certified Job Search Trainer	Career Masters Institute	
CMP: Certified Career Management Practitioner	International Association of Career Management Professionals	
CPC: Certified Personnel Consultant	National Association of Personnel Services	Expertise in staffing and placement
CPRW: Certified Professional Resume Writer	Professional Association of Resume Writers and Career Coaches	Knowledge of resume strategy development and writing
CPS: Certified Professional Secretary	Professional Secretaries International	Expertise in business communications
CRW: Certified Resume Writer	Professional Resume Writing and Research Association	Successful passage of all requirements of the Certified Resume Writer examination
CSS: Certified Search Specialist	Search Research Institute	Advanced knowledge of personnel law, recruitment, and placement
CTMS: Certified Transition Management Seminars	William Bridges and Associates	Comprehensive training program on transitions
CTSB: Certified Targeted Small Business	Individual states	Qualifying small business

Credential	Awarded by	Recognizes
CWDP: Certified Workforce Development Professional	National Association of Workforce Development Professionals	
Ed.S.: Educational Specialist in Counseling	Accredited university	Graduate-level education
FJST: Federal Job Search Trainer	Maryland Institute for Employment and Training Professionals	Expertise in the nuances of federal job search
GCDF: Global Career Development Facilitator	Center for Credentialing and Education, Inc.	Advanced certification for career development professionals
JCTC: Job and Career Transition Coach	Career Planning and Adult Development Network	Training and expertise in job and career coaching strategies
IJCTC: International Job and Career Transition Coach	Career Planning and Adult Development Network	Training and expertise in job and career coaching strategies
LPC: Licensed Professional Counselor	Individual states	Master's in counseling plus three years of supervised counseling experience
MA: Master of Arts degree	Accredited university	Graduate-level education
MAT: Master of Arts in Teaching	Accredited university	Graduate-level education
MBA: Master of Business Administration degree	Accredited university	Graduate-level education
MBTI: Myers-Briggs Type Indicator	Various training organizations	Qualification to interpret the MBTI assessment
MCDP: Master Career Development Professional	National Career Development Association	Post-master's-level certification in career counseling
M.Ed.: Master of Education degree	Accredited university	Graduate-level education
MFA: Master of Fine Arts degree	Accredited university	Graduate-level education
MRW: Master Resume Writer	Career Masters Institute	Advanced expertise in resume strategy, writing, and design
MS: Master of Science degree	Accredited university	Graduate-level education
M.S.Ed.: Master of Science in Education	Accredited university	Graduate-level education

(continues)

Credential	Awarded by	Recognizes
NCC: National Certified Counselor	National Board for Certified Counselors (affiliated with the American Counseling Association and the American Psychological Association)	Qualification to provide career counseling
NCCC: National Certified Career Counselor		
NCRW: Nationally Certified Resume Writer	National Resume Writers' Association	Knowledge of resume strategy development and writing
Ph.D.: Doctor of Philosophy degree	Accredited university	Post-graduate education

Jennifer N. Ayres
President, Nell Personal Advancement Resources
P.O. Box 2
Clarkston, MI 48347
Phone: (248) 969-9933
Fax: (248) 969-9935
E-mail: jennifer@nellresources.com
URL: www.nellresources.com

Ann Baehr, CPRW
President, Best Resumes
122 Sheridan St.
Brentwood, NY 11717
Phone: (631) 435-1879
Fax: (631) 435-3655
E-mail: resumesbest@earthlink.net

Jacqui D. Barrett, CPRW, CEIP
President, Career Trend
11613 W. 113th St.
Overland Park, KS 66210
Phone: (913) 451-1313
Fax: (801) 382-5842
E-mail: jacqui@careertrend.net
URL: www.careertrend.net

Janet L. Beckstrom, CPRW
Owner, Word Crafter
1717 Montclair Ave.
Flint, MI 48503
Phone: (810) 232-9257
Toll-free: (800) 351-9818
Fax: (810) 232-9257
E-mail: wordcrafter@voyager.net

Mark Berkowitz, MS, NCC, NCCC, CPRW, IJCTC, CEIP
Executive Master Team—Career Masters Institute™
President, Career Development Resources
1312 Walter Rd.
Yorktown Heights, NY 10598
Phone: (914) 962-1548
Fax: (914) 962-0325
E-mail: cardevres@aol.com
URL: www.careerdevresources.com

Debi Bogard, CCMC
Principal, Career Formulas
11835 Carmel Mtn. Rd., Ste. 1304-175
San Diego, CA 92128-4609
Phone: (858) 592-9406
Toll-free: (877) 460-7271
Fax: (858) 592-7271
E-mail: careerformulas@san.rr.com
URL: www.careerformulas.com

Rima Bogardus, CPRW, CEIP
President, Career Support Services
P.O. Box 2026
Garner, NC 27529
Phone: (919) 779-9772
Toll-free: (877) 939-1099
E-mail: rima@careersupportservices.com
URL: www.careersupportservices.com

Arnold G. Boldt, CPRW, JCTC
Arnold-Smith Associates
625 Panorama Trail, Bldg. 1, Ste. 120C
Rochester, NY 14625
Phone: (585) 383-0350
Fax: (585) 387-0516
E-mail: Arnie@ResumeSOS.com
URL: www.ResumeSOS.com

Kathryn Bourne, CPRW, JCTC
President, CareerConnections
5210 E. Pima St., Ste. 130
Tucson, AZ 85712
Phone: (520) 323-2964
Fax: (520) 795-3575
E-mail: Ccmentor@aol.com
URL: www.BestFitResumes.com

Carolyn Braden, CPRW
President, Braden Resume Solutions
108 La Plaza Dr.
Hendersonville, TN 37075
Phone: (615) 822-3317
Fax: (615) 826-9611
E-mail: bradenresume@comcast.net

Nita Busby, CPRW, CAC, JCTC
Owner/General Manager, Resumes, Etc.
438 E. Katella, Ste. G
Orange, CA 92867
Phone: (714) 633-2783
Fax: (714) 633-2745
E-mail: resumes100@aol.com
URL: www.resumesetc.net

Freddie Cheek, M.S.Ed., CPRW, CWDP, CCM, CRW
Cheek & Cristantello Career Connections
4511 Harlem Rd., Ste. 3
Amherst, NY 14226
Phone: (716) 839-3635
Fax: (716) 831-9320
E-mail: fscheek@adelphia.net
URL: www.CheekandCristantello.com

Jean Cummings, MAT, CPRW, CEIP
President, A RESUME FOR TODAY
123 Minot Rd.
Concord, MA 01742
Phone: (978) 371-9266
Fax: (978) 964-0529
E-mail: jc@aresumefortoday.com
URL: www.AResumeForToday.com

Norine T. Dagliano, BA, CPRW
Principal, ekm Inspirations
616 Highland Way
Hagerstown, MD 21740
Phone: (301) 766-2032
Fax: (301) 745-5700
E-mail: ndagliano@yahoo.com
URL: www.ekminspirations.com

Robert A. Dagnall
President, ResumeGuru.com
1010 University Ave. #674
San Diego, CA 92103
Phone: (619) 297-0950
Fax: (619) 297-7409
E-mail: robert@resumeguru.com
URL: www.resumeguru.com

Laura A. DeCarlo, CCM, CERW, JCTC, CCMC, CECC
President, A Competitive Edge
Career Service, LLC
1665 Clover Circle
Melbourne, FL 32935
Toll-free: (800) 715-3442
Fax: (321) 752-7513
E-mail: getanedge@aol.com
URL: www.acompetitiveedge.com

Anne-Marie Ditta, CEIP, CPRW, CCMC
Owner, First Impression Career Service, LLC
58 Lincoln Ave.
Tuckahoe, NY 10707
Phone: (914) 961-0579
Toll-free: 877-HIRED-11
Fax: (360) 287-3434
E-mail:
amditta@firstimpressioncareerservices.com
URL: www.firstimpressioncareerservices.com

Kirsten Dixson, JCTC, CPRW, CEIP
President, New Leaf Career Solutions
P.O. Box 963
Exeter, NH 03833
Phone: (866) 639-5323
Toll-free Fax: (888) 887-7166
E-mail: info@newleafcareer.com
URL: www.newleafcareer.com

Nina Ebert, CPRW
President, A Word's Worth
Plumsted/Jackson Townships
NJ 08533/08527
Phone: (609) 758-7799 or (732) 349-2225
Fax: (609) 758-7799
E-mail: keytosuccess@magpage.com
URL: www.keytosuccessresumes.com

Cory Edwards, CRW, CECC, CCMC, MBTI
Principal, Partnering For Success
P.O. Box 650042
Sterling, VA 20165
Phone: (703) 444-7835
Fax: (703) 444-2005
E-mail: ResumeWriter@aol.com
URL: www.resumes4results.com

Debbie Ellis, MRW, CPRW
President, Phoenix Career Group
Toll-free: (800) 876-5506
International: (859) 236-4001
E-mail: debbie@phoenixcareergroup.com
URL: www.PhoenixCareerGroup.com

Donna Farrise
President, Dynamic Resumes of Long Island, Inc.
300 Motor Pkwy., Ste. 200
Hauppauge, NY 11788
Phone: (631) 951-4120
Toll-free: (800) 528-6796 or (800) 951-5191
Fax: (631) 952-1817
E-mail: donna@dynamicresumes.com
URL: www.dynamicresumes.com

Dayna Feist, CPRW, JCTC, CEIP
President, Gatehouse Business Services
265 Charlotte St.
Asheville, NC 28801
Phone: (828) 254-7893
Fax: (828) 254-7894
E-mail: gatehous@aol.com
URL: www.bestjobever.com

Debra Feldman
President, JobWhiz
21 Linwood Ave.
Riverside, CT 06878-1929
Phone: (203) 637-3500
Fax: (203) 637-3500
E-mail: Debra@JobWhiz.net

Art Frank, MBA
President, Resumes "R" Us
1991 Diamond Ct.
Oldsmar, FL 34677
Phone: (727) 787-6885
Fax: (727) 786-9228
E-mail: AF1134@aol.com
URL: www.powerresumesandcoaching.com

Roberta F. Gamza, JCTC, CEIP, CJST
President, Career Ink
Louisville, CO 80027
Phone: (303) 955-3065
Fax: (303) 955-3065
E-mail: roberta@careerink.com
URL: www.careerink.com

Louise Garver, MA, JCTC, CMP, CPRW, MCDP, CEIP
President, Career Directions, LLC
115 Elm St., Ste. 203
Enfield, CT 06082
Phone: (860) 623-9476
Fax: (860) 623-9473
E-mail: TheCareerPro@aol.com
URL: www.resumeimpact.com

Wendy Gelberg, M. Ed., CPRW, IJCTC
President, Advantage Resumes
21 Hawthorn Ave.
Needham, MA 02492
Phone: (781) 444-0778
Fax: (781) 444-2778
E-mail: WGelberg@aol.com

Susan Guarneri, MS, CCM, NCC, NCCC, LPC, CPRW, CEIP, IJCTC, MCC
President, Guarneri Associates/Resumagic
1905 Fern Lane
Wausau, WI 54401
Phone: (866) 881-4055
Fax: (715) 355-1935
E-mail: Resumagic@aol.com
URL: www.resume-magic.com

Michele Haffner, CPRW, JCTC
Advanced Resume Services
1314 W. Paradise Ct.
Glendale, WI 53209
Phone: (414) 247-1677
Fax: (414) 247-1808
E-mail: michele@resumeservices.com
URL: www.resumeservices.com

Loretta Heck
President, All Word Services
924 E. Old Willow Rd. #102
Prospect Heights, IL 60070
Phone: (847) 215-7517
Fax: (847) 215-7520
E-mail: siegfried@ameritech.net

Peter Hill, CPRW
President, Distinctive Resumes
1226 Alexander St. #1205
Honolulu, HI 96826
Phone: (808) 306-3920
E-mail: distinctiveresumes@yahoo.com
URL: www.peterhill.biz

Andrea J. Howard, M.S.Ed.
Employment Counselor, NYS Department of Labor—Division of Employment Services
175 Central Ave.
Albany, NY 12054
Phone: (518) 462-7600, ext. 124
E-mail: USAAH3@labor.state.ny.us
URL: www.labor.state.ny.us

Gayle Howard, CPRW, CRW, CCM
Founder/Owner, Top Margin Resumes Online
P.O. Box 74
Chirnside Park, Melbourne, Australia 3116
Phone: +61 397266894
Fax: +61 397265316
E-mail: getinterviews@topmarginonline.com
URL: www.topmargin

Lynn Hughes, MA, CPRW, CEIP
A Resume and Career Service, Inc.
P.O. Box 6911
Lubbock, TX 79493
Phone: (806) 785-9800
Fax: (806) 785-9800
E-mail: resume@aresumeservice.com
URL: www.aresumeservice.com

Deborah S. James, CPRW, CCMC
President, Leading Edge Resume & Career
Services
1010 Schreier Rd.
Toledo, OH 43460
Phone: (419) 666-4518
Toll-free: (800) 815-8780
Fax: (419) 791-3567
E-mail: djames@leadingedgeresumes.com
URL: www.leadingedgeresumes.com

Marcy Johnson, CPRW, CEIP, NCRW
President, First Impression Resume & Job
Readiness
11805 U.S. Hwy. 69
Story City, IA 50248
Phone: (515) 733-4998
Fax: (515) 733-9296
E-mail: firstimpression@iowatelecom.net
URL: www.resume-job-readiness.com

Bill Kinser, CPRW, JCTC, CEIP, CCM
President, To The Point Resumes
4117 Kentmere Square
Fairfax, VA 22030-6062
Phone: (703) 352-8969
Fax: (703) 352-8969
E-mail: bkinser@tothepointresumes.com
URL: www.tothepointresumes.com

Jeanne Knight, JCTC
Career and Job Search Coach
P.O. Box 828
Melrose, MA 02176
Phone: (617) 968-7747
E-mail: jeanne@careerdesigns.biz
URL: www.careerdesigns.biz

**Myriam-Rose Kohn, CPRW, IJCTC, CCM,
CEIP, CCMC**
President, JEDA Enterprises
27201 Tourney Rd., Ste. 201
Valencia, CA 91355-1857
Phone: (661) 253-0801
Fax: (661) 253-0744
E-mail: myriam-rose@jedaenterprises.com
URL: www.jedaenterprises.com

Rhoda Kopy, BS, CPRW, JCTC, CEIP
President, A HIRE IMAGE®
26 Main St., Ste. E
Toms River, NJ 08753
Phone: (732) 505-9515
Fax: (732) 505-3125
E-mail: rkopy@earthlink.net
URL: www.jobwinningresumes.com

Cindy Kraft, CCMC, CCM, CPRW, JCTC
President, Executive Essentials
P.O. Box 336
Valrico, FL 33595
Phone: (813) 655-0658
Fax: (813) 653-4513
E-mail: careermaster@exec-essentials.com
URL: www.exec-essentials.com

Bonnie Kurka, MS, CPRW, JCTC, FJST
President, Resume Suite
5171 Waterway Dr. #139
Montclair, VA 22026
Phone: (703) 730-3649
Toll-free fax/voice: (877) 570-2573
E-mail: bonnie@resumesuite.com
URL: www.resumesuite.com

**Richard Lanham, MDiv, MA, CCM, CECC,
CCRP**
Regional Manager, R.L. Stevens & Associates,
Inc.
8888 Keystone Crossing #950
Indianapolis, IN 46240
Toll-free: (888) 806-7313
Fax: (317) 846-8949
E-mail: rlanham@rlstevens.com
URL: www.myexecutiveweb.com/rlanham

**Rolande L. LaPointe, CPC, CIPC, CPRW,
IJCTC, CCM, CSS, CRW**
President, RO-LAN Associates, Inc.
725 Sabattus St.
Lewiston, ME 04240
Phone: (207) 784-1010
Fax: (207) 782-3446
E-mail: RLapointe@aol.com

Chandra C. Lawson (May), CPRW
President, A Standard of Excellence
193 E. Main St., PMB 205
Chillicothe, OH 45601-2507
Toll-free: (877) 772-6240
Fax: (740) 634-3004
E-mail: chandra@astandardofexcellence.com
URL: www.astandardofexcellence.com

Lorie Lebert, CPRW, IJCTC, CCMC
President, The Loriel Group—Coaching
ROI/Resume ROI
P.O. Box 267
Novi, MI 48376
Phone: (248) 380-6101
Fax: (248) 380-0169
E-mail: Lorie@DoMyResume.com
URL: www.DoMyResume.com

Nick Marino, USN-Ret., MA, CPRW, CRW, CFRWC, CEIP, CFCM
Principal, Outcome Resume Career Service
710 Aurora Dr.
Bishop, TX 78343
Toll-free: (866) 899-6509
Fax: (707) 248-1578
E-mail: outcomerez@earthlink.net
URL: www.outcomeresumes.com

Peter S. Marx, JCTC
3208 Wallace Ave.
Tampa, FL 33611
Phone: (813) 832-5133
E-mail: marxps@aol.com

Wanda McLaughlin, CPRW, CEIP
President, Execuwrite
314 N. Los Feliz Dr.
Chandler, AZ 85226
Phone: (480) 732-7966
Fax: (480) 855-5129
E-mail: wandaj@cox.net
URL: www.execuwrite.com

Jan Melnik, CPRW, CCM, MRW
President, Absolute Advantage
P.O. Box 718
Durham, CT 06422
Phone: (860) 349-0256
Fax: (860) 349-1343
E-mail: CompSPJan@aol.com
URL: www.janmelnik.com

Nicole Miller, CCM, CRW, CECC, IJCTC
Mil-Roy Consultants
1729 Hunter's Run Dr.
Orleans, Ontario, Canada K1C 6W2
Phone: (613) 834-4031
E-mail: resumesbymilroy@hotmail.com

Sue Montgomery, CPRW, IJCTC
President, Resume Plus
4130 Linden Ave., Ste. 135
Dayton, OH 45432
E-mail: resumeplus@siscom.net
URL: www.resumeplus.com

Doug Morrison, CPRW
President, Career Power
2915 Providence Rd. #250-B
Charlotte, NC 28211
Phone: (704) 365-0773
Fax: (704) 365-3411
E-mail: dmpwresume@aol.com
URL: www.careerpowerresume.com

William G. Murdock
President, The Employment Coach
7770 Meadow Rd., Ste. 109
Dallas, TX 75230
Phone: (214) 750-4781
Fax: (817) 267-2115
E-mail: bmurdock@swbell.net

Ellen Mulqueen, MA, CRW
Vocational Counselor, The Institute of Living
200 Retreat Ave.
Hartford, CT 06106
Phone: (860) 545-7202
Fax: (860) 545-7140
E-mail: emulque@harthosp.org
URL:
www.instituteofliving.org/Programs/rehab.htm

Carol Nason, MA, CPRW
Career Advantage
95 Flavell Rd.
Groton, MA 01450-1536
Phone: (978) 448-3319
Fax: (978) 448-8948
E-mail: nason1046@aol.com

John M. O'Connor, MFA, CRW, CPRW, CCM, CECC
President, CareerPro Resumes & Career
Management
3301 Woman's Club Dr., Ste. 125
Raleigh, NC 27612-4812
Phone: (919) 787-2400
Fax: (919) 787-2411
E-mail: john@careerproinc.com
URL: www.careerproinc.com

Helen Oliff, CPRW, Certified Executive Coach
TURNING POINT
2307 Freetown Ct. #12C
Reston, VA 20191
Phone: (703) 716-0077
Fax: (703) 995-0706
E-mail: helen@turningpointnow.com
URL: www.turningpointnow.com

Don Orlando, MBA, CPRW, JCTC, CCM, CCMC
Executive Master Team—Career Masters
Institute™
President, The McLean Group
640 S. McDonough St.
Montgomery, AL 36104
Phone: (334) 264-2020
Fax: (334) 264-9227
E-mail: yourcareercoach@aol.com

Teresa L. Pearson, CPRW, JCTC, FJST, Master in Human Relations
President, Pearson's Resume Output
Meriden, KS
Fax: (503) 905-1495
E-mail: pearsonresume@earthlink.net

Sharon Pierce-Williams, M.Ed., CPRW
President, The Resume.Doc
609 Lincolnshire Ln.
Findlay, OH 45840
Phone: (419) 422-0228
Fax: (419) 425-1185
E-mail: TheResumeDocSPW@aol.com

Rich Porter
CareerWise Communications, LLC
332 Magellan Ct.
Portage, MI 49002-7000
Phone: (269) 321-0183
Fax: (269) 321-0191
E-mail: careerwise_resumes@yahoo.com

Christine Robinson
P.O. Box 422
Lima, NY 14485
Phone: (585) 624-4232
Fax: (208) 979-3621
E-mail: christine_robinson@frontiernet.net

Jane Roqueplot, Certified Behavioral Consultant, CECC
President/Owner, JaneCo's Sensible Solutions
194 N. Oakland Ave.
Sharon, PA 16146
Phone: (724) 342-0100
Toll-free: (888) 526-3267
Fax: (724) 346-5263
E-mail: info@janecos.com
URL: www.janecos.com

Teena Rose, CPRW, CEIP, CCM
Resume to Referral
7211 Taylorsville Rd., Office 208
Huber Heights, OH 45424
Phone: (937) 236-1360
Fax: (937) 236-1351
E-mail: admin@resumetoreferral.com
URL: www.resumebycprw.com

Jennifer Rushton, CRW
Keraijen
20 Enfield Ave.
N. Richmond NSW, Australia 2754
Phone: 612 4511 1123
Fax: 612 4571 1971
E-mail: vbss@keraijen.com.au
URL: www.keraijen.com.au

Jennifer Rydell, CPRW, NCRW, CCM
Principal, Simplify Your Life Career Services
6327-C SW Capitol Hwy., PMB 243
Portland, OR 97239-1937
Phone: (503) 977-1955
Fax: (503) 245-4212
E-mail: jennifer@simplifyyourliferesumes.com
URL: www.simplifyyourliferesumes.com

Janice Shepherd, CPRW, JCTC, CEIP
President, Write On Career Keys
2628 E. Crestline Dr.
Bellingham, WA 98226-4260
Phone: (360) 738-7958
Fax: (360) 738-1189
E-mail: janice@writeoncareerkeys.com
URL: www.writeoncareerkeys.com

Igor Shpudejko, CPRW, JCTC, MBA
President, Career Focus
23 Parsons Ct.
Mahwah, NJ 07430
Phone: (201) 825-2865
Fax: (201) 825-7711
E-mail: ishpudejko@aol.com
URL: www.CareerInFocus.com

Makini Siwatu, CPRW, IJCTC, CEIP, CJST
Executive Director
Career Success Partners
1426 Harvard Ave., Ste. 419
Seattle, WA 98122
Phone: (206) 760-9334
Fax: (206) 760-9077
E-mail: careersuccess@citycom.com

Billie Ruth Sucher, MS, CTMS, CTSB
President, Billie Ruth Sucher & Associates
7177 Hickman Rd., Ste. 10
Urbandale, IA 50322
Phone: (515) 276-0061
Fax: (515) 334-8076
E-mail: betwnjobs@aol.com

Gina Taylor, CPRW
President, A-1 Advantage Career Services
1111 W. 77th Terrace
Kansas City, MO 64114
Phone: (816) 523-9100
Fax: (816) 523-6566
E-mail: GinaResume@sbcglobal.net
URL: www.GinaTaylor.com

Sharla Taylor
Principal, At Home With Words
P.O. Box 1513
Collierville, TN 38027-1513
Phone: (901) 853-6007
Fax: (901) 853-2071
E-mail: athomewithwords@msn.com
URL: www.athomewithwords.com

Vivian Van Lier, CPRW, JCTC, CCMC
President, Advantage Resume & Career Services
6701 Murietta Ave.
Valley Glen, CA 91405
Phone: (818) 994-6655
Fax: (818) 994-6620
E-mail: vvanlier@aol.com

Pearl White, CEIP
Principal, A 1st Impression Resume Service
41 Tangerine
Irvine, CA 92618
Phone: (949) 651-1068
Fax: (949) 651-9415
E-mail: PearlWhite1@cox.net
URL: www.a1stimpression.com

Amy C. Whitmer, CPRW
President, Envision Resume Services
P.O. Box 7523
Louisville, KY 40257
Phone: (877) 879-6638
Fax: (877) 879-6638
E-mail: writer99@bellsouth.net
URL: www.theresumestore.com

Janice Worthington, MA, CPRW, JCTC, CEIP
President, Worthington Career Services
6636 Belleshire St.
Columbus, OH 43229
Phone: (614) 890-1645
Toll-free: (877) 973-7863
Fax: (614) 523-3400
E-mail: janice@worthingtonresumes.com
URL: www.worthingtonresumes.com

INDEX